TO HIL AND PETER

## United Nations Agencies

| | |
|---|---|
| ECLA | Economic Commission for Latin America |
| ECOSOC | Economic and Social Council |
| EPTA | Expanded Program of Technical Assistance |
| FAO | Food and Agriculture Organization |
| IAEA | International Atomic Energy Administration |
| IBRD | International Bank for Reconstruction and Development |
| ICAO | International Civil Aviation Organization |
| IDA | International Development Association |
| IFC | International Finance Corporation |
| ILO | International Labor Organization |
| IMF | International Monetary Fund |
| ITO | International Trade Organization (never established) |
| ITU | International Telecommunications Union |
| SUNFED | Special UN Fund for Economic Development (never established) |
| UNCAST | UN Conference on the Application of Science and Technology to Developing Areas |
| UNCTAD | UN Conference on Trade and Development |
| UNDP | UN Development Program (formerly Special Fund and EPTA) |
| UNESCO | UN Educational Scientific and Cultural Organization |
| UNIDO | UN Industrial Development Organization |
| UNITAR | UN Institute for Training and Research |
| UNRRA | UN Relief and Rehabilitation Administration (defunct) |
| WHO | World Health Organization |
| WMO | World Meteorological Organization |

## Other International Agencies

| | |
|---|---|
| CENTO | Central Treaty Organization |
| CIAP | Inter-American Committee for the Alliance for Progress |
| COMECON | Council for Mutual Economic Assistance (East European) |
| EEC | European Economic Community |
| EFTA | European Free Trade Association |
| ENDC | Eighteen-Nation Disarmament Conference |
| EURATOM | European Atomic Energy Community |
| GATT | General Agreement on Tariffs and Trade |
| IA-ECOSOC | Inter-American Economic and Social Council (of the OAS) |
| IDB | Inter-American Development Bank |
| LAFTA | Latin American Free Trade Association |
| NATO | North Atlantic Treaty Organization |
| OAS | Organization of American States |
| OECD | Organization for Economic Cooperation and Development |
| OEEC | Organization for European Economic Cooperation (defunct) |
| SEATO | Southeast Asian Treaty Organization |

# TANGLE OF HOPES

# TANGLE
# OF
# HOPES

American commitments and world order

**ERNST B. HAAS**

*University of California, Berkeley*

PRENTICE-HALL, INC.

Englewood Cliffs, New Jersey

PRENTICE-HALL INTERNATIONAL, INC., *London*
PRENTICE-HALL OF AUSTRALIA, PTY. LTD., *Sydney*
PRENTICE-HALL OF CANADA, LTD., *Toronto*
PRENTICE-HALL OF INDIA PRIVATE LTD., *New Delhi*
PRENTICE-HALL OF JAPAN, INC., *Tokyo*

Illustrations by Judith L. Winthrop

Library of Congress Catalog Card No.: 69-14548

Current printing (last number):
    10  9  8  7  6  5  4  3  2  1

Printed in U.S.A.

# PREFACE

America cautiously entered the world of universal and regional international organizations in the 1930's when she joined the International Labor Organization and solidified the nascent Inter-American system. With the founding of the United Nations system in the last years of World War II, she took a giant step toward full involvement. The United States supplied the main impulses for growth of regional organizations after 1948 in founding the North Atlantic Treaty Organization, as well as the Organization for European Economic Cooperation, and in encouraging the unification of Western Europe.

Neither these organizations nor the aims of the United States in joining or founding them progressed according to a single design. American hopes and expectations, far from remaining constant, were modified by unintended and unanticipated new forces. Nor did these hopes flourish consistently once the isolationist stance had been weakened. The unity of the allied nations facing Germany, Japan, and Italy gave way to the Cold War. The bipolar confrontation between the American and the Soviet world constellations yielded to forces released by the process of decolonization in Africa and Asia—forces that found their international fortune in the formula of nonalignment. All military-diplomatic constellations then made way, to some extent, to the voices clamoring for a redistribution of the world's wealth, as the division between the industrialized world of the "North" and the developing nations of the "South" achieved salience.

One major purpose of this book is to recapitulate what happened to American expectations of the network of international organization and to American objectives in joining it. How did the United States, its government, people, and interest groups adjust to disappointment? What did they do and demand when initial expectations of global peace and democracy were not achieved by the United Nations and NATO? What did American public opinion and public policy learn from repeated unintended and unanticipated changes in the international system? Did the lessons generated by disappointment result in more, or less, reliance on international organizations?

The historical portion of our argument stresses the reality of a process of unwitting further enmeshment that may result from an effort to realize in a new setting the achievements that were not possible in the previous one. We shall see how the interplay of American policies and the expectations of other nations in the network of international organizations evolved successive constellations, institutional patterns that we call systems. Once brought into being, how did these systems then shape the next series of American moves and demands?

The lives of systems grow shorter as the pace of technological, scientific, and human innovation gathers speed. The current pattern of international institutional confrontation is certainly not a permanent one. What will the "next" international system be like? Will it have more or fewer alliances? Economic blocs that coincide or overlap with military forces? Will it permit the United Nations to do more or less peacekeeping than the present system allows? Can the evolution of a new technology influence the character of international politics? Many of the features of coming systems may indeed be undesirable for—even destructive of—American aims and values. It is the second major purpose of this book to throw into relief, and submit to our judgment, aspects of evolving international systems that clash with our aspirations.

A hiatus between our aims and the reality of the international system begs the question of what American policy should be in the future when we deal with other nations in the UN, the Organization of American States, or the World Bank. The final task of this book is to criticize current American policy toward international organizations as probably destructive of the chief values we cherish, and to demonstrate that the continuation of this policy will not meet the challenges and demands of future international systems. We therefore present a series of institutional and policy recommendations for a more appropriate American policy, recommendations designed to enable us to work for a world in which human dignity and welfare can flourish without our having to resort to future Vietnams.

In the attempt to carry out these tasks I have found it necessary to make use of a number of devices that call for a word of explanation. The effort to link transformations in American policy with lessons learned from the encounter with the international system utilizes a number of public opinion polls to determine the consistency of American mass attitudes, even though it is generally agreed that certain interest groups, the Executive branch, and the Congress are much more important in shaping foreign-policy decisions. The use of public opinion data, however, was necessary to demonstrate that policy was *not* changed very often because of fluctuations in the mood of the public and that lessons learned by elites from encounters with the external world were central in determining policy. On the other hand, when we discuss the future choices confronting American policy, the range of alternatives permitted by public opinion must be fixed. Even lessons learned abroad cannot find their way into new action unless the public is prepared to pay its taxes and permit its sons to be drafted. My treatment also makes use of categories of regimes and of abstractly ordered patterns of interaction more familiar to the study of comparative politics and development than to the analysis of international organizations. This, too, had to be done, in order to explore the range of future activity likely to bear fruit in a world setting that is heavily populated with underdeveloped, unstable, and authoritarian nations. If the preoccupations of states in a system are partly determined by their domestic institutions and ideologies, these had to be brought into focus in the economical way permitted by systems theorizing. Finally, my concern with the future persuaded me to write or to adapt a number of "scenarios" which may jar the reader who is accustomed to hard data derived from the past. No foreknowledge and no precision can be claimed for these scenarios. Consistency with presently discernible trends, however, can be postulated. Only the very timid or the supremely self-confident among us can afford to forego such stabs at the easily conceivable fates that face us.

I have always been extremely fortunate in working with a group of dedicated collaborators. This book is no exception. My work could not have been done without the generous financial support of the Institute of International Studies of the University of California (Berkeley). Space, equipment, and facilities made available by the institute also proved most important, as marshalled by the good will of Cleo C. Stoker, the institute's central *force motrice*.

It is a deep pleasure to acknowledge gratefully the energetic and devoted research assistance and perceptive criticism provided by Cynthia Frey and Robert Catlett. Kathleen Wilson not only gave additional research assistance of superb quality but also took responsibility for typing and editing. Mary Arnquist was good enough to do the bulk of the typing. To James Murray of Prentice-Hall, I owe a great debt for stimulating and encouraging me to undertake the writing of this book.

ERNST B. HAAS

Berkeley, California

# CONTENTS

# PART THREE

The strength of the web of interdependence

# PART ONE

The nation
in the international system

# CHAPTER ONE

# THE WEB OF INTERDEPENDENCE:

## Two Perspectives

Nations, like individuals, are held in a web of affiliations. Nations form part of a network of ties—willed and unwilled, deliberate or fortuitous—which makes them interdependent to the point of being unable to deal with epidemics, mail, diet, culture, cherished beliefs, and peace except through common institutions. This we are told often; but is it really true? Governments seem often to have acted as if every nation were full master of its own fate. Is there, then, a web of interdependence if the authors of foreign policies deny it?

This tension is illustrated by statements we encounter every day. Many say that times are changing, whether we will it or not, that a new road will be taken, no matter what the statesman perceives and does. Yet, a long-time United States delegate to the United Nations tells us that "at the present time the important thing is to find ways and means of making sovereign national states conscious that in this nuclear age their most vital national interest, their survival, depends not upon the evasion or nullification but the revitalization of the law of the Charter." [1] Apparently, his fellow statesmen are *not* likely to take the new road unless they are made to perceive that this course is in their own interest.

There are three different perspectives that determine whether there is, in fact, a web of interdependence: the reformer's, the actor's, and the observer's. The reformer, obsessed with the roadblocks to interdependence, equates their removal with Utopia; he is of interest to us only if we can demonstrate his ability to shape events. If we can show that he lends a hand for changing the times, only then need we take seriously his complaints that to write of military strategy is to condone war, and to send troops to Asia is to be imperialistic. The actor, on the other hand, is our central concern: his decisions shape the chain of events that affirm—or deny—interdependence.

What about the observer? Scholars see large and impersonal forces unfolding before our eyes. They prefer to uncover laws of development and change. They neither advocate shaping nor act to shape events; but they claim to be able to understand the course of history, to sketch its possible or probable futures. Take, for example, the common view that we are now living through several "concurrent revolutions" that impose certain "unmistakable facts" on our human environment, facts that American policy must tame. What are these revolutions? [2] First, we can all agree that the number of nations is constantly growing, as is the network of special organizations linking them and us. We can also agree that this poses new problems of assimilating and understanding information created by mutually antagonistic demands. Further, a rapidly accelerating technological revolution is clearly engulfing us. What, for example, is the relationship between our military security, space exploration, genetic manipulation, and automated decision-making? And people everywhere seem no longer content with traditional ways of life as rising expectations affect more and more nations and their leaders. We all know that these are real facts and changes. We, as observers, know it. But unless we can also be sure that the actors know it, we

[1] Benjamin V. Cohen, "The United Nations in Its Twentieth Year," *International Organization,* XX, No. 2 (Spring, 1966), 207.
[2] This argument follows Andrew M. Scott and Raymond H. Dawson, eds., *Readings in the Making of American Foreign Policy* (New York: Macmillan, 1965), pp. 3-8.

can no more claim the relevance of these revolutions to the world of international politics than can the reformer.

Is there, then, a web of interdependence only if the makers of foreign policy so perceive it? Yes, but the observer and the actor see things in much the same way concerning the short run: tomorrow's decisions will shape the events of the day after tomorrow; policy-maker and commentator can agree on how and why the decisions will be made and what their probable immediate consequence will be. Why is this agreement possible?

Short-term analysis ignores independent social processes such as economic development, demographic evolution, changing class relations, or scientific breakthroughs. It assumes that a certain rationality inheres in international decision-making and that this rationality—known and observed by the actors—can also be understood by the observer. But this is possible only if three conditions hold: (1) the immediate aims underlying the actor's policy must be unambiguous; (2) the constraints operative on the actor must be clear to him, so that his field of maneuver is as obvious to him as to the observer; and (3) the actor's longer-range objectives can be identified, including the means left to him by the constraints he recognizes.[3] One of these constraints may be the web of interdependence represented by the network of international organizations.

Events that are not correctly comprehended within these three limiting conditions of course interfere with the ability of the observer to understand the actor and his world. Because the United States is not certain which constraints the Chinese Communist leaders recognize, neither scholar nor diplomat can take full satisfaction in knowing that in the long run Mao wants to communize the world and in the immediate future help "liberate" South Vietnam. That gap in knowledge leaves room for chance events, though the chance is much smaller than it would be if we had no knowledge governing immediate and long-range objectives.

Thus the perspective of the actor is the most important datum of political analysis. The world is what it is because the immediate choices of statesmen make it so. What the actor sees as real *is* real because of the policy consequences of his vision. The observer, as long as he is able to follow the rationality of the actor, has no difficulty in identifying and plotting these data. How then can we know whether there is, in fact, a web of interdependence?

[3] This argument follows the telling demonstration of Saul Friedländer, "Forecasting in International Relations," in Bertrand de Jouvenel, ed., *Futuribles*, II (Geneva: Droz, 1965), pp. 57 ff.

One observer, Stanley Hoffmann, suggests that there is none.

> The UN impact on world affairs remains necessarily limited. The
> UN does not reach domestic opinion, does not affect the choice
> of a regime, the selection of alliances, the military policies of main
> powers. . . . whenever the UN hits (deliberately or accidentally)
> a vital interest of a state, and in particular whenever the UN
> seems to threaten what a nation considers to be its very fabric or its
> essential values—in other words, the image the citizens have of
> their nation—the reaction is bound to be violent and bitter. . . .[4]

Yet another observer, incidentally also an actor, thought that the
UN compelled the United States to exercise restraint "and the restraint that we have to exercise in that ethical frame is a restraint
that we welcome." Moreover, "in the post-colonial period the United
Nations will have a lot to do with the problem of the nature of
government and how these wonderful words that have been put
into ratified and unratified conventions can be made to take effect." [5]
Can both be right?

The web of interdependence—its strength, its very existence—can
be judged from a second perspective, that of the long run as seen by
the observer alone. While two observers rarely agree in their analyses, they do share a stance here that differentiates them from the
actor. They do take into account the independent sources of change
that are implicit in large social and economic trends. How do they
know that such trends influence decisions? They must study the
*consequences* of daily decisions, the intended and unintended, and
thus arrive at a conclusion. The question of whether there is a web
of interdependence is then answered by tracing when, where, and
how the earlier decisions of actors have triggered new relationships—
wanted and unwanted—which reaffirm dependence on other nations
and even call for more enmeshment with them. But the observer
alone possesses the detachment and the knowledge to achieve these
linkages of knowledge: the actor is too preoccupied with daily
choices, and the reformer is busy with overcoming daily evils.

We must not think that these two perspectives on international
interdependence must forever remain apart and situated on differ-

---

[4] Stanley Hoffmann, "An Evaluation of the United Nations," *Ohio State Law
Journal*, 22, No. 3 (Summer, 1961), 487.

[5] Harlan Cleveland, "The Capacities of the United Nations," in Francis O.
Wilcox and H. Field Haviland, eds., *The United States and the United Nations* (Baltimore: Johns Hopkins, 1961), pp. 141, 148.

ent levels of analysis. Visions and images covering the long run do not become relevant to concrete reality unless their implications are somehow realized by political actors. The short run and the long run must merge analytically somewhere if the musings of the observer are to be more than just musings. The analytical link between the two perspectives is the notion of *social learning*. With the aid of this notion we are able to explain how both actor and observer can be "right" in their views of the world and how the actor's view comes to approximate the observer's over the long haul. In thus meeting at a different level we are also describing how the international system "changes," owing to social learning on the part of the actors. That change, to be sure, may imply a tighter as well as a looser web of interdependence.

How do political actors learn? We can conceptualize two different learning processes. One is purely national and thus autonomous of international influences. Political actors may learn simply on the basis of successes and failures at home, as reinforced by the demands made upon them by their own citizens. For example, success in dealing with economic crises through a certain method of planning may induce an attitude of international planning predicated on the same principles; failure in stemming a political revolt of an ethnic minority at home may imply a new attitude on internationally fomented internal war. There is, of course, no guarantee that separate national learning processes in different countries will proceed along similar, symmetrical, or parallel courses; one country's lesson may be the opposite of her neighbor's—as illustrated by the contemporary cases of Cambodia and Thailand.

The other learning process is "systemic"; i.e., the impulse proceeds from an international experience to a national reaction. Experience in international dealings, encounters with the "system" of international relations and institutions causes national policy-makers to react differently than they did before the experience, to adapt or to revise their expectations—thus possibly changing the system itself because of a new pattern of demands and response.

Henry Kissinger provides us with a half-real and half-hypothetical demonstration of both learning processes at work.[6] In the years since 1945, the number of independent states has multiplied; the scope of national power has become more diffuse; the reach of ideas has grown downward into previously inert layers of all socie-

---

[6] Henry Kissinger, "Domestic Structure and Foreign Policy," *Dædalus* (Spring, 1966), pp. 518-24.

ties; communication across and within nations has become instantaneous; ideologies have become universal: in short, everybody influences everybody else all the time. This much is seen clearly by the observer and reflects long-run forces. But it is only dimly and intermittently recognized in the perceptions and policies of political actors.

Short-run political action is determined by three styles of leadership, each typical of a particular kind of national society active in the post-1945 international scene. The styles breed mutual distrust. The most familiar style is the bureaucratic-pragmatic mode of leadership familiar to the West, stressing practical aims, the rational choice of means, quiet consultation, and negotiation. Almost equally familiar is the more ideological style of Communist nations, with its claim to an objective "science of society" which gives them a "certain" purchase on social reality, contrasting sharply with the skewed vision of reality attributed by Communist actors to their "bourgeois" counterparts. Finally, there is also a charismatic-revolutionary style typical of many new nations, as exemplified by a Castro or a Sukarno. Such leadership is interested in a vision of the future that is purely political—everything else is instrumental toward the "political kingdom" of which Nkrumah always spoke. The state must hold together a fragmented society and hence must be authoritarian. Its leadership then seeks to solve intractable domestic problems by using foreign policy more extensively than Western and Communist leadership uses it.

Consequently, in the short run the activities of the international system will stress conflict because these three types of actors find it impossible to negotiate meaningfully. They cannot agree on the definition of an issue, on what constitutes a reasonable proposal. Each depends heavily on immediate success as measured by domestic repercussions, on the short-term goal of immediate survival. The more they become conscious of the long-run forces mentioned above, the greater their striving for immediate success is likely to become.

Thus far in our example, a domestic setting has induced a type of "learning" that conditions the actor to distrust his opposite number in the international system. But what if the process of encountering his opposite number year after year, with constantly mounting dangers *perceived equally by all*, induces him to abandon some aspect of his previous stance? What if a shared sense of danger develops and begets a more trusting pattern of response? Were that to happen, systemic learning would be at work. There is some evidence that this has indeed happened in the United Nations and elsewhere in recent years.

We hear more and more of yet a third type of learning, akin to the perspective of the reformer in world politics, both in content and in epistemological value. This is learning induced by the scholar-reformer, imparted directly to the actor. Thus Tinbergen, an international economist, believes that there is an "official recognition that national autonomy, as the cornerstone of international politics, simply does not work and must be given up if the economic interests of the world's population are to be served in an efficient way." Therefore, he continues, "I submit that it is the economist's task *to guide the politicians* in the elaboration of the proper international policies and their preparation, that is international economic planning." [7] Tinbergen's plea can no more be given a central place in our study than can the reformer's perspective, because the scholar who is to do the guiding is still dependent on the actor's perception. He cannot plan the international economy, promote disarmament, preserve world peace, or assure racial equality in South Africa *unless* the actor accepts his guidance. The analytical linchpin, therefore, is the actor and his capacity to learn, whether from domestic or international stimuli.

But our central problem is the position of the United States in a web of interdependence. Do its leaders perceive the United Nations, the North Atlantic Treaty Organization (NATO), or the Organization of American States (OAS) as facilitating or decreasing American global influence? Has that perception changed since the birth of our contemporary organizations in the years immediately following World War II? If so, has the change in perception been due to domestic or systemic learning? If learning was systemic, have United States' attitudes and policy been adapted to reflect the long-range independent change factors we noted above? If so, what does that suggest with respect to the "rules" and "constraints" of a future international system?

That both scholars and actors, writing fifteen or twenty years after the birth of the UN, see new American perceptions is not difficult to prove. In 1945 most Americans thought of the UN Charter and institutions as devices to make the world safe for basi-

---

[7] Jan Tinbergen, "International Economic Planning," *Dædalus* (Spring, 1966), p. 545. Emphasis supplied. On the other hand, see the argument of Ivan Malek, a Communist Czech scientist, in defense of a growing and peaceful web of interdependence following the systemic-indirect learning model, *Dædalus* (Spring, 1966), pp. 663-65.

cally peaceful, satisfied, and progressive—if not entirely democratic —nations. The UN Charter implied the American Way of Life writ large. By 1960 there was a widespread recognition that "we cannot value the United Nations, in general terms, as a pro-Western agency, and expect the Soviet Union to value it, at our occasional convenience, as an impartial agency of the international community."[8] "We should recognize that there will be times, many times, when the interests of the United Nations, an organization devoted more and more to the needs and wishes of the small states, will not be identical with ours."[9] "The price of participating in any political institution is that you cannot get your way all of the time. . . . The central question is whether the credits exceed the debits, whether as a whole the institution is making a net contribution to the national interest."[10] "And the notion persists that agreement or disagreement among nations at any given time is total—that you cannot hold opposing views on subject A and simultaneously cooperate on subject B. This, of course, is nonsense. . . ."[11] The long-run trends spotted by observers seem clearly to have been recognized by actors. Apparently the United States did learn the rules of a new system as 'a result of lessons taught *by the system itself*.

Our question now is: what choices are open to the United States as a national entity with changing demands and expectations in the international arena? The point of departure for giving an answer must be the vision of the past, present, and future international systems, long-range views rising above the maelstrom of immediate events and crises, those that have already passed and the ones yet to come. In other words, choices are limited by the international constellation of trends, influences, and forces we label the "system." Why cannot the United States simply cut loose from these influences and, by a supreme act of will, dictate its terms to the world? It can—but it won't. As long as actors seek to maximize gains and minimize losses, they will avoid dramatic moves. And they are therefore the prisoners of history. The logic of compromise and adjustment, as mediated through the way actors perceive their inter-

---

[8] Inis L. Claude, "The Containment and Resolution of Disputes" in Wilcox and Haviland, *The United States and the United Nations,* p. 124.

[9] Joseph E. Johnson, "Helping to Build New States" in Wilcox and Haviland, *ibid.,* p. 7.

[10] Richard Gardner, *In Pursuit of World Order* (New York: Frederick A. Praeger, Inc., 1964), pp. 119-20.

[11] Harlan Cleveland in Foreword, *ibid.,* p. ix.

ests, will predispose the United States toward a continuing learning process. It is the duty of the observer, the scholar, to recapitulate past lessons learned and to suggest the outlines of future ones.

Still, without escaping the prison that is history, the policy-maker is free to react in any of three ways to the options sketched by the observer. These ways of adapting—or reacting—are open to him without his making the gesture of supreme defiance, which is to say, "I shall act as if no constraints were imposed on me and do what I think right. . . ." The United States can recognize basic new forces and influences, large-scale trends identified by the observer, and can oppose their coming to fruition. It is able to adopt a stance of seeking to freeze the international *status quo*. To do so would be to attempt a "break in the web of interdependence." Alternatively, policy-makers can neglect to pay close attention to long-range trends and continue to follow along the lines of crisis-by-crisis international accommodation. If they follow this road, they are likely to "strengthen the web" because the accommodations will imply more complex and more numerous institutional and financial ties with other countries and organizations. Finally, the United States is able to recognize the implications of basic change and identify those that are desirable. It can then respond by weakening its participation in some international activity while strengthening it in others. This response would be to "confuse the web of interdependence." One aim of this book is to discuss whether the United States will strengthen, break, or confuse the web.

The discussion must combine the perspectives of the actor and the observer. Our first step must be a description of the web over the last fifty years as it appears to the observer. Successive international systems must be sketched. But we must understand that these systems are not the figment of the observer's imagination but the *resultants* of short-range views and policies adopted by successive actors—as interpreted by the observer. Nations and their statesmen provided the decisions that shaped the events that produced the successive patterns that the observer sketches as systems. Sketching these systems is the task of the next chapter.

Next, the character of the United States as a collective actor on the world scene will be thrown into relief, compelling us to show that our participation in the web is related to the military, Congress, the Executive, pressure groups, public opinion, and all other institutions and forces of a pluralistic democracy. Again, it is the stance considered appropriate by the observer that shall inspire this effort, because we are interested in presenting a synthesis of the varied analyses purporting to explain how and why the United States in world affairs acts in terms of its internal dynamics.

We shall therefore treat the hallowed topic of power with some measure of disrespect. The scholar who singles out the perceptions of politically significant actors as the linchpin of his treatment cannot very well assume that an abstract quantity called power is the ultimate determinant of national demise or glory. Neither can he argue that the constraints of the international system which limit the actor's perceptions and choices are identical with the iron law of power. Nor can he take solace in the proposition that social learning on the part of his actors is another way of talking about understanding this iron law.

Power is the special form of political influence that involves the threat of coercive sanction by one party against another. Influence, more generally, is the ability of one party to get another to do something that the second would not otherwise do.[12] Since we usually have no certain way of knowing the extent to which the second party was unwilling, initially, to do the first's bidding, we cannot speak with any precision about the amount or scope of American world influence. This is all the more true as the means at the disposal of American policy-makers in seeking to influence other nations vary in persuasiveness from issue to issue. Nor are we in any clearer position regarding power, the ability to exercise influence by threat of punishment. Normally it is assumed that the militarily and industrially stronger nation has "more power" than the weaker nation and can threaten sanctions accordingly. But the real question is: *Will the stronger readily use this power?* Britain in Rhodesia, the Soviet Union in Rumania, and the United States in Cuba all suggest that the answer must be "not necessarily." The *capability* of a nation to coerce should never be confused with the *will* to do so. Will depends on the perception of actors, on their ability to learn the character of constraints. We can discuss changing perceptions without complicating our analysis with the elusive notion of power.

By placing the United States into a global systemic vision we can then determine how American groups and policy-makers formulate specific policy demands in international organizations. The issue areas of concern to us include the following: maintenance of collective security by the United Nations; regional defensive alliances; disarmament and arms control; economic development and

[12] These definitions and the associated discussion rely heavily on Robert A. Dahl, *Modern Political Analysis* (Englewood Cliffs: Prentice-Hall, 1965).

technical assistance; world trade and finance; the protection of human rights; decolonization; science, technology, and international planning. We are here concerned with how the actors see these issue areas in various periods of time. Have demands changed over time? Have the actors learned to tone down certain demands and voice others? Have policies associated with new demands brought forth results intended by the actors? If so, with what consequences for American satisfaction or dissatisfaction? Have these policies, on the other hand, resulted in unintended and unforeseen results? If so, with what consequences for the degree of American content-ment with the web of interdependence? We suspect that the web can be broken, confused, or strengthened in large measure because unintended results occur far more commonly than expected ones. But we also suspect that the strength of the strands owes more to the inability of actors to see beyond the short range than to any commitment on their part to the glory and the virtue of the web.

# CHAPTER TWO

# MODERN INTERNATIONAL SYSTEMS

International organizations appeared on the stage of history with some force and effect in 1919. Since that time we can see the total network of international relations—the strands of the web that pass through the League of Nations, the International Labor Organization (ILO), the United Nations, the World Health Organization (WHO), and many others—as divided into seven "systems." What is a system? It is a period in the history of international relations during which the crucial characteristics of the web of interdependence differed in some specifiable way from similar characteristics before and after. The characteristics we must observe are: (1) the number of actors and their internal attributes, (2) the international distribution of actor capabilities, (3) the goals they pursue, the methods they adopt, and (4) the outcomes of their conflicting goals and methods which they impose on the common structures they have set up; i.e., the "tasks" assigned to international organizations.

## 1. Number and Character of Actors

We shall confine the notion of "actor" to states that appear as members of universal international organizations: the League of Nations and the United Nations. Occasionally, as with modern China, we also consider as "actors" important states that have not joined such organizations but still influence their decisions. The number of actors grew from about 50 in the early life of the League to the present 125 in the UN. But the character of the member states changed even more dramatically and frequently. Their characteristics cluster so that they produce six types of nations: reconciliation polities, mobilization polities, modernizing autocracies, authoritarian polities, modernizing oligarchies, and traditional oligarchies.[1]

A reconciliation polity distributes governmental authority as in a pyramid of power. The values held dear by its citizens are secular, flexible and subject to instrumental evaluation. Government possesses much information regarding the society and economy and uses little coercion against it. Norms are sanctioned by the constitution and by custom; history serves as a central symbol; public policy is carried out by a bureaucracy working in close conjunction with private groups; and national identity rests on the satisfaction of the populace, which is "participant" in character. Government is highly accountable; elites are recruited on the basis of individual skill and merit as well as on the basis of access; enforcement of norms is flexible; resources are allocated by market forces or wide consultation with private enterprise; and important private groups are co-opted into the governing structure.

A mobilization polity is the exact opposite. Official values are rigid and almost sacred. Authority is organized hierarchically downward. The single "party" serves as the source of norms and the governing mechanism. A "political religion" provides the central symbol and national identity. There is little accountability; recruitment into the elite rests on loyalty to the party; norms are rigidly enforced, resources allocated according to a plan, and consent

---

[1] The discussion of types of polities and of their capabilities is based on the adaptation of materials taken from David E. Apter, *The Politics of Modernization* (Chicago: University of Chicago, 1965); Edward Shils, *Political Development in the New States* (The Hague: Mouton, 1962); Gabriel Almond and Sidney Verba, *The Civic Culture* (Princeton: Princeton University, 1964); Wolfram F. Hanrieder, "The International System: Bipolar or Multibloc?" *The Journal of Conflict Resolution*, IX, No. 3 (September, 1965), 299-308; Henry A. Kissinger, "Domestic Structure and Foreign Policy," *Dædalus* 95, No. 2 (Spring, 1966), 503-29.

groups manipulated. All national energies are "mobilized" to achieve dramatic and rapid modernization.

A modernizing autocracy attempts to attain rapid modernization by more modest means. The traditional ruler seeks to use and adapt traditional symbols, norms, and sources of identity to cajole his subjects into modernity. The established religion is pressed into service if this is feasible in terms of the norms of that creed. Kingship is stressed; personal loyalty to the king determines recruitment; there is little accountability; consent groups are manipulated; and the allocation of resources is planned by the ruler to the extent that his limited skills permit. Modernizing autocracies frequently fail in controlling the social forces released by modernizing policies and thus become victims of their efforts at planned adaptation.

Authoritarian polities are milder and more relaxed forms of mobilization polities; sometimes they emerge after a harassed populace has succeeded in overthrowing a mobilizing regime which had failed to plan and manipulate consent groups successfully. Authoritarianisms hinge around the person of a "presidential monarch," an "elected" ruler who claims legitimacy on the basis of popular acclaim but who surrounds himself with the trappings of a court. Flexible values dominate, but authority is organized hierarchically. Moderate amounts of coercion are used. The president himself attempts to be the source of new, modernizing, and progressive norms; he seeks to shape the new tradition, using a single party and a bureaucracy as the integrating device. National identity rests on the people's identification with the "new tradition" and also on the degree of satisfaction they experience. Personal merit and skill are important in recruitment, some accountability is maintained, and norms are enforced with moderation. While consent groups are both co-opted and manipulated, the allocation of resources preserves a large sphere for private enterprise and mixed corporations. The modernizing policies of such a regime are relatively relaxed. Dissent is not tolerated officially, but dissenting views can be heard privately and incorporated into the hierarchy through various informal devices. Authoritarianisms are the reasonably efficient dictatorships that can grow up in societies in which the bulk of the people have not yet evolved from the status of subjects to that of participants and where reconciliation polities were introduced prematurely, only to be overthrown.

A modernizing oligarchy lacks the structure and purpose of the authoritarian polity. It is led by a junta of dedicated civilians or military people ruling over largely pre-modern people only dimly aware of their formal citizenship in a state. Formal links between government and society and economy are tenuous; the civil or military bureaucracy is neither large nor efficient, though committed to modernization. Modernizing oligarchies have no clear source of norms; only when young officers make up its personnel can the ethos of the army sometimes meet this requisite. Only then can army life serve as a source of national identity. There is no accountability, consent groups are ignored, the enforcement of norms is rigid in principle but haphazard in practice, and recruitment to the elite rests on bureaucratic or personal identification with the junta seizing power. Modernizing oligarchies have little staying power; they readily develop into authoritarian or mobilization polities.

A traditional oligarchy has been spared the pangs of modernization. It is a polity in which a small group of people, related in terms of family and status, control government, society, and economy. The bulk of the people live in tribal or village units under traditional rules and are outside the political system altogether. The small urban population is in the position of subjects rather than participants—except through occasional unstructured outbreaks. Real public values do not exist. The authority structure is hierarchical, and the oligarchy simply seeks to keep things the way they are. There is little information about the society and little coercion because there is so little government.

No source of norms other than the Church and the status values of the oligarchs exists. Certainly there is no national identity. Nor can one speak of consent groups or accountability outside the oligarchic circle. Resources are allocated purely on the basis of private—mostly foreign—market forces; recruitment into the elite rests on family ties. When modernization arrives, it is borne by the winds of accident and private enterprise, not by public policy.

## 2. Distribution of Capabilities

Actors differ in their ability to influence one another's behavior. Apart from its will to exercise influence, each nation is endowed with military capability—conventional, nuclear, or both—industrial and scientific capacity, and the ability to launch effective ideological, propaganda, and subversive offensives. These kinds of capabilities may be distributed symmetrically, heterosymmetrically or asymmetrically among nations. In a period characterized by symmetry, all kinds of capability are distributed so that two actors or two blocs share them about evenly. In a period of heterosymmetry, some third force possesses the kinds of power that *reduce* the aggregate ability of the major blocs to maneuver freely on the international stage in *equal proportions*. And in a period characterized by asymmetrical distribution of capability, the third force or forces reduce in *unequal proportions* the capability of the major centers.

Further, we must specify how the distribution of these kinds of capability is clustered around poles or into blocs. When single states "lead" or "dominate" (through alliances or otherwise) large segments of the globe, we speak of a polar distribution: bipolar from 1947 until 1955, tripolar in the immediate aftermath of the Bandung Conference, and multipolar since the mass admission of African nations. Note that this multipolarity implied the introduction of a heterogeneous distribution of capability *even though* the third pole possessed neither the nuclear nor the conventional military power to cut into the slices possessed by the United States and the Soviet Union. Symmetry was destroyed because of the ideological-subversive capability of the third bloc and because of its ability to make claims on the economic-industrial capacity of the large nations. The third bloc, however, was led by a changing group of nonaligned nations—including Indonesia, India, Egypt, and Yugoslavia—rather than by a single bloc leader. With the possible decline in the ability of single states to "lead" alliances, we may have to start speaking of "multibloc" clusterings of power in preference to "poles."

The changing distribution of capability and the growing proportional share of all types of nations other than traditional oligarchies and reconciliation polities are apparent from Table 2.1 (p. 20). These two sets of characteristics taken together set the scene for the action that nations impose on the web of interdependence.

### 3. Aims and Methods of Actors

The objectives of national foreign policy have always been classified as "revisionist" or *"status quo"* oriented. States either wish to keep things as they are or work for a change favoring their goals. What major substantive issues of modern international relations cause states to behave as *status quo* or revisionist powers?

The legitimacy of existing political boundaries is one such issue. States demanding territorial adjustments, cessions of provinces, the removal of colonial administrations, and tribal reunifications are

TABLE 2 · 1
International Settings
1919-1968

| | Members of League of Nations or UN | | | | | | |
|---|---|---|---|---|---|---|---|
| | Polities (per cent of total membership) | | | | | | |
| Period and number | Rec. | Mob. | M.A. | T.O. | M.O. | Auth. | Capability distribution |
| 1919-31 League: 55 members (1925) | 51 | 2 | 5 | 35 | 2 | 5 | Unipolar victor group; isolated dissenters |
| 1932-40 League: 57 members (1935) | 33 | 7 | 10 | 37 | 2 | 10 | Bipolar asymmetrical |
| 1945-47 UN: 53 members (1946) | 43 | 11 | 6 | 34 | 4 | 2 | Unipolar victor group |
| 1948-51 UN: 60 members (1950) | 50 | 13 | 5 | 25 | 5 | 2 | Tight bipolar symmetrical |
| 1952-55 UN: 61 members (1953) | 46 | 13 | 7 | 19 | 8 | 7 | Loose bipolar hetero-symmetrical |
| 1956-60 UN: 82 members (1958) | 43 | 19 | 15 | 10 | 6 | 7 | Tripolar heterosym-metrical |
| Since 1961 UN: 116 * members (1965) | 41 | 19 | 13 | 6 | 8 | 9 | Multipolar hetero-symmetrical |

* Includes six African states which were not classified for lack of data. UN membership figures (and the percentage for mobilization systems) do not include Ukraine and Byelorussia.

| | | | |
|---|---|---|---|
| Rec. | — Reconciliation Polity | T.O. | — Traditional Oligarchy |
| Mob. | — Mobilization Polity | M.O. | — Modernizing Oligarchy |
| M.A. | — Modernizing Autocracy | Auth. | — Authoritarian Polity |

revisionists; governments taking their stand on the legitimacy of existing borders—a position usually cloaked in the phrase, "respect for international obligations and treaties"—are not. The expansion of a specific ideology, whether by conquest or propaganda linked with externally supported subversion, is another aspect of the same larger issue. Another issue is international economics. Should there be a "natural" division of labor between raw material producers and industrial countries? Should there be a concerted effort to make everybody industrialize? Is the most-favored-nation clause an instrument of economic oppression or a device to assure equality? A revisionist state aims at the reduction of the superiority of the industrialized West; the West itself has taken a *status quo* position much of the time. The universal protection of human rights, through international legal obligations and possibly intervention, is another issue area. Revisionists stress such a role; *status quo* powers emphasize the domestic character of such questions. One may quibble over whether the disarmament and arms control question is a sub-aspect of the territorial and ideological security issue or whether it should be considered as an issue in its own right. Revisionists stress the danger of arms—the arms of other powers—while *status quo* powers emphasize the need for caution and the demands of security. Finally, the promises and dangers of science and its relationship to social change have emerged as an international issue area; *status quo* countries here tend to defend the promise of science and the need for unfettered diffusion of techniques and ideas while the revisionists are more alive to the implicit dangers. Note, however, that on this issue it is the developed countries who act as the revisionists.

The types of methods available to nations do not change very rapidly. What matters to us is which methods are predominant in any one historical system. Means have included the marshaling of national armaments (both nuclear and conventional), strategic planning and counterplanning, resulting in the eventual institutionalization of the nuclear balance of terror. Mutual thermonuclear deterrence thus came to be the major method relied upon by the superpowers. Conventional capability for fighting local or limited wars has been cultivated by almost all nations, large and small. In the inevitable confrontations which have ensued, the dominant methods have been alliance-building, threat, and appeasement. In the realm of ideological technique we have seen the flowering of systematic propaganda, large-scale "international information" programs designed to praise the home state and to defame the opponent, the encouragement of dissident movements in the opponent's territory, and the support of subversive activity. In the field of economics, the methods have included bilateral and multilateral technical assistance, international lending, emergency relief, and the granting of long-range development funds. Human rights have been extolled, by and large, as a way to hurt the opponent's image and to cater to the ideological commitments of third blocs. Disarmament negotiations have been featured to eliminate threats perceived symmetrically by all parties as well as to score propaganda points. Large-scale scientific conferences and much technical work by international agencies, including international inspection of scientific installations, have been the way of dealing with the issue area of science.

### 4. Tasks of International Organizations

The number and character of the nations in each period, when combined with the distribution of capability to influence each other, set the scene for international interaction; their objectives and the methods at their disposal determine the interaction itself. Various combinations of actor characteristics, capability, objectives, and methods, in turn, produce typical bundles of tasks for the international organizations created by the nations. These bundles contain different ingredients, according to the period in question; moreover, the potency of each ingredient is a function of the interissue bargaining process in which the member nations engage in defining tasks for their organizations.

Thus, collective security is an ingredient of each historical system. But it is vital to know whether security decisions rest on a big power consensus, on bargaining with third forces, or on overwhelming majority support. Do the bargains struck involve other issue areas? How important are collective economic decisions favoring the revisionists in shaping collective security policy? Must human rights be protected in the process? Do third forces extract disarmament or national self-determination concessions in voting for a United Nations police force? In other words, we wish to know whether decisions on any one ingredient overlap with the other issue areas. If so, a widening of the scope of bargaining, discussion, and international activity takes place; if not, the maintenance of collective security is an autonomous task perhaps unrelated to the growth or decline of United Nations influence.

We expect, of course, that the web of interdependence enmeshing the United States and other countries will be stronger to the extent that issues do overlap in the bargaining process, whereas the autonomy of each issue and each partial task will continue to give each member nation a great deal of freedom of national initiative outside the web. Multipolarity and heterosymmetry may be the basis of a stronger web.

Successive tasks involving different bundles of ingredients, of course, cannot be explained without also wondering how the actors perceive the previous task, what they have learned from experience with it. This problem leads us back to the learning processes associated with international systems and their transformation. Before undertaking this discussion, however, it is better to sum up the characteristics of the seven historical systems we have sketched. Table 2.2 summarizes the aims and methods of states and describes the bundle of ingredients that made up the task of each period. The periods, in turn, were defined by the capability distribution that we used in Table 2.1.

Clearly, the trend toward the multipolar, heterosymmetrical system, populated with an ever larger number of mobilization, authoritarian, and modernizing oligarchical polities, has been associated with a larger and more variegated task for international organizations. As far as American elite perceptions are concerned, they were foretold in a way by perceptions already discernible in the period 1952-1955. At that time there was general satisfaction with the anti-Communist emphasis in United States foreign policy and the determination to use all possible means to maintain the West's world position. Many influential Americans, however, were also advocating continuous negotiation with the East and a pragmatic issue-by-issue approach to the Communists, which would not require a rigid insistence on "good faith" on all possible issues.

By 1961, the tasks of international organizations were being undertaken with this pragmatic orientation. The tasks had expanded, but not because member nations—including the United States— were demonstrating more loyalty to UN principles or more determination to abide by rules of international law. The UN had become more important, perhaps, because the repeated invocation of the principles of self-determination, economic welfare, human freedom, and world peace had resulted in the addition of many new and vocal actors restraining nuclear alliances of the U.S. and those of the Soviet Union. Both alliance leaders came to reject total war and both showed a low tolerance for any changes in the distribution of capabilities. Both found it desirable to invest more in economic activity—bilateral and through international organizations—as they both downgraded the military objectives of the alliances they lead. The United States and the Soviet Union undertook reciprocal arms control obligations, each knowing that a major ally would not agree, thus straining each alliance to the breaking point. Relations between smaller member states of opposing alliances improve as the nonmilitary tasks of the UN grow in scope and ambition. The result, in 1968, was a world in which NATO and the Warsaw Pact were rapidly declining in military significance, in which the Sino-Soviet alliance had crumbled, and in which the Southeast Asian and Central Treaty Organization were losing their relevance. As for the OAS, its economic and human rights tasks have grown as many Latin American members developed an acute discomfort in regard to United States leadership in the military and antisubversion fields. The question then is: *How* do systems change in the manner suggested here? *How* do actors learn to contribute and adapt to international systems change?

TABLE 2 · 2

Aims, Methods, and Tasks
in International Systems, 1919-1968

| Period | Aims of states | Methods of states | Tasks of international organizations |
|---|---|---|---|
| 1919-1931 | Victors: preservation of political *status quo*, colonial system, global free enterprise. | Alliances, arms reduction, improvement of collective security against occasional protest from dissenters. | Achieve collective security based on a Big Power consensus to preserve victors' peace settlement of 1919; give short-term financial aid and emergency relief to victims of World War I; promote arms reduction; preserve free trade and freedom for private financial transactions. |
| | Dissenters: territorial revisionism. | | |

TABLE 2 · 2
(continued)

| Period | Aims of states | Methods of states | Tasks of international organizations |
|---|---|---|---|
| 1932-1940 | Victors: preservation of entire *status quo*. | Victors: appeasement, slight rearmament | None of importance to world politics and economics. |
| | Dissenters: territorial enlargement, autarky. | Dissenters: subversion, propaganda, aggression. | |
| 1945-1947 | Victors: preservation of new political *status quo*, colonial system, global free enterprise. | Development of collective security through Big Power consensus; indoctrination and reform of vanquished states; return to competitive world trade and investment. | Achieve collective security through Big Power concert; give emergency relief to victims of World War II; promote world trade rules stressing non-discrimination and unfettered investment; promote arms reduction. |
| | Dissenters: not heard | | |
| 1948-1951 | West: preservation of total *status quo*. | Alliances, bilateral economic aid, multilateral technical aid, propaganda, collective security *against* East, limited war. | Achieve collective security through authority delegated to U.S. and its allies; give technical assistance; do some regional economic planning for industrialization; advocate Western-controlled human rights. |
| | East: expansion into Europe and Asia; support of nationalist and communist revolts. | Subversion, aggression, propaganda, limited war, alliances. | |

TABLE 2 · 2

(continued)

| Period | Aims of states | Methods of states | Tasks of international organizations |
|--------|----------------|-------------------|-------------------------------------|
| 1952-1955 | West: preservation of *territorial status quo;* catering to third forces otherwise. | Alliances, bilateral military and economic aid, nuclear buildup, propaganda. | Achieve collective security through third-world mediation between East and West; give more technical assistance; advocate more general human rights; provide more varied technical services for underdeveloped countries. |
| | East: aid to nationalist and communist revolts. | Propaganda, subversion, nuclear buildup, alliances. | |
| | Others: profit from Cold War, for further national and economic development. | Agitation, revolts, economic planning | |
| 1956-1960 | West: adaptation to third force by winning or neutralizing it. | Stabilization of balance of terror; multilateral economic aid; UN stabilization of third force. | Achieve collective security through cautious supranational leadership of UN Secretary-General; give much more extensive economic aid; institute ambitious technical aid programs; intervene collectively for decolonization and human rights. |
| | East: adaptation to third force by winning or neutralizing it; support for decolonization. | Stabilization of balance of terror; bilateral military and economic aid to new nations; some support for UN aid programs, limited war; propaganda in new states. | |
| | Others: profit from Cold War for further national and economic development; containment of Cold War and nuclear arms; dislodgment of colonial powers. | Aggression, limited war, more external military and economic aid; legitimation of total national self-determination. | |

TABLE 2 · 2
(concluded)

| Period | Aims of states | Methods of states | Tasks of international organizations |
|---|---|---|---|
| Since 1961 | West: same as above, with Europe more eager than U.S. to adapt; mute Cold War. | Stabilize balance of terror; arms control, decolonization, supranational economic aid, encouragement of trade; less stress on alliances, military aid, propaganda. | Achieve collective security through supranational leadership and Big Power concert; massively promote human rights and decolonization; establish new world trade norms; control arms; explore implications of science; greatly expand investment aid to developing countries. |
| | East: same as above, with USSR most eager to adapt; mute Cold War; reduction of involvement in new countries while stress is laid on decolonization. | Balance of terror; arms control; encouragement of trade; economic aid; less stress on alliances, military aid, propaganda (*after* nuclear bid in Cuba). | |
| | Others: same as above (with several different blocs of unaligned states); reorganization of world trade and finance systems. | Subversion, limited war, aggression, regional economic bloc formation. | |

## 5. Systems, Learning, and Perception

States "learn," not according to stimulus-response theory, but by adapting their objectives and methods to what can be conceived as attainable by their decision-makers. Learning is a rational process of redefining objectives and changing methods—though the original objectives may ultimately be traced back to "irrational" causes—as leaders discover that persistence with the initial aims is self-defeating or too costly. Hence international bargaining serves as a school in which such lessons are learned.

Considered from the vantage point of the international system itself, we can express the process differently. The initial objectives of states, as determined by their internal characteristics, are the explicit purposes that lead to demands made of other states in international organizations. In order to gain acceptance of these purposes, a price has to be paid to the purposes of other states, perhaps in a different issue area. The purpose, once accepted by the organization, becomes its immediate task, and its program is built around it. Programs, however, cannot be fully realized, because of faulty planning, inadequate power, low budgets, or national opposition. Disappointment and the hope for better performance in the future are a consequence unintended by those who first framed the task. The lessons of what could and could not be achieved are fed back into the national states. They then propose new purposes. These can either increase or decrease the task of the organization. In either event, learning has taken place through the feedback process triggered by unintended consequences.

Two brief examples will illustrate this process. Frustrated by Soviet opposition to meeting the demands of Western collective security, the United States sponsored, and the UN adopted, the Uniting for Peace Resolution. In 1950 it was thought that a Western-controlled General Assembly would vote the appropriate powers to a coalition of states eager to take on enforcement duties. As an unintended consequence of this sudden catering to the small powers —especially as more were admitted in 1955—these states proved exceedingly uninterested in meeting the purpose the United States had in mind in 1950. Hence, contrary to intentions, no new constitutional powers were bestowed on the General Assembly. The Uniting for Peace Resolution languished from disuse. As a second unforeseen consequence, however, the Secretary-General assumed prominence in the collective security issue area. With the Security Council deadlocked and the General Assembly unwilling or unable to act rapidly, the Secretary-General, in dispute after dispute after 1956, assumed the initiative with a certain measure of autonomy in organizing UN collective measures.

The role of the General Assembly in making new international law illustrates a deceptive trend toward functional adaptation. As part of Cold War and anticolonialist propaganda, various states at various times assumed the responsibility for having the General Assembly adopt declarations on human rights. Whatever the original intent, these declarations were soon used by other countries to press for changes in national policy, often in political contexts which had not been in the minds of the original sponsors. Some even argued that these declarations possess the force of law, if and when invoked often enough and respected in state practice. In short, as an unintended consequence of an immediate and expediential motive, new comprehensive international law is said to come into existence. In fact, the reluctance of states to ratify conventions resulting from the process—indeed, the insistence that the declarations be transformed into conventions—suggests that the claim is exaggerated. But it illustrates the process of international learning.

This model of international system transformation credits the international organization with the capacity to produce feedbacks that result in changed perceptions on the part of national actors. The alternative model puts the emphasis on autonomous changes within nations. Developments in the various domestic social, economic, and political sectors are conceived as proceeding more rapidly and decisively than the learning of lessons fed back from the international system. New demands will then be put on the system also. These will still encounter other new or opposing demands. The system may not gain any net power at the expense of the member nations but will be transformed, just the same, because it is given new tasks.

System transformation can be due to either or both processes. But only the "feedback" model gives rise to tighter interdependence. The "autonomous internal change" model—in isolation—results in a system that remains largely static. When feedbacks result in adaptive learning among elites, the result is likely to be a stronger system with more autonomous power. When new tasks evolve from rapidly changing domestic impulses, the system's powers have barely a chance to keep up with the changing mixture of demands. In the actual history of the United Nations and the specialized agencies, the second model comes closer to describing the truth.

But what if actors were to say, "We defy the international system to influence our national way of life; we have no demands of the international system except to be left alone"? Mao's China and

Sukarno's Indonesia suggest that the attempt at full withdrawal from international life may still appear desirable and feasible to statesmen. The reaction of statesmen and peoples to external and internal demands and lessons is not simply a function of the intensity of the stimulus. The frame of mind, the values, the doctrines and institutions of each nation are important in determining whether the feedback model, the autonomous internal change model, or outright isolationism provides the mechanism for strengthening or breaking the web of interdependence.

Much depends on whether statesmen make decisions according to the bureaucratic, charismatic, or ideological style of thinking. All are able to learn, unless they are possessed of suicidal or paranoid traits. These three styles have different implications for system transformation, because each also describes a different way of perception. Ideological and charismatic views are imbued with consummatory qualities. They refer to cherished beliefs, passionate hopes, and hallowed traditions. Bureaucratic views are highly instrumental, and policies produced by them lend themselves to bargaining and accommodation. It follows that the more adaptable international systems are made up of states whose leaders respond to bureaucratic-pragmatic impulses. Difficulty in carrying on negotiations is typical of systems made up of a large number of countries professing passionate views that blame foreign "enemies" and "obstacles" for blocking the realization of national hopes. The League of Nations suffered accordingly after 1935, and the UN between 1948 and 1956. Peaceful transition of international systems, to strengthen the web, is facilitated if (1) the actors, or at least the most powerful, think and learn in bureaucratic terms; and (2) the actors are overwhelmingly devoted to the perfection of their own societies without making dramatic claims on foreigners.

When peoples and their leaders think more in charismatic and ideological terms, they tend at the same time to involve themselves more readily in making claims on foreigners: they demand capital, know-how, and independence. They also want protection against "imperialist" or "racist" or "Communist" enemies, and they blame their shortcomings and misfortunes at the national level on their foreign "enemies." When this is the case, learning depends almost entirely on autonomous changes taking place internally in such countries, and the web of interdependence becomes confused rather than strengthened.

Have Americans "learned" to respond primarily to systemic impulses and adjust to the web so that they reinforce it? There is some evidence that they have. When asked in 1965 whether international or domestic problems facing the United States were most important, 58 per cent stressed international problems. A maximum of 11 per cent, since 1950, thought that the United States should leave the UN. In 1963, 82 per cent felt that the United States must work with other nations. And only 31 per cent felt in 1966 that the United States should withdraw from the UN if Communist China were admitted to the organization.

# CHAPTER THREE

# AMERICAN DEMOCRACY AND THE INTERNATIONAL SYSTEM

### 1. Democracy and Foreign Policy: Three Models

Whether we look at the phenomenon of American foreign-policy-making from the perspective of the actor or the observer, there is no unambiguous and universally accepted view on the exact relationship among public opinion, political parties, the State Department, the President, Congress, and the United Nations. We think we know the general thrust of influence, but our intuitive knowledge soon evaporates under the heat of some searching questions. Yet we must know, so that we may discover how, if at all, America adapts to changes in the international system.

In a general way, we all agree that in a democracy public opinion significantly influences policy. Or are we merely saying that it *should* influence policy but that actually it may fail to do so? We also agree that public opinion is the sum of individual opinions. These, in turn, are the attitudes we, as citizens, hold toward the role the United States should (or does?) play with respect to other countries. Our attitudes, in turn, are said to be determined by our personalities; but they are also shaped by the values we imbibed. Are individual attitudes crucial in shaping generalized public opinion? The experts disagree. But they confirm that attitudes are brought to bear on policy-making only in the mold of some specific "situation," such as a crisis or an election, which focuses the attention of the citizen on a choice to be made.

Attitudes and public opinion, it is agreed, do not influence government in a direct way. What intervenes? Certain special groupings of citizens—interest groups, community groups, respected commentators ("opinion leaders")—speak to and for the individual citizen. Especially influential groups of citizens—elites—are admitted to exist even in democracies, and somehow they intervene between the public and government. But how and when?

Policy is clearly "made" in Washington. Congress discusses policy and votes funds; political parties, in and out of Congress, channel divergent policy demands; officials in government agencies study the needs and position of the United States and make proposals for action; and the President selects from these proposals the course of action he then puts before Congress, the public, and the world. Is he influenced by public opinion, by the parties, by elites? At least three different views exist on *how* public opinion, elite groups, and government are interconnected.

One such model we may call "pure democracy." Individuals are expected to be interested in public issues and the role of America abroad. They are also expected to inform themselves by reading, discussion, and attention to information and interpretations provided by the communication media. United in their local world affairs council, they express their opinions in their votes for congressional and presidential candidates and in the letters they write to their elected representatives. The policy proposed by the President or Congress, then, reflects the sum of informed opinion thrust upward and the balance of informed views. When the American representative in the UN speaks in the name of the United States, he truly speaks for the American people.

What is wrong with this model? Forty per cent of Americans never bother to vote; not less than 75 per cent are ill-informed, emotional in reaction to public affairs, disinterested in foreign policy. Only the more spectacular crises or situations—major wars or space exploits—manage to excite as many as 75 per cent of Americans to a shallow and temporary interest in world affairs. Occasionally, a dramatic crisis suddenly makes the general public wake up. The people may then impulsively embrace a total solution and call for drastic foreign action, or they may break up into several passionate camps, each advocating contradictory total solutions. Perhaps 3 per cent of Americans think about foreign affairs in a way that meets the minimal criteria of rational action: make sure that an individual's attitudes are internally consistent and bear a good correspondence to objectively determined facts. Probably less than 1 per cent combine rational attitudes with a willingness to lobby and influence the government.[1]

In each community there are, of course, people who combine information, interest, influence, and the willingness to act—the active membership of world affairs councils, committees, and centers. Do they speak for public opinion? Studies of foreign policy decision-making suggest that such community and opinion leaders often act as *downward* transmission belts of information, attitudes, and policy desires that originate in government. The opinion-transmission process frequently starts at the top and utilizes local opinion leaders to persuade the public, rather than taking the reverse route.

Even then there is no consistent and reliable link between public opinion and congressional or presidential action. For example, Congress voted military aid to Greece, passed the Marshall Plan, and approved U.S. membership in several technical international organizations, even though public opinion polls showed initial majority opposition to these steps. The President acquiesced in the UN's intervening in internal Congolese affairs even though the majority of opinion-makers in the media disapproved of this step. "Democracy is like nearly everything else we do; it is a form of collaboration of ignorant people and experts. . . . The power of the people in a democracy depends on the *importance* of the decisions made by the electorate, not on the *number* of decisions they make." [2] In foreign affairs, at least, the number is too small and the importance too questionable to support the "pure democracy" model.

Hence why not stress the role of elites intervening between public and government? This brings us to the "pluralist" model. The public is admitted to be as inert as it seems to be. Government then is held to be influenced by myriad organized groups—economic, religious,

---

[1] For these and similar statistics, see Alfred O. Hero, *Americans in World Affairs* (Boston: World Peace Foundation, 1959); James N. Rosenau, *Public Opinion and Foreign Policy* (New York: Random House, 1961). Ninety per cent of Americans do not consider world affairs a major determinant of their vote for President. Fewer than 15 per cent have ever written to an individual or agency in government. For a discussion of rationality, see William A. Scott, "Rationality and Non-rationality of International Attitudes," *Journal of Conflict Resolution* (March, 1958).

[2] E. E. Schattschneider, *The Semisovereign People* (New York: Holt, 1960), pp. 137, 140.

ethnic, military, professional. Each group defends its own viewpoint on policy, as articulated through the values explicitly shared by the membership, through the ideology professed by each group. Economic, professional, and communication elites at the apex of each group enjoy the support of the mass membership and access to the government—these elites are the brokers between the public and Washington. Democracy is maintained because each coalition of groups is held to bring into being an opposing coalition with which the first has to bargain before policy is made. Public policy, then, is the product of countervailing power wielded by interest groups through their elites.

One possible objection to this model is the undeniable fact that interest and commitment with respect to foreign affairs are consistently and highly correlated with advanced education and high socioeconomic status, irrespective of occupation or group affiliation. It is the educated and highly placed in their respective communities who lead opinion and profess concern for world affairs. Yet it is also true that the same people sometimes hold elite positions in interest groups and may thus meet the demands of the model. A stronger objection is the role claimed for interest groups. Do they really persuade a determined President or a committed majority in Congress? Do all interest groups figure in this process? If not, which ones, how often? Do they really match power with power, coalition with opposing coalition, or does the advice of the expert—the military or civilian bureaucrat in the Pentagon and State Department—count more heavily than the weight of group pressure? When public opinion polls uniformly tell us that in grave international crises, confidence in the President always rises—regardless of who occupies the office, or the locale of the crisis—we may wonder what happened to countervailing power. To many partisans of the peace movement in the United States, the pluralist model appears merely as a façade behind which the "Establishment" rules without check by any opposing force of opinion.

Undeniably, there has usually been a strong American consensus cutting across groups and regions. This fact has led dissenters from this consensus to advance a third model of American democracy, the "power elite" model. It argues that foreign policy decisions are made by an inner clique of industrialists and military men unable and unwilling to depart from a rigid commitment to the economic, racial, and ideological *status quo* — nationally and internationally. Congress, the bureaucracy, and the President are merely the creatures of this Establishment. International peace demands that the power elite be checked and defeated by the masses who are not committed to the *status quo* and who must make themselves into a true countervailing power in order to penetrate and reform the Establishment.[3]

If the argument of the power elite school sounds like the complaint of the groups that have failed to make themselves prevail within American democracy, the complaint nevertheless points up some weak spots in the pluralist model. The model is correct in pinpointing the role of interest groups and opposing elites, but it errs in exaggerating the degree of opposition. It is right in minimizing the influence of individuals and of public opinion on foreign policy; it goes too far by ignoring the mood of the public altogether. Pluralism accurately reflects the practice of American democracy in stressing the influence of interest groups on government; it distorts reality by depriving the government of the undeniable capacity to manipulate groups and to ignore them. Between the decision-makers in Washington and the public throughout America, there intervene groups and institutions that "make" and "submit" opinions. The opinion-makers are the communication media and the leaders of groups. At the same time, the leaders of interest groups also submit opinions to government, whether or not the opinions are based on the views of the membership. Which leaders—and which groups—can be regarded as influential? If decision-makers and observers consider a given group important and if the opinions submitted to government by that group tend to prevail as policy, we are entitled to infer that such groups are important in foreign policy-making. We can affirm the existence of these processes in American democracy; we cannot assert with precision when and where the influence of any one actor will prevail, though we must review the regularities in public opinion and individual attitudes that do recur.

## 2. Society, Attitudes, and Public Opinion

Are Americans predisposed toward joining with other nations in common institutions? Are they willing to

[3] The literature on this topic is extensive. For a moderate version of this model, arguing that because of the pervasive consensus the United States *is* a military-industrial complex unable to meet the requisites of peace unless challenged by "the Movement," see Marc Pilisuk and Thomas Hayden, "Is There a Military-Industrial Complex Which Prevents Peace? Consensus and Countervailing Power in Pluralistic Systems," *Journal of Social Issues* (July, 1965).

commit themselves to contractual obligations and joint enterprises with foreign nations? Do they accept aid to developing countries, military alliances, intervention abroad, increased trade, and immigration as natural and desirable? Studies linking personality with opinion toward isolationism and nonisolationism suggest that Americans are overwhelmingly so disposed and do accept interdependence—at least in the international systems that have prevailed since 1945. Isolationism in modern America is a deviant stance.

The same studies, however, also show that "isolationist beliefs are far more common among the general population than they are among the political leaders. Similarly, isolationism is more frequently expressed among the less educated than the more educated. . . . Isolationism increases as political and social awareness decline: it is more common among the unthinking than among the informed segments of the electorate, stronger among the poor, the culturally deprived, and any other groups who have been cut off from the mainstreams of the articulate culture." [4]

If leaders tend to be less isolationist than the mass of Americans are, Republicans and conservatives generally are more likely to be so inclined than are Democrats and liberals. In fact, socioeconomic conservatism has in the past been a good predictor of isolationist beliefs, though this is probably no longer true.

Much the same lesson can be inferred from the way isolationists and nonisolationists respond to specific policy issues. Among political leaders, nonisolationists also overwhelmingly favor strengthening the UN, increasing immigration, and relying on military alliances. Isolationist leaders favor decreases in defense spending and foreign aid—an issue on which nonisolationist leaders feel at least ambivalent. Contrast this with opinion at the mass level. Here things cannot be neatly dichotomized; isolationist preferences do not correlate cleanly with unambiguous policy positions. Again, however, socioeconomic conservatism on domestic issues does go hand in hand with isolationist policy preferences abroad.

These findings applied fully to the UN during the 1950's. The educated and higher status groups overwhelmingly supported the UN as a meaningful method of advancing American foreign policy and world peace—though they tended to equate the two. While all strata of the population supported the UN in a general way, only these groups combined knowledge with a deeper commitment and constituted a firm base of supporting opinion.

After 1955, the United States was less and less able to use the

[4] Herbert McClosky, "Personality and Attitude Correlates of Foreign Policy Orientation," in J. Rosenau, ed., *Domestic Sources of Foreign Policy* (New York: Free Press, 1967), p. 63.

UN for the realization of national policy. As the world grew multi-polar and as different kinds of power were diffused asymmetrically, the United States had to yield to unfriendly majorities and compromise its preferences on many occasions. Did the legitimacy of the UN in the eyes of the American public suffer as a result? Did the authority of the UN over the will of the informed and concerned American decline, as one might suspect? It did not.

Support for the UN has run far ahead of support for foreign aid, lower tariffs, coexistence with communism, cultural exchange programs. Support for the UN was less and less linked with specific preferences for items in American foreign policy. Since 1960, never less than 92 per cent of Americans have supported the UN, compared with 86 per cent in 1951. Eighty per cent feel that the UN is doing a good job and is important to the United States. Over half of all Americans believe the UN prevented World War III and 66 per cent want the UN to have a stronger role in peace-keeping with military forces. In 1966, there were 25 per cent who would have admitted Communist China; only 11 per cent in 1951. With exceptions to be noted, by 1966, class, occupation, sex, status, urban or rural residence, and region no longer accounted for any significant variation in support for the UN. But education continued to predict the most world-minded. The educated everywhere, however, also manifested a greater readiness to distinguish between support for the UN and attitudes on specific international issues, and supporters of the UN were no longer necessarily sanguine that the UN would assure peace and plenty. Further, popular support for the UN was more consistent and stronger than congressional enthusiasm for the world organization.

What are the exceptions to this astounding state of affairs? While significant regional differences in attitudes have disappeared, the South continues to be somewhat less reconciled to interdependence than the rest of the country. Moreover, southern opposition to the UN in particular and international cooperation in general has increased in proportion to the intensification of the civil rights struggle. Lower- and lower-middle-class people are somewhat more likely to oppose the UN; and among all religions, Jews are most likely to favor it. Negroes, before 1960, tended to be indifferent to UN issues but since that time have grown to favor the organization.[5]

[5] For the period 1945-1955, the most comprehensive treatment of public opinion toward the UN was made by William A. Scott and Stephen B. Withey, *The United States and the United Nations* (New York: Manhattan Publishing Co., 1958). For the period 1955-1966, a complete review is provided by Alfred O. Hero, "The American Public and the UN, 1954-1966," *Journal of Conflict Resolution* (December, 1966). My treatment is a summary of both studies.

Since we are concerned with the interplay between the system as seen by the observer and the actor, we must be particularly sensitive to shifts in perception and attitude characteristic of different age groups. Do the young see the world and the UN as do the older generations? Are they less or more willing to live in a differently ruled world? As a whole, the young are more willing to give up sovereignty and to make concessions to opinions and demands contrary to American policy. Table 3.1 recapitulates general shifts in willingness to dismantle the sovereign nation and highlights the views of the young.[6]

This survey of opinion clearly supports a generalization ventured ten years ago:

> Repeated surveys of the attitudes of the American public toward the United Nations have disclosed two principal and paradoxical facts: (1) The large majority of Americans approve the United Nations as a vital instrument in dealing with the great problems of the day and this support is not easily shaken by occasional adverse developments. (2) This support is not, however, solidly based on intelligent understanding of what the United Nations is, what it can realistically be expected to do, what its relationship is to the personal life of the average citizen. The public's faith in the United Nations is the result of a vague quest to fulfill ill-defined emotional requirements rather than an appreciation of the importance of the world organization in today's complex civilization.[7]

Public opinion, then, cannot use specific and consistent terms to tell elites or governments what our foreign policy should be. At best, it forms dikes "which channel public action or which fix a range of discretion within which government may act or within which debate at official levels may proceed." [8] Public opinion defines large substantive areas of consensus that *permit* the government to act and to justify itself after the event. Being permissive, public opinion can be aroused after an action committing the United States has already been taken. Only very rarely—in the field of foreign affairs—does the consensus prohibit the government from taking action.

---

[6] Adapted from Hero, "The American Public and the UN, 1954-1966," *ibid.*
[7] Carnegie Endowment for International Peace, *The United States Public and the United Nations: Report on a Study of American Attitudes on the U.N. and the Communication of Information to the U.S. Public* (New York: Carnegie Endowment for International Peace, 1958), p. 9.
[8] V. O. Key, *Public Opinion and American Democracy* (New York: Knopf, 1961), p. 532.

TABLE 3 · 1
Ways of Achieving Peace

*"While everyone seems to agree that peace is an important thing, there are a good many different views as to how to bring it about. Here are some different ideas. . . . Will you . . . tell me which one you come closest to agreeing with?" (From "A Study of Attitudes Concerning Closer Ties Among Democratic Nations." New York: Elmo Roper Assoc., mimeographed, September, 1963, p. vi.)*

| Selected as best way to bring about peace | July 1953 (N = 3502) Per cent | July 1963 (N = 3007) Per cent | July 1963 21-34 yr.-olds Per cent |
|---|---|---|---|
| We shouldn't get tied up in any more alliances or joint commitments with other countries and we should aim at getting out of as many as we can as soon as we can. | 9 | 6 | 3 |
| We should continue to work along with the United Nations just about as we have been, gradually trying to make it better as time goes on. | 21 | 22 | 22 |
| We should immediately get behind *strengthening* the United Nations and do everything necessary to give it more power and authority than it has—enough to actually keep even a strong nation from starting a war. | 35 | 39 | 44 |
| In addition to continuing with the United Nations, we should also unite with the friendly democratic countries into one government in which each member nation would in effect become a state, somewhat like the different states in this country. | 6 | 6 | 6 |
| We should start now working towards transforming the United Nations into a real world government of *all* nations of the world, in which every nation would in effect become a state, somewhat like the different states in this country. | 11 | 11 | 13 |
| Some of these ideas are good, but we won't get any of them working in time to prevent war, so we'd better not rely on them. | 7 | 6 | 6 |
| Don't know or no answer. | 11 | 10 | 6 |

Gabriel Almond has called the areas of consensus delimited by the dikes of public opinion the "mood" of the American people. That mood is as shallow as the opinions of which it is made up, and as changeable. It fluctuates between the extremes of indifference to foreign affairs and oversimplification of foreign threats, between optimism and pessimism, the desire to withdraw from the web of interdependence and the determination to intervene regularly abroad. The mood wavers between pessimistic and cynical tolerance of other nations, and optimistic, idealistic intolerance designed to make the world more American through American aid and sacrifice.

Naturally, a sharply experienced crisis can trigger a radical shift in mood. Since many people who support the UN also oppose foreign aid and express a desire to increase domestic welfare without raising taxes, a depression or a war or a housing crisis can possibly trigger an isolationist revival. Intensified racial strife might bring about the same thing. In fact, some contemporary dissenters from the general consensus identify with neither of the two main moods, favoring an active American policy identifying with the revolutionary Third World instead; however, such people are committed to an explicit ideology rather than to a mere mood. A mood, unlike an ideology, hardly provides a firm ground for a consistent policy approved by the public; but it permits leaders great leeway in action and legitimates a broad range of specific steps.

Weak opinions can easily be channeled, if not changed, by strong sources, by persuasive opinion-makers. When President Eisenhower proposed a more active role for the UN, he was heartily applauded by editors, columnists, and TV commentators; but when Nikita Khrushchev proposed the troika formula for the UN, the makers of public comment rallied to the support of the UN as constituted. Leadership and the dissemination of the leader's opinions by the opinion-makers are particularly important in a setting in which shallow and shifting moods account for the bulk of the inattentive public's reaction. Because the moods are shallow, they respond to manipulation by respected authorities. Hence we turn to a discussion of elites, interest groups, and foreign policy.

### 3. Interest Groups, Elites, and Politics

That America is a nation of joiners has been known for some time. Americans join permanent, large, multi-purpose groups like fraternal organizations; durable, large, but single-purpose efforts such as labor unions and trade associations; and small, less durable, but intensely committed groups, such as *ad hoc* committees to advance this or that momentary cause. All such efforts at organized political action belong to the genus "interest group"; but they vary as to the *scope* of their interests, the *intensity* of the interest, and the *duration* of effective interest. We know little that is systematic and beyond question about interest-group influence on foreign policy. Let us make the effort to list what we do know, enumerating typical organizations and classifying them according to the three dimensions mentioned. We can then attempt to assess the effectiveness of each type on foreign policy.

The groups most familiar to everyone are the large civic, fraternal, and educational groups such as the world affairs councils, Masons, women's clubs, the National Federation of Business and Professional Women, and—in many communities—the senior and junior Chambers of Commerce. These groups are intended to be permanent, and they devote their attention to a very wide spectrum of issues, ranging from local charity and improvement to the UN and world peace. The wider the spectrum of their concern, the lower is the intensity of their attention for any one issue. The League of Women Voters is rarely successful in organizing a local community on single foreign policy issues, such as the 1962 Trade Expansion Act. The American Association of University Women maintains national and local committees on legislation; but they are rarely heard, even though they stand for a clear policy in favor of a strong UN. The American Legion has failed for decades in trying to make the government downgrade the UN. Masons, Elks, Rotarians number many millions of Americans among their members, but their size and diversity of interests condemn these organizations to a passive role in foreign policy-making.

But these are the groups that contain the local "notables" of American politics. Individuals with status, education, and concern —the attentive public—generally belong to such groups. They respond first to appeals coming from the government; they join the special committees and commissions designed to arouse public concern when Washington considers a major shift in foreign policy; they are the prime recipients and participants in a *downward* flow of influence. On the other hand, they may also influence that policy by virtue of their membership on the major citizens advisory bodies associated with government programs, such as the Freedom from Hunger Foundation or the General Advisory Committee of the U.S. Arms Control and Disarmament Agency. Their beliefs cluster at the internationalist end of the attitude spectrum.

Groups of notables tend to facilitate government initiatives rather than launch innovations of their own. A second type of group, however, does take the initiative. Here we think of multipurpose organizations of a permanent nature or "attention groups" that experience an intense commitment to certain single issues. Predominantly, this includes American religious bodies and ethnic groups. The Ancient Order of Hibernians is not greatly interested in foreign policy unless the issue of Ulster is raised. American Jews focus on the UN only when Israel and the fate of Jews abroad seem to matter. The Catholic Church is active in foreign affairs—as an organized group—only when the issue seems to be atheistic communism. The American Friends Service Committee is particularly active when the issue is one of international understanding and conciliation. Groups of this character also include notables and local elites. They are sometimes of crucial importance in initiating and demanding specific *single* actions or bills in Washington, but not in consistent and long-range foreign affairs activity.

Thirdly, we have the major economic and occupational interest groups. They are permanent organizations, with the single, major purpose of advancing the economic well-being of workers, farmers, businessmen or professional people, and an intense commitment to those aspects of foreign policy that are related to the main organizational purpose. Like the civic and fraternal groups, their leaders are part of the elite that has access to government and communicates between the mass membership and the inattentive public, on the one hand, and the makers of policy, on the other. Like the notables, leaders of these interest groups are the nongovernmental elites of American society who participate in fashioning the public consensus in support of policy; unlike those leaders, they take a continuous and active part in initiating suggestions and demands for policy.

These groups display more of an ideological structure in their approach than do unorganized individuals or multipurpose organizations, though they are not typically rigid. The American Federation of Labor–Congress of Industrial Organizations has supported a militant anticommunist policy and is committed to the stimulation of free trade unions abroad, cast in the pluralist mold. The National Students Association has generally supported government policy, though it has demanded stronger and more radical steps in favor of decolonization and human rights in Africa and Latin America—blaming the United States for faltering in this area. The major business groups—U.S. National Chamber of Commerce, National Association of Manufacturers, Committee for Economic Development—have all supported the general line of policy since 1945, including increasing participation in the UN and other international organizations. Regarding general policy, then, these groups are not necessarily significant or powerful.

Their influence is much stronger on specific issues, such as a fisheries agreement, tariff negotiations, immigration of farm labor, and certain aspects of foreign aid (e.g., the rule that half of American aid must be shipped on American vessels). Here, influence can be attributed to the fact that congressmen and administrative officials close to the group's concerns are accessible to lobbying and that these policy-makers sometimes depend on information and arguments from the lobbyists for their ammunition. Further, the demands are often precise, clearly linked to the welfare of an identifiable group or voting bloc, and not really contested by any other group. Under those circumstances, specific economic group demands can often see enactment. Yet on other, or more general, issues, the same groups are powerless because neither congressmen nor administrators need pay any attention to them.

Businessmen tend to be more and more committed to freer trade and to international competition, an attitude that is correlated with a belief that an open world and an open United States contribute to strengthening democracy at the expense of communism. The larger and better-informed business groups and firms display these commitments to a greater extent than the smaller ones. Yet even these "people fail to see where their self-interest lies." [9] Assessments and calculations of interest are couched in immediate short-run terms; they are seldom based on careful analysis, even when they are made by single-purpose interest groups with intense and focused commitments. American interest groups—whether business or labor—are far from constituting a single-minded, powerful, and consistent bloc in favor of free enterprise and anticommunism.

Our final type of interest group differs from the three we have analyzed, in that its members usually are part of the opposition to government policy and that its leaders are not typically part of the opinion-making elites who occupy powerful positions in American life. We here deal with single-purpose groups of intense commitment, usually temporary in nature and organized around a single, burning issue. United World Federalists (membership: 20,000) is such a group. The China Lobby of the 1940's was another one. At the end of the 1930's, two *ad hoc* groupings opposed each other actively: one determined to keep the United States out of World

[9] Raymond A. Bauer, Ithiel de S. Pool, and Lewis A. Dexter, *American Business and Public Policy* (New York: Atherton, 1963), p. 128.

War II, the other determined to intervene on the side of Britain and France. The isolationist grouping tended to be the political "outs." The interventionists—in this instance—were broadly representative of the urban notables and important economic interest groups. They sought to influence Washington in favor of intervention, and the government gladly availed itself of the group's resources and prestige, to steer the country toward involvement, to exploit the shallow and diffuse mood prevailing at that time. In the late 1960's, the Peace Movement is the most significant grouping of this type.

As long as the movement simply sought to prepare antigovernment statements and projects and present these directly to policymakers, very little attention was paid to its efforts. These demands hinged mostly around disarmament, opposition to racial discrimination abroad, and the encouragement of "popular" regimes in Africa and Latin America. Much of the effort became irrelevant with the arms control agreements accepted by the superpowers and the end of colonialism (except in southern Africa). Even the World Federalists merely advocated piecemeal reform—the establishment of the Arms Control Agency, repeal of the Connally reservation, more financial support for the UN—and ran out of steam when many of them were enacted. The Peace Movement, however, regained relevance to foreign-policy-making when the Vietnam war became the central issue and tactics changed to mass action at the local level, including civil disobedience and violence. The effort was designed to fuse commitment to civil rights, pacifism, "people's liberation from imperialism," Negro nationalism, and general left-wing opposition to the style of American politics—and to fuse them at the mass level. Foreign policy became *the* issue on which disaffected groups sought to build a coalition of opposition forces, thus running counter to the pluralist-elitist flavor of public opinion and interest group action in the foreign-policy field. If the Peace Movement were to succeed, it would be the first time in American history that an *ad hoc* group of intense commitment—not part of the circle of regularly participating elites—signally affected the course of policy.

What about the military in this array of publics and groups? It is sometimes argued that the military constitutes an interest group of its own, advocating and implementing policy to protect its investment in weapons systems, strategic ideas, and foreign enemies—thus protecting its status and prestige in American life. It is undeniable that military experts do suggest strategies and influence decisions opting for this weapons system or that, thus committing the country to new strategies. Further, the identity of present and future enemies may be left to the judgment of the military professionals. The facts that we possess suggest, however, that the military is divided internally, that services squabble over strategies, missions, and weapons and that they do not necessarily see eye to eye on the character of the enemy. Even though the public is certainly excluded from military-political decisions, there is a great measure of internal pluralism among military organizations and among their civilian superiors, thus arguing against the unambiguous dominance of an "industrial-military complex."

Yet the military, like other segments of the federal bureaucracy, must maintain a typical political relationship with an appropriate civilian group. For the Department of Labor, this special constituency is the AFL-CIO; for the Department of Agriculture, it is the Farm Bureau Federation; and for the military and the Department of Defense, it is those segments of industry that specialize in manufacturing the weapons on which American military strategy is based. Does this give the aerospace industry, the steel industry, the merchant marine, or the field of electronics a special position of influence? Only if each were not subject to countervailing influence or check from above and were to profit consistently from its special relationship with the military. In point of fact, these branches of industry compete against one another and against still different constituencies of the Department of Defense, such as the National Guard Association, veterans' and patriotic organizations. War industry may be influential in determining which kind of missile or what type of reactor or submarine is to be made; its role in determining tactics and strategy abroad, in deciding on escalation or de-escalation is very much smaller. Finally, even this influence is subject to check by the ever more powerful office of the Secretary of Defense and the committees of Congress charged with supervising the Department of Defense.

Do businessmen or Protestants or Irishmen run American foreign policy? No single group—and no coalition—seems to be predictably influential on more than a single issue. All groups are more or less ineffective, unless welded into a special coalition for a great purpose consistent with the ideological commitments of the major elites and the government. Even business groups, which are the most effective of all the organizations we have surveyed, "are nevertheless only mildly influential and then only with respect to a rather narrow range of economic issues which comprise only a small proportion of the fundamental issues of American foreign policy." [10] We see

[10] Bernard Cohen, *Influence of Non-Governmental Groups on Foreign Policy-Making* (Boston: World Peace Foundation, 1959), p. 20. Also, Bauer, Pool, and Dexter, *op. cit.*, p. 488.

little hint of domination when we observe the successful efforts of a single-purpose, small and focused interest group, such as the Pacific Coast fisheries industry, to insert clauses favorable to it in a peace treaty. Indeed, the very flow of communications and messages is so complex and runs in so many diverse directions that the policy-maker is bombarded with not one set of demands or ideas, but with a plurality of clashing ones. The access of interest groups, in turn, is a competitive phenomenon. One group must fight with others for time; indeed, some studies suggest that interest groups spend a great deal of time seeking merely to arouse their own members to put pressure on the policy-maker. Many congressmen deliberately expose themselves to a cacophony of ideas through questionnaires addressed to their constituents or through community conferences held for them.

As for interest groups and the UN, the record shows the institutional logic of imperfect pluralism at work. For some years a Conference Group of national organizations attempted to speak for all major interests on matters relating to the UN. The Conference Group spoke for large, permanent, single-interest groups as well as for the larger multipurpose groupings, in addition to some *ad hoc* organizations. Since the UN was the only common denominator among the interests represented, the denominator was so low that it precluded effective action—and the Conference Group languished. Diverse membership implies diffuseness and lack of power. No single interest is triumphant; indeed, it would be more accurate to say that neither individual attitudes nor organized groups shape foreign policy in any regularly discernible fashion. Is there, then, a power elite that links the government to key persons in society and in the economy, and is it this elite that runs things?

## 4. Government, Bureaucracy, and the President

"In the realm of foreign policy there has not been a single major issue on which Presidents, when they were serious and determined, have failed." [11] An examination of how foreign policy decisions have been made over the last quarter of a

[11] Aaron Wildavsky, "The Two Presidencies." Copyright © 1966 by Washington University, St. Louis, Mo. Reprinted from *Trans-Action* magazine (December, 1966), p. 7.

century will permit no other conclusion. But how can that be, when Congress has the power to vote or withhold appropriations for all foreign and defense programs, when the Senate must approve treaties by a two-thirds majority, and when the committees of both Houses can, and do, investigate the operations of the Executive in foreign affairs? How can the President—as a person—dominate so completely when he has the State and Defense Departments as expert assistants, the National Security Council, the Joint Chiefs of Staff, and the foreign policy demands of less involved agencies such as the Atomic Energy Commission and the Department of Labor and Agriculture? How can one man prevail over several armies of specialists and professionals in foreign and defense questions?

Let us examine the presidential dominance thesis first with respect to Congress. Table 3.2 shows the degree of presidential suc-

TABLE 3 · 2

Congressional Action
on Presidential Proposals from 1948 to 1964

| Policy area | Congressional action % Passed | % Failed | Number of proposals |
|---|---|---|---|
| Domestic policy (natural resources, labor, agriculture, taxes, etc.) | 40.2 | 59.8 | 2499 |
| Defense policy (defense, disarmament, manpower, misc.) | 73.3 | 26.7 | 90 |
| Foreign policy | 58.5 | 41.5 | 655 |
| Immigration, refugees | 13.2 | 86.0 | 129 |
| Treaties, general foreign relations, State Department, foreign aid | 70.8 | 29.2 | 445 |

Source: Aaron Wildavsky, "The Two Presidencies." Copyright © 1966 by Washington University, St. Louis, Mo. Reprinted from *Trans-action* magazine (December, 1966).

cess in dealing with Congress. But that is to assume that Congress *wishes* to oppose the President. James A. Robinson found that

the scope of congressional influence varies with the constitutional provisions governing the making and conduct of foreign relations. The Senate, with an advantage in confirming diplomatic appointments and approving treaties, has not exploited the former and is finding the latter less and less an important instrument of policy. The House, with an advantage deriving from its constitutional position with respect to appropriations, awaits the executive budget and reacts to it by legitimating or cutting it, but rarely by raising it. . . . Finally the domain of Congressional influence, especially when it is initiative, tends to be on marginal and relatively less important issues.[12]

Thus congressmen tend to react to presidential initiatives, recommendations, messages, and instructions, rather than to assert themselves independently. Senators, more often than not, consider it their job to facilitate the President's leadership, rather than to oppose or modify his initiatives. Though the President must evaluate the likelihood of congressional opposition to his plans—and in this sense Congress has a deterrent effect—the legislators on the *whole* and as a *bloc* do not wish to oppose him or detract from his leadership. Still, individual senators commonly oppose him; occasionally a congressional committee or a strong minority on it takes the initiative in blocking or criticizing an aspect of foreign policy. But as long as the President vigorously fights for his preferences, these challenges rarely succeed.

The normal play of party politics, in short, does not operate clearly and consistently in foreign policy-making. The two major parties do not frontally and consistently disagree on foreign and defense policy questions. There is, at the center of the political spectrum in Congress, a considerable overlap among liberal Republicans and the bulk of northeastern moderate Democrats, and this coalition has provided the "foreign policy consensus" in the last twenty years. Neither party is a disciplined entity, and prolonged negotiations within each party are necessary before the party caucus takes a firm position. Thus a skillful President can rule with the help of shifting coalitions of party factions; his manipulative talents can exploit congressional incoherence, division, and desire to defer to a more knowing source of information. This means that conservative Republicans and southern Democrats who advocate some version of withdrawal from, or all-out offensive in, world affairs have been more or less consistently deprived of influence. It also means that radical Democrats who favor retrenchment in military affairs and a foreign policy exclusively dedicated to "peace" have suffered the same fate.

[12] James A. Robinson, *Congress and Foreign Policy-Making* (Homewood, Ill.: Dorsey, 1962), p. 14.

There are several reasons for this nonpartisanship. Congressmen, as a rule, are under minimal pressure from their constituents on questions of foreign policy, thus permitting each legislator to vote as he pleases or respond to presidential initiatives. This naturally gives respected experts or persuasive advocates greater influence than they have on many domestic issues. It is true, as former Secretary of State Dean Acheson said, that administration officials spend as much as one-sixth of their time appearing before congressional committees to explain and advocate foreign policy measures. While the President's men must justify themselves continuously, they almost always have their way.

Although congressional committees have been accommodating in accepting administration requests for regional and collective security measures, there are nevertheless some sharp limits to congressional compliance. The formidable Joint Committee on Atomic Energy has gone its own way, and the administration has respected its autonomy by seeking to avoid international nuclear steps that would require the committee's approval. Congress has rarely disputed the creation of new international organizations or America's membership in them. Nor have the legislators as a group quarreled with the principle of foreign aid, bilateral or multilateral. They have, however, balked sharply at the amounts of aid, the sums contributed by the United States to international organizations, and the creation of world trade rules considered to impinge on congressional prerogatives with respect to tariff policy. We will note these limits on American learning and participation later. Congressional insistence on financial caution in supporting international commitments is clearly apparent in the oft-asserted rule that the United States provide no more than a fixed share of the budgets of the United Nations system—ranging between 32 and 50 per cent—and in the sharp cuts in foreign aid appropriations imposed by Congress on the President in recent years. But this limit on presidential leadership tends to operate without party influence.

Nonpartisanship, rather than bipartisanship, seems to be a proper term for this situation. Parties are not united internally or collectively in value preferences, nor are they regularly and punctiliously consulted by the President prior to new foreign policy initiatives. Because the legislature lacks long-term cohesive majority and minority positions on foreign policy and because the organization of the parties and of Congress does not foster clarity and coherence on foreign affairs, the hand of the President is strengthened. Sometimes he consults the opposition party; often he does not. Usually he takes his own party for granted; occasionally he must conciliate and persuade influential members. Optimally, he wishes to have a "bipartisan policy" that consists of merely being able to demonstrate publicly that influential members of the opposition talk to him, support him, and seek to influence their colleagues on his behalf.

The State and Defense departments have more than one million civilian officials. Do these men, then, make the policies that reenforce, confirm, or destroy the web of interdependence? In a general way, the answer is "yes." Initial thought about what future policy should be and what immediate measures should be taken to implement existing policy does come from these departments in the Executive Branch. But they have their way only if the President and his personal staff do *not* have ideas and wishes of their own. Presidents can, and do, override, outflank, and ignore their Secretaries of State; they direct and prod the Foreign Service and the military services—and they play them off against each other on occasion. Since 1952, at any rate, the persons who have held the offices of President, Secretary of State, and Secretary of Defense at any one time have been so close to each other in values and judgment that little occasion for conflict arose.

Are the two giant departments monoliths of bureaucrats who go their own professionally-sanctioned ways when permitted to do so by the President? Public *control* over either is absent; but *consultations* with the public are routine. Thus the State Department carefully follows press and public opinion on foreign affairs questions. Its officials routinely talk to representatives of interest groups, both in Washington and at meetings of the organizations concerned. In addition, panels of distinguished private experts are consulted by the professionals in government.

None of this is true in the same way of the Department of Defense or the Central Intelligence Agency. Occasionally, conflict among officials is "resolved" by referring a question of high strategy to a panel of distinguished private citizens. Technical studies of alternative strategies are undertaken by civilian research institutes related to the department. And representatives of armaments firms, of course, regularly seek to influence the department in favor of this or that weapons system. By and large, however, Defense goes its own professionally-sanctioned way, subject only to the will of the President. As for the CIA, only major failures in operations exposed fully its freedom from control.

We must add, finally, that certain private interests exercise an inordinate amount of influence on certain other departments of government marginally related to foreign affairs. Thus organized labor is most important in shaping the position of the Department of Labor with respect to international issues; farmers' organizations are equally powerful in using the Department of Agriculture in this way. The medical profession and public health officials exercise a similar role through the Department of Health, Education, and Welfare. We do not know enough of the role of the Atomic Energy Commission to assess the leverage exercised by it or by private groups associated with it.

What about the Joint Chiefs of Staff and the National Security Council? Doesn't the prestige of these organs predetermine the President's choices? The Joint Chiefs scrupulously avoid making firm recommendations; instead, they tend to adopt resolutions with generalities that simply plaster over interservice disagreements. Even when they do make firm recommendations, the President does not necessarily accept them; Eisenhower, for example, ignored the Joint Chiefs' recommendation to intervene in the 1954 Indochina war. The National Security Council, the President's chief advisory body on foreign and defense matters, groups all the cabinet officials concerned, as well as the Central Intelligence Agency. The consensus of observers is that the council is little more than a forum for negotiating interagency differences; furthermore, Presidents vary in the extent to which they use the council. The President makes policy, essentially, on the basis of direct access to him, open to crucial officials in the two main departments. There is no firm military policy determined by professionals on "rational" or technical grounds; there is only interservice and interagency bargaining using all the normal political techniques for attracting allies and building coalitions—so long as the President has not made up his own mind on what course to follow.

All roads of inquiry, then, lead to the President as the fountainhead of foreign policy-making power. This power, first of all, does have the sanction of the Constitution. In addition, the diffuse state of public opinion and the incoherence of interest group activity, coupled with the willingness of Congress to be led on foreign policy questions, provide the President with the political setting in which to exercise his constitutional powers. The fact of the matter, of course, is that some Presidents seize the opportunity consistently and others do not. Strong leadership, appeals to the public; the skillful use of the press and television, energetic nonpartisan persuasion of Congress usually yield acquiescence to the policy desired by a President; the failure to exercise leadership results in widespread attack and opposition. The election in which a foreign policy issue defeated the governing party—the contest of 1952 and the Korean war—illustrates this rule: a confused and divided electorate mirrors an equally confused and irresolute Administration's policy. An active President remains abreast of public moods by means of polls and surveys; he seeks to shape the moods through press conferences and television appearances. A passive President neglects these channels and pays the price in opposition. Both kinds suffer from public ill will if they are unable to shape a coherent and understandable policy, to be clearly communicated to the people. And such is the mood of the American public that neither an active nor a passive President can long have his way unless the policy he follows appears to be successful. Prolonged sacrifices will not be tolerated by the American public unless visible success attends them.

This discussion suggests that presidential leadership is restrained only by the natural limits of the chief executive's energy and motivation. Additionally, perhaps, the entrenched bureaucratic power and *expertise* of federal agencies act as a brake on presidential initiatives. Each agency, being a complex organization in its own right, tends to act as a self-sufficient goal-seeking and goal-attaining unit with needs and demands of its own, not subject to simple control by way of presidential wish or formal interagency coordinating machinery. How then can we conceptualize more formal limits on presidential power? A survey of the *types of decisions* Presidents must make will help matters, as will a look at the *kind of consensus* required to make such decisions effective. We distinguish between emergency decisions, the initiation of major new programs, and the planning or evaluation of ongoing policy.

Emergency decisions are made in secret by the President's closest collaborators: the White House staff, the Secretaries of State and Defense, the Director of the CIA. Such decisions may, and do, involve war and peace, the use of nuclear weapons, escalation and de-escalation, appeals to the UN or to NATO, interpreting ambiguous radar blips, extending emergency aid to an attacked nation, recognizing or not recognizing a regime resulting from a coup or a revolution abroad. They must be made rapidly, and they require immediate and coordinated implementation. No consensus outside the inner circle can be built. If the decisions made require money and lives and if success is not rapidly achieved, this very lack of consensus may spell the failure of the decision, particularly when it runs counter to the prevalent public mood.

Major new policies are discussed in the public arena, which includes Congress, the press, interest groups, and the whole attentive public. Major new policies usually demand additional resources, financial and human. Money must be appropriated, new missions abroad constituted, thinking patterns changed. Consensual bridges among all parties affected become essential. A President eager to launch such a program must build coalitions of supporters in the interest group and congressional world if he wishes to succeed. Major new programs, then, are in effect negotiated among all parties concerned before being formally voted on by Congress. The terms of major departures such as the Marshall Plan, the Alliance for Progress, and NATO are defined through the process of bargaining, because they trigger group, class, and regional interests that demand a hearing and that command votes. Experts make recommendations and studies, but these are filtered through the prism of intergroup and interparty bargains; they do not stand on their professional merits alone. Congress therefore often ignores and counters the President's suggestions in the politics of approving foreign aid and defense production—*unless* the President has taken care to build the proper supporting coalitions with appropriate package deals. Opposition to foreign aid has grown quite consistently since 1961, a trend matched by increasing lack of cohesion and agreement among executive departments dealing with foreign aid. The larger the programs have grown, the more opposition and greater lack of administrative focus have developed, as segments of the public and of government have been pitted against each other concerning who gets what and how much.

But the President's own executive agencies can give him plenty of trouble on the way. "Officialdom, whether civil or military, is hardly ever neutral. It speaks, and inevitably, it speaks as an advocate. The Army battles for ground forces, the Air Force for bombers, the 'Europe faction' in the State Department for policy benefiting NATO, and the 'Africa faction' for anti-colonial policies unsettling to our relations with Europe." [13] The result is "policy" only in the sense that continuing bargaining and negotiation among executive agencies eventually result in a compromise among them. Not even the best-informed and strongest-willed President can impose his own preferences unless he can be sure that his decision will be faithfully and rapidly carried out. There is very little planning of policy in Washington. Policy emerges incrementally, step-by-step, from crisis to crisis, as a result of interagency confrontation and compromise mediated by the President. Hence it is of the greatest importance to the representative principle in American government that the leaders of executive agencies, the major "front men" of Washington, be people who command confidence and fol-

[13] Roger Hilsman, *To Move a Nation* (Garden City, N.Y.: Doubleday, 1967), p. 8.

lowers among important interest groups, whether they be "liberals" like Adlai Stevenson and Arthur Goldberg or "conservatives" with ties in law, business, and industry like John McCone, John J. McCloy, or Dean Acheson. A President legitimates his leadership over his own agencies by staffing them with such front men. He limits the interagency conflict and bargaining by this technique.

Decisions involving evaluation are semipublic. Typically they involve high-level presidential commissions or panels charged with evaluating the success of past policies and making suggestions for the future. Initially, these steps are secret. But as the results come to affect competing federal agencies, leaks to the public occur, and the President's final choice is influenced by the expectations and fears aroused by these unauthorized disclosures. If funds and much new thought are involved in implementing a new policy, the President is still constrained to build supporting coalitions in Congress and in the interest-group world. Moreover, he must still persuade his federal agencies to do his bidding, though he usually attempts to do this in the first place by including their representatives on the commission. Organizational structures brought into being by earlier, important departures from policy—like the various foreign aid agencies and various divisions of departments dealing with specific international organizations—now become defenders of the status quo and must be negotiated with before another new departure in policy can be undertaken. This process is illustrated by studies and negotiations in Washington leading to the creation of foreign aid programs, civilian defense outlays, strategic missile planning, and the use of subversion abroad.

## 5. The Imperfect Pluralist Model Recapitulated

Unless we understand how democracy relates to foreign-policy-making, we will be unable to demonstrate how Americans influence the international system and learn from it. The web of international interdependence rests on an imperfect pluralist domestic process insofar as American-initiated demands and American-learned lessons are concerned.

The imperfect pluralist model recognizes that public opinion plays a very limited role in this process. Opinion at the mass level is characterized by pervasive moods, not by structured and strongly held beliefs. The mood is shared by a large majority of Americans at any one time: it is consensual. It stresses the superiority of the American Way of Life, and it equates our policy in international organizations with its growing legitimacy abroad. Foreign aid, alliances, collective security, the protection of human rights—all these are ways of making the American and the World ways of life coterminous. The opposing mood, no longer pervasive, dictates withdrawal from the world, to safeguard the superior Way of Life. A polarization into several rival moods—all equally shallow and short-lived—comes into being when a given policy clearly lacks success, imposes sacrifices, and deeply frustrates people in their daily lives. The Vietnam issue is a clear example of this otherwise unusual trend. A single pervasive mood imposes limits on political leadership; the coexistence of several competing moods offers opportunities for political bargaining, shifting, and manipulating.

Organized interest groups, though more consistently active and effective in policy-making than public opinion is, differ widely among themselves in terms of influence. Only groups with specific, permanent, and intensely held views succeed in being heard regularly in Washington, and their influence is on specific issues of concern to them. Interest groups also act as two-way communication channels between their members and Washington, insofar as their leaders are part of the attentive public in their home communities. But interest groups are far from constituting a monolith. They oppose one another frequently and bitterly. Evidence, however, does not bear out the pluralist argument that groups tend to approximate each other in opposing power, to be arranged in countervailing power. Interest groups, disproportionately, have instead been part of a general internationally-minded but anti-Communist consensus.

While political parties, or at least regional factions in them, do aggregate the demands of interest groups, they do not do so very consistently or effectively in the field of foreign policy. Nor does Congress reflect a clear pattern of countervailing power. Congress tends to be passive in international matters unless new programs are being planned. It also tends to be behind the President. Dissent from the consensus is concentrated on single issues and demands, rather than on broad principles.

This leaves us with the federal bureaucracy as the major force in policy-making. The bureaucracy is made up of complex organizations, each determined to survive, each eager to make policy for itself in the formal setting of dependence on the executive and legislative branches of government, each eager to do the job it can do best without much thought for a total plan, a long-range design, a global vision. Agencies oppose one another, and "interagency coordination" is a euphemism for diplomacy and bargaining among competing departments. Policy is the result, then, of negotiated compromise—often mediated by the President—in which the interest groups most closely associated with given departments have participated indirectly. This compromise is then presented to Congress for its ratification in terms of legislative approval and funding.

The President can take a more direct and authoritative position if he wishes. He does so only in emergencies. Normally he lets the process of consultation, bargaining, indirect participation, and downward communication go its way, feeding his own preferences and ideas in at the proper time. Policy, then, is incremental. It "is made" by moving from package deal to package deal without much thought for an over-all scheme, a total design that takes in immediate crises, intermediate trends, and long-range probable developments in the broad field of human ecology. And thus policy is always an approximation of rational and comprehensive thought, just as it is merely an approximation of a pure pluralistic democratic pattern.

In fact, it has been argued that the process is not democratic at all, because it does not provide for consistent mass or elite participation. To argue thus is to insist on procedures that presume equal commitment, intelligence, and knowledge on the part of all the people. Alternatively, it would give disproportionate powers to the minority that actually has these attributes, rather than to the people's elected representatives and to the professional specialists chosen on the basis of their competence. Pluralism, though imperfect, remains democratic as long as the leaders must bargain for support among the elites and the public, and as long as segments of the public have the ability to influence policy by means of access to the bureaucracy. Shallow as the public mood may be, the fact that it does act as a constraint on leadership confirms the persistence of popular force. But as long as the mood remains shallow, arguments in favor of better and more profound modes of public participation in policy-making are more likely to result in more effective downward manipulation than in genuine and informed democratic control from below. If the power elite model gives a grotesquely inaccurate picture of American policy-making, the pure democratic model yields a house built on sand.

Therefore, when America learns to adapt to new complications abroad and fashions new strands in the web of interdependence, the learning most often originates in the bureaucracy and among those elites who experience the international system most profoundly, such as industrialists, bankers, lawyers, and cultural leaders. Overwhelmingly, foreign events, not domestic trends and crises, have caused an American adaptation. America did not turn toward interventionism in the late 1930's because of the Depression; nor did the containment policy in 1947 owe much to internal American developments.

But the late 1960's taught us the limits of this rule. When painful failure abroad combines with massive domestic crises such as racial insurrection, the decay of cities, and large-scale unemployment, a change in foreign policy *can* be attributed to essentially domestic events. Dissenters from the ongoing foreign policy use these events to impress upon policy-makers the connections between failures at home and abroad. The government's response in terms of new policy then constitutes adaptive learning, forced by a new coalition of domestic political forces. Congress may come into its own again. So may leaders who were not previously part of the inner policy-making circle.

Yet, while such learning does occur, it is just as piecemeal and incremental as the previous round of learning. The dissenters will succeed in teaching the government that it is impossible to have both guns and butter, to fight costly wars abroad and improve the fundamental conditions of twenty million people at home. But they will fail in having butter take the place of guns. They will make us question the rules of the international system and challenge us to fit together many new pieces in the jigsaw puzzle of policy. But will the search for a more tolerable international system result in a dramatic breakthrough? Even if incrementalism makes possible such drastic changes, should we look for them and welcome them indiscriminately?

# PART TWO

The strands
of the web of interdependence

In Part I, we used the actor's and the observer's types of knowledge to examine the web of interdependence. With the observer's tools, we summarized the main lines of world development during the last three decades. And we sketched the traits and habits typical of an America seeking to find its way, enmeshed in interdependence and attempting to master it.

Webs are made up of single strands. In world politics they include the search for military and political security through the United Nations and through regional alliances and treaty organizations—though it is not always clear whether we are talking of the world's security or America's. Another and closely related strand is the attempt to abolish, limit, or control armaments. Efforts to spur and support the economic development of the impoverished two-thirds of the world provide a constantly thickening strand; some of these efforts are made by the UN and its specialized agencies, while others are the preserve of Organization for Economic Cooperation and Development (OECD) and the Organization of American States (OAS), to mention only those in which the United States enjoys membership. Further, the rules governing world trade, competition, access to foreign markets, lending, borrowing, and monetary policy constitute an area of obvious interdependence in which UN agencies are the dominant international actors. The international protection of human rights and the abolition of the colonial system are twin objectives and activities that have generated strands of interdependence in recent years. The United Nations is the chief actor here, too. Finally, the scientific and technological breakthroughs are becoming increasingly important in international life, because they suggest perhaps new, improved ways of doing things while also propelling us toward new and more frightening challenges to an orderly and humane world. We must inquire whether the possible consequences of such breakthroughs, consequences unintended by governments and elites, may not lead to a species of worldwide planning that might fundamentally transform the character of the web.

These are the strands of the web in which the United States and all other countries, in varying degrees, are enmeshed if not entrapped. Clearly, when the outlines of the contemporary system took shape in the minds of Western policy-makers in 1945, these issues and concerns were not all intended or foreseen. American officials sought to build a world order in which the preservation of military and political security on the basis of the frontiers of 1945 was to be the fundamental aim. Economic development, decolonization, regional alliances, and the protection of human rights were not considered central parts of the new order. When in 1947, Communist expansion came to be perceived as the main threat to that order, the United States countered by attempting to use the UN as a vehicle in the policy of containing communism. At the same time, a network of anti-Communist regional organizations was constructed to make up for the weakness of the UN, while the bulk of American energies went into unilateral military efforts to contain Russia and to deter her through the threat of massive nuclear punishment. Only insofar as it seemed necessary to cater to neutrals and make them friends, did the United States turn to international organizations to spur economic development and to end colonial rule.

These countering trends resulted by 1956 in the emergence of a multipolar world system rather than the earlier bipolar confrontation dominated by the cold war. Unwittingly, the major powers had stumbled into the new system in their efforts to please the third world. International organizations had been one major medium through which the transformation had occurred. Would the major powers now withdraw from them, as the harbingers of unintended consequences? Would they adjust to them by learning how to construct and manipulate new strands in the web?

The period since 1955 is our major concern in this book. We wish to know *how* the United States adjusted to the multipolar world and its multiplying issue areas and concerns. We want to know *what* the United States learned that kept it from leaving the system that had failed fully to contain communism and preserve the *status quo* of 1945.

# CHAPTER FOUR

# NATIONAL SECURITY, WORLD PEACE, AND DISARMAMENT

## 1. World Peace and American Security in the Bipolar System

In the wake of World War II, the victor powers set up the UN, to prevent a repetition of the violent tragedies that had engulfed the world since the middle of the 1930's. There cannot be the slightest doubt that the American people, in the mass and in opinion-making groups, gave overwhelming support to the idea of a world organization with peacekeeping power. Majorities in excess of 70 per cent in 1944 and 1945 favored an organization with power to stop all wars, to fix the military power of individual nations, earmark national forces for global peacekeeping, decide on the merits of disputes between nations, make binding laws, and even examine schoolbooks to eliminate nationalist biases.

These opinions—subject to all the strictures set forth in Chapter 3 about the role of public opinion—were expressed while the war was still in progress. A few years later, the internationalist ardor of the American public had cooled a bit. In the words of the most comprehensive study of this period:

When support for the United Nations is presented without reference to other means of maintaining peace and security, a large majority [of the people interviewed] is in favor of it. When presented as an alternative to other policies, sizable proportions of people continue to advocate support for the United Nations, but the alternatives of strengthening US defenses and developing separate alliances with friendly nations attract about as many advocates.[1]

TABLE 4 · 1

Choice of Alternative
US Foreign Policies (NORC)

|  | Nov., 1949 | June, 1950 | July, 1950 | Mar., 1951 |
|---|---|---|---|---|
|  | | | Per cent | |
| US should rely mainly on: | | | | |
| The United Nations Organization and do what it can to make it more effective | 28 | 27 | 40 | 32 |
| Alliances with other democratic countries, and work toward closer unity with them | 27 | 35 | 30 | 31 |
| Its own armed forces, and stay out of world affairs as much as possible | 38 | 32 | 26 | 30 |
| No opinion | 7 | 6 | 4 | 7 |

Source: National Opinion Research Center. Quoted in Scott and Withey, *The United States and the United Nations*, p. 24.

The decline of enthusiasm for UN peacekeeping efforts coincides with the intensification of the Cold War after 1948. But in the immediate aftermath of World War II, even the American Legion,

[1] William A. Scott and Stephen B. Withey, *The United States and the United Nations* (New York: Manhattan Publishing Co., 1958), p. 23.

always concerned with stressing the unique role of American armed forces in maintaining peace, strongly favored the UN and saw in it the forum for the deployment of American troops. In 1947, when President Truman bypassed the UN in coming to the aid of Greece and Turkey, 66 per cent of the public disapproved and 51 per cent thought the UN was able to cope with the situation. Why, then, did not the government, fully and without reservation, combine the American desire for peace with the work of the UN?

Obviously, the government did not think that the UN could handle the situation. That, however, is another way of saying that measures undertaken by the UN would not have corresponded to American wishes and objectives. In other words, action would not have been in conformance with the national interest. Policy in international organizations is still part of national policy, and usually only a subordinate part at that. One test of the sturdiness of the web of interdependence is the extent to which policy in international organizations is one of many means, or *the predominant* means. United States foreign policy uses purely national initiatives —military, economic, cultural, and diplomatic—alongside multilateral steps through regional organizations as well as the UN. The calculation of whether to use the UN as the mainstay of policy involves (1) the types of action the UN can take, (2) the type of military confrontation which the action is to meet and control and (3) the price of a UN operation in terms of international consensus. We know that such calculations conform to the type of international system in which the country finds itself, whether bipolar, multipolar, or multibloc. The United States never deliberately defined her interests as being identical with the success of the UN, but the process of learning taught Washington how to mix UN objectives with America's in everchanging proportions as the bipolar system gave way to the multibloc world. In fact, the learning changed the system.

The Charter to which the world agreed in 1945 banned the use of force and the threat of it in international relations and guaranteed each member nation its territorial integrity and security. How? Two types of action were enumerated in the Charter, and a third developed immediately in practice. Elaborate procedures for peacefully settling disputes among nations are prescribed, using the Security Council as well as the General Assembly. These procedures involve the collective mediation and conciliation of the UN between antagonists but they are not binding on them. In the event of a breach of the peace or act of aggression in defiance of "peaceful settlement" procedures, the UN is able to order binding "enforcement" measures, military as well as nonmilitary, against the guilty state. But as the Kashmir (1947), Palestine (1948), and Indonesian (1949) cases soon demonstrated, a third way of keeping the peace was the establishment of a truce by order of the Security Council and the creation of neutral forces for "truce supervision," a step short of enforcement. Enforcement was ordered by the Security Council only once, ineffectively against Rhodesia in 1966. "Peacekeeping" by means of forces temporarily contributed by small countries and placed under UN command seeks to separate the combatants physically and contain them without forcing the peacekeepers to fight. This is a development not foreseen in the Charter and improvised by the Secretary-General under the very different conditions of the multipolar system that made its advent after 1955.

How do the members reach agreement on which kind of action to take, when? Before replying, the various types of possible military confrontations should be set forth. The most general type of confrontation conceivable is a general thermonuclear war between the Western and Communist blocs; this type is by definition beyond the scope of UN action, since the countries designed to guarantee peace under the Charter would then become the antagonists that call peace into question. A limited war between the two camps, on the other hand, might be amenable to UN intercession, and a limited war among other countries certainly should be amenable to intercession. The same is true of small and carefully controlled probing attacks designed to test the enemy's strength and will to resist. Local wars fought by nations outside the major ideological camps contribute heavily to the number of actual military conflicts; when these are in danger of escalating into larger conflicts, they become natural targets of UN action and concern. Some local wars, however, are so far removed from becoming sources of escalation or general concern that neither the great powers nor the UN is likely to be able to intercede successfully, because nobody is sufficiently concerned to make the necessary effort. Finally, there is the type of conflict we call "internal war," or civil strife tied to international ideological conflict and indirectly supported from the outside. This type of conflict is not "aggression" in the sense of the UN Charter, and it presents some of the chief difficulties in the decision of whether to use the UN or sidestep it in the attainment of a national objective.

But who would provide the counterforce needed for UN action? In 1945 the maintenance of peace and security was lodged in the Security Council in which each of the major nations—United States,

Soviet Union, France, Britain, and China—has the power to veto a resolution: the major powers have to be unanimously in favor of a given course of action before anything can be done to stop aggression. Since nobody expected the great powers themselves to submit voluntarily to being policed by their peers, this meant that the machinery could work only if war was threatened by a smaller nation. In short, the security of mankind depended on the maintenance of a concert of confidence and power among the large nations. The institutional and symbolic proof of this understanding lay in the fact that the military enforcement machinery of the UN—the still-born Military Staff Committee and national forces earmarked for its use—was to be made up entirely of personnel furnished by the major powers. By 1948 the basic assumptions underlying a successful functioning of the UN were no longer met, the Cold War was under way, and the implication was that a "concert" of the major powers could be effectively mobilized only in conflicts of a local nature. If the conflicts did not involve the interests or direct commitments of Washington, Moscow, London, or Paris, the UN Security Council could continue to work. There were as many such conflicts then as there are now, and the cease-fires and truce supervision procedures adopted in the Middle East, South and Southeast Asia illustrate the continued importance of a big power consensus that could prevail despite, or because of, the Cold War.

In crises involving a direct confrontation with communism, however, the Security Council was deadlocked, and UN action became impossible. The United States, disappointed with the built-in limits of the UN machinery, looked for ways to use its majority in the world body to subject the Soviet Union itself—though one of the original guarantors of world peace—to the enforcement procedure. It did so by bypassing the Security Council and relying on a two-thirds majority in the vetoless General Assembly instead. Such a majority could *recommend*, not order, enforcement and other security measures, and the recommendation would then lend the UN's mantle of legitimacy to the military operations undertaken by the member nations. The United States government, encouraged by the undifferentiated and shallowly held public view supporting the UN, thus "learned" to adapt the rules of the world organization to suit the anti-Soviet purposes of American foreign policy. The Greek and Korean interventions authorized by the United Nations followed. By 1950 the UN seemed to have become an instrumentality of United States policy in the pursuit of the Cold War. But instead of the Charter-sanctioned consensual principle for enforcement action, the new principle involved simply the delegation of enforcement power by the UN majority to the United States and its allies. Enforcement, instead of being collective and binding, became permissive and selective.

But only so long as the UN forces in Korea were winning. As soon as China entered that conflict and threatened to trigger American escalation, the bulk of the UN membership sought to limit the anti-Communist mandate earlier given the United States. The bipolar confrontation that had prevailed between 1948 and 1951 altered as an Arab-Asian grouping of states mediated between the two poles, using the UN as a balancer between hostile blocs rather than as an enforcement agency. And thus a new consensual principle evolved *ad hoc:* the negotiation through parliamentary diplomacy in the General Assembly of a compromise agreement between the antagonists, even though one fought under the UN flag, a process we label "balancing." The principle could be successfully used to end the fighting of localized and probing wars among the major powers and their allies. It could not be used, any more than any other consensual principle, to end direct and major military confrontations among the large powers.

## 2. National Security, World Peace, and the Multipolar System

In 1955, Washington and Moscow negotiated a "package deal" by virtue of which sixteen additional nations were admitted to UN membership, seven of them not allied to either East or West. By 1958, six more nonaligned nations had been admitted. By 1966, forty more new nations were members, all but four or five nonaligned. The United States, because of the procedures on enforcement of security used in the Greek and Korean cases, had committed itself to upgrade sharply the peace maintenance powers of the General Assembly. More nonaligned members meant more restraints on America's ability to manipulate the UN procedures. The original lesson learned—upgrading the General Assembly at the expense of the veto-bound Security Council—produced unintended results in that the American freedom of maneuver was once more circumscribed by an unreliable majority. How, if at all, would the United States adapt to this new environment in its pursuit of the containment policy through the UN?

It bears stressing that the UN by no means always facilitated the attainment of American foreign policy objectives in the years since the bipolar world broke up. In 1956 the UN failed in stopping Soviet intervention in Hungary; nor did it resolve the Suez Canal crisis fully in line with American preferences. In 1958 the UN operated at cross purposes with American objectives in Lebanon. In 1960 operations in the Congo did not always correspond to United States policy, though they did in 1962. The Cuban missile crisis of 1962 was resolved without UN help, even though mediatory services were proffered. Opponents of American policies in the Western Hemisphere sought to use the UN to counter American measures in Panama (1964) and the Dominican Republic (1965). Communist and nonaligned states attempted to oppose American policy in Vietnam on several occasions, and Secretary-General U Thant, in 1965 and 1966, sought to mediate that war without American encouragement. In short, the UN increasingly appeared as an opponent rather than as an instrument of the national interest as defined by the government.

Did the public perceive, approve, or condemn this changed role? The American public, by almost uniform two-thirds majorities, recorded its approval of UN peacekeeping operations since 1956, even advocating the creation of strong, standing, peacekeeping contingents not under American control. Approval was expressed even at times of setbacks suffered by UN forces and by American policy. Furthermore, general expressions of opinion more and more saw the UN as the proper agency for dealing with "brush-fire wars," local conflicts not related to the Cold War or other big power confrontations. The reduced military participation of the large powers in UN peacekeeping operations was apparently welcomed by the public. Again, therefore, the mood and elite perceptions of the national interest proved permissive, allowing the government to take new initiatives. The mood allowed for something more than all-or-nothing solutions; limits on the possibility of action were admitted; there was more and more recognition that some issues were not capable of solution in the short run and that palliatives of temporary utility were all anybody could offer.

But not all segments of elite opinion shared in this passive, permissive frame of mind. The advent of African-Asian economically underdeveloped nations and the strident tone they lent to debate did not go unnoticed. The shift in power from the Security Council to the General Assembly was deplored by some people because it gave strength to "rampant nationalism, fuzzy and irresponsible resolutions, and the violation of domestic jurisdiction" [2] in the UN. The

2 Raymond A. Moore, ed., *The United Nations Reconsidered* (Columbia, S.C.: University of South Carolina, 1963), p. 11.

West was increasingly urged not to underwrite all UN operations while the Afro-Asian states indulged in "financial irresponsibility" by voting for large programs and then refusing to pay for them. The Afro-Asian states were asked to "grow up" politically. Some kind of weighted voting formula was suggested to compensate the West for the numerical preponderance of new and small nations in the Assembly. Most important, the government was asked not to use the UN as a substitute for national policy, to continue to seek the attainment of American objectives outside the UN as well as in.

A subtle combination of perceptions accounts for this critical stance. Domestic unrest in the United States increasingly involved the twin themes of race relations and equality; international unrest seemed to follow a similar pattern. In domestic relations, the volume of the dissenting and reforming voices seemed proportional to the enactment of concessions in the form of the civil rights and anti-poverty programs; in the General Assembly, the non-Western dissenters and reformers, apparently, could do no wrong. When they claimed territory by force (India in Goa, Indonesia against Malaya), the UN took no action; when they intervened in the domestic politics of their neighbors (in the Congo, South Africa, Angola, Rhodesia) the protection of human rights took precedence over the rule against intervention. Subversion, outside support for subversives, "indirect aggression," and race relations assumed the quality of a single syndrome of threat that seemed to link events in American ghettos to conditions in Africa. Conditions that would otherwise seem remote became a source of considerable malaise. There was, therefore, considerable opposition to the UN's role in the Congo, because it was played to support some foes of Western influence. Since neither Rhodesia nor South Africa directly threatened world peace with their restrictive racial policies, some Americans could not see why they should be condemned as aggressors simply to give satisfaction to the new African nations. In Latin America and Southeast Asia, where civil strife in many countries went hand in hand with externally supported Communist subversion, appeals to the United Nations on behalf of the rebels were sometimes seen by these critics as direct challenges to American interests.

The United States government at first reacted negatively to the new tone of militant nonalignment, even though it bowed to it in Korea. President Eisenhower and Secretary of State Dulles condemned as "immoral" any attempt at neutrality between democracy and communism. They developed the formula of "indirect aggression"—the Eisenhower Doctrine—whereby the United States assumed the right to come to the assistance of any government calling for help against civil strife aided by external forces. Since the UN was not convinced that such situations represent classic cases of aggression, the containment policy had to be implemented bilaterally. The Southeast Asia Treaty Organization and the Central Treaty Organization of the Middle East were created as a method of implementing the doctrine. Marines were landed in Lebanon as a more direct way of supporting a shaky government. President Kennedy followed the same course in Vietnam, and President Johnson in the Dominican Republic.

In the UN, however, the doctrine was not accepted, and the United States quickly learned that direct intervention can be dangerous and embarrassing unless it succeeds rapidly or commands general support. Hence in conflicts of a local nature, outside the Cold War entirely or to be kept outside it to prevent escalation, the United States soon proved amenable to a new type of UN action and a new consensual principle for launching it. The action originated in the 1956 Suez-Sinai war, and it featured UN peacekeeping forces, contributed entirely by small nations, with the mission to separate the combatants and to fight only in carrying out this mandate. Such forces have since been used also in Cyprus (1964-68), the Congo (1960-63), and West Irian (1962); their withdrawal from Sinai in 1967 triggered the Arab-Israeli war of that year. Although no American troops were ever used, the United States provided transportation and financial support, sometimes of crucial proportions. In the Congo, at any rate, the United States felt that the UN operation successfully stopped internal war as well, even though the pro-American influence of the UN was stressed only by the "new Africa" section of the State Department (led by G. Mennen Williams) against the opposition of the "old Europe" wing.[3]

"Permissive engagement," the consensual principle on which these operations rested, involves the Secretary-General, rather than a single great power or a bloc of members as the initiator, organizer, and inspiration. But the UN membership must still "permit" the Secretary-General to "engage" the organization. Hence the procedures we identified as "balancing" and as the big power "concert" still remain appropriate as alternative ways through which an active Secretary-General can provide himself with a working majority. Balancing confirms dependence on the nonaligned; the concert obviates this but compels agreement with Moscow and Washington.

Because the other members of the UN—especially the nonaligned countries of Africa and Asia whom the United States desperately

[3] Roger Hilsman, *To Move a Nation* (Garden City: Doubleday, 1967), chaps. 17, 18, 19.

wished to keep out of the Communist orbit, whether Chinese or Russian—strenuously opposed intervention by the West, the United States learned to tolerate peacekeeping by the military forces of small countries as a way of protecting the national interest in local conflicts. This acceptance, however, brought with it two further consequences not clearly anticipated. First, operations of this kind cost a considerable amount, and few nations outside the West were anxious to pay for them. The Soviet Union and France objected to two such operations (Suez and the Congo) because they rested on "permissive engagement" and "balancing" rather than the Charter-inscribed concert. They declined to pay their shares. Second, because the procedure for passing peacekeeping resolutions demanded a strong Secretary-General or a two-thirds majority in the General Assembly the special role of big powers seemed seriously threatened. How did the United States respond to these developments?

The prolonged financial crisis engendered by the dispute over peacekeeping and permissive engagement marks the high-water point of American commitment to collective security not controlled from Washington. The United States sought to rely on a decision of the International Court of Justice, which held that all UN members were *bound* to contribute to the expenses incurred in peacekeeping operations, whether they had voted for them or not. Had this decision become a law of international conduct, both permissive engagement and balancing would have become dominant; however, France, the Soviet Union, and many smaller nations opposed the American and the Court's position. By 1965 the United States had abandoned its position and admitted that future peacekeeping operations would have to depend heavily on *voluntary* contributions, primarily from industrial countries. Further, the Security Council rather than the General Assembly or the Secretary-General would once more be the legitimate source of action and consensus. In coming to this conclusion, Washington in effect came to agree with Moscow and Paris that emphasis should once more be shifted to the concert of the powers. And those who deplored excessive dependence on the votes of inexperienced Asian and African nations thus adapted to the multibloc world by resuscitating the Security Council, thereby seeking to escape the restraints of catering to the nonaligned.

By the mid-sixties the United States had learned that the UN, no matter which system and which consensual formula prevails, is no substitute for national policy. But it also learned that because the UN was unable to end the Cold War, the mere winning of propaganda votes at Turtle Bay was no great boon. Instead, America had come to understand that UN action is able to neutralize trouble spots, prevent escalation, keep Cold War probes limited, and thus keep the Cold War from spreading. But the web of interdependence woven by these lessons is a frail one. An America determined to realize its vision abroad, in a Cold War setting, will not be enmeshed, as proved by Vietnam above all else. Direct confrontations between the big powers will be solved directly by them, not by the UN.

And so the lessons have been selective, and the resulting rules full of loopholes. There has been a minimum of learning that results in institutionalization. At most, the United States has learned when *not* to use the UN as a tool of its policy and how to play the UN for its greatest effectiveness when it is used. The criterion of effectiveness, for the United States as for any other nation, remains the service rendered for advancing national objectives. The hallmark of political development for any human association may very well be the degree of "institutionalization" achieved by the collectivity. Institutionalization must mean more than stability and adaptation, for the UN's organs and procedures have been both stable and adaptive. It must mean more than mere growth in task and competence, for the UN has experienced steady growth. *Institutionalization must mean that the organs and their procedures become valued and accepted by the member nations as legitimate sources of policy even when that policy is not favored by the member.* In this sense, the United States has not revalued the UN for the maintenance of world peace. What can we hazard about the future?

### 3. The UN and the Future of World Peace

It is most probable that the future will bring more local conflict, more border disputes among new nations, more civil strife supported from beyond a country's borders. It is equally probable that the great powers, especially the United States, will continue to be confronted with international radical and revolutionary movements unwilling to respect national sovereignty and official frontiers, particularly in Latin America and Southeast Asia. What would be the reaction of the American public to an increased peacekeeping task on the part of the UN in such a situation? How legitimate would the UN be as an institution if it were to interpose itself between the United States and its foreign antagonists?

Gallup Poll data accumulated in 1965 and 1966 suggests some answers. It is a striking fact that 59 per cent of Americans believe that the UN saved the world from another major war. Seventy-four per cent approved of a general move to ask the UN to try to work out *its own* formula for peace in Vietnam. And 62 per cent approved of a specific proposal involving UN-supervised elections, reciprocal troop withdrawals, and a standby American force offshore. However, when the public was asked pointedly whether the United States should abide by *any* UN decision regarding a solution in Vietnam, only 49 per cent were favorable.[4] It appears, therefore, that, as before, much blind faith continues to inhere in the UN *and* in Washington, thus bestowing considerable legitimacy on the procedures that flourish along the East River and the Potomac.

Elite opinion, however, does not match this picture entirely. While the major labor unions and business organizations follow the lead of the government in defending American moves, whether inside the UN or through external channels, many individual business and labor leaders do not. Many favor UN action on principle, even when in opposition to policy in Washington. Others tend to be more and more skeptical of international organizations not controlled by the West. Some say bluntly that if Communist China were admitted to the UN, the United States should leave the organization. Church leaders increasingly espouse internationalist positions perceived as conflicting with government policy, as do students and many professionals.

Congressional majorities, on the other hand, have been far more skeptical and reluctant to embrace the UN as a guarantor of American security. This became very apparent in 1962 when President Kennedy sought to persuade Congress to authorize the purchase of $100 million worth of UN bonds in order to finance peacekeeping operations. In fact, the financial crisis of the UN was in some measure the result of congressional insistence that other nations assume a heavier burden in financing UN military operations. Congress, by narrow committee majorities, approved a very restrictive measure authorizing the conditional purchase of bonds, linked to the withholding of interest and amortization payments from the annual American contribution to the UN budget. Events since have done little to increase congressional respect for, and reliance on, UN security operations.

There is then considerable evidence that the earlier American consensus on the UN and American policy toward world peace, a consensus that blindly equated UN peacekeeping and enforcement with the American national interest, is about to break up. Contradictions between the two positions are becoming more ap-

---

[4] Gallup Polls, June 25, 1965; August, 1965; February 9, 1966; April 17, 1966.

parent as the United States engages in military action not condoned by the world forum. They also become sharper as the organization intercedes in disputes in ways not considered acceptable by all sections of the American public. As the influence of the non-Western and economically underdeveloped members rises, some sections of the American public will become alienated from the UN; others will come to embrace it more passionately. Some people tend to argue in favor of more national initiatives and more multilateral ties, both economic and military, among the North Atlantic nations, and they tend to oppose American involvement in all military crises elsewhere—whether by way of intervention or in response to UN decisions. In short, the permissive and benevolent mood of the last twenty years is no longer to be taken for granted.

Nor can we rely on the continuity of the present system of blocs, even though neutralism has become respectable in the eyes of Washington. Instead of one nonaligned bloc of Africans and Asians, we will have an increasing trend toward bloc proliferation in the UN, involving committed Asians against nonaligned ones, pro-Western Africans as against neutral or pro-Communist ones, radical Latin Americans as against those favoring the United States. At the same time, these proliferating blocs tend to agree on less and less regarding the substance of world peace. The procedures of UN intercession, based on neutralist balancing between the major blocs and the creative initiatives of Secretary-General Dag Hammarskjöld, may be losing, rather than gaining, relevance here.

Yet both major political parties seem to advocate steps more appropriate to the past internationalist system than to the one we are entering. Republicans have been advocating the strengthening of the Secretary-General's capacity to mount peacekeeping forces, prepare military plans, and be ready to administer strife-torn new nations. They feel that the UN's financial independence ought to be strengthened and voting power should be made more proportional to the voting country's real strength. A high Republican group stated their position:

> Republicans take a realistic view of what the UN can and cannot
> do. We do not believe, as do some, that it is a panacea for the
> problems of the world; nor do we believe it works against our
> national interest. Experience has shown that the UN on many
> occasions has been useful in easing international tensions and in
> implementing our own foreign policy objectives.[5]

[5] Report of the Republican Coordinating Committee, meeting in Washington on June 27-28, 1966. *San Francisco Chronicle*, July 12, 1966.

Democrats do not differ greatly in approach. They, too, favor strengthening UN military planning capacity and the Secretary-General (even though the Johnson Administration had less than complete confidence in the incumbent, U Thant). They also favor the creation of additional national standby forces, capable of being turned into peacekeeping personnel at short notice. Although neither Democrats nor Republicans envisage any drastic institutional innovations approaching some species of world government, Democrats tend to favor increased powers for the International Court of Justice through repeal of the Connally Reservation. And in order to escape both the programmatic and financial "irresponsibility" of the General Assembly, the Democratic Administration has favored a return to the pre-eminence of the Security Council in matters relating to world peace, a course it favors over the introduction of a weighted voting formula.[6]

Undoubtedly, the United States is more enmeshed in the web of interdependence now and for the future than was thought possible in 1945 or 1950. The consequences of the containment policy pursued in the United Nations were far from expected, and the lessons learned by American policy-makers resulted in additional interdependence in the period that followed. The consequences that developed from decolonization likewise resulted in institutional accretions to the UN that had not been planned or even advocated by the United States. Yet the desire for peace and for the exclusion of the Soviet Union from Africa and Asia seemed to leave Washington little choice, unless it wished to intervene on its own. When it did intervene, the cry was loud enough to discourage a unilateral repetition of the episode, because it seemed to cost too many friends and render unneutral too many neutrals. Expediency alone dictates continued dependence on the web, and expediency alone supports policies designed to create standing, well-trained, easily transportable, nonfighting UN forces able to intercede in the minor squabbles outside the Cold War framework.

But bipolar nuclear deterrence will continue to be the tamer of the Cold War itself, not the UN. And as nuclear weapons become more and more widely accessible, the role of the UN in keeping the peace may be called into question. If, at the same time, peacekeeping and enforcement will increasingly take place at the expense of the West and only in the service of the UN majority, the desire to break the fragile bonds of the web may become irresistible in the United States. Hence we must round out our analysis of national

[6] For views of the Johnson Administration, see Richard N. Gardner, *In Pursuit of World Order* (New York: Frederick A. Praeger, Inc., 1964), pp. 94 ff.

and collective security by examining the UN's efforts to tame the nuclear threat. Perhaps disarmament can finally enmesh nation and world, to protect both.

### 4. The Protecting Wing or the Universal Embrace? Disarmament Negotiations until 1958

The large powers have been engaging in disarmament negotiations almost continuously since 1921, interrupted only by major wars among them. These negotiations have overwhelmingly failed to achieve the objective of making the world secure. Why? Chief Soviet negotiator Maxim Litvinov taunted the West in 1932 by asking, "Why don't you just abolish your armies and navies if you are serious about establishing peace?" To which Salvador de Madariaga replied:

> The animals decided to disarm, and held a Conference for that purpose. The eagle, with an eye on the bull, suggested that all horns should be razed off. The bull, with a squint at the tiger, thought that all claws should be cut short. The tiger, glaring at the elephant, was of opinion that tusks should be pulled out or at any rate shortened. The elephant, staring at the eagle, thought it indispensable that all wings should be clipped. Whereupon the bear, with a circular glance at all his brethren, cried out: "Why all those half-way measures? Let all weapons be done away with, so that nothing remains in the way of a fraternal, all-embracing hug." [7]

Clearly, then, collective security and disarmament are closely related. Total disarmament involves complete mutual trust. To abolish national arms implies a willingness to secure peace by way of international police forces; that is, enough confidence in the UN to delegate peacekeeping to someone else's soldiers. Completely successful collective security is inconceivable without significant disarmament; disarmament is inconceivable without mutual trust. Since the bipolar and multipolar systems have not been characterized by large quantities of confidence and good faith among nations, the

---

[7] Salvador de Madariaga, *The Burning of the Parthenon* (New York: Frederick A. Praeger, Inc., 1960), p. 70.

failure of disarmament is easily explained. Yet this is too simple an answer, because it does not explain why the negotiations nevertheless continue and what, if anything, the parties learn from them. Nor does the failure of complete disarmament explain when and how more limited steps, wholly compatible with improved collective security, can be insinuated into the international system.

Basically, the policy of the United States after the end of World War II was to pursue negotiations that would disarm the Soviet Union while leaving intact the American superiority in nuclear weapons. The Soviet Union's policy, not irrationally, was the mirror image of America's. To disarm, then, meant to disarm your enemy. It would be useless and tiresome to set forth, even in summary form, the many disarmament proposals advanced in the various UN committees. None were approved prior to 1958. All foundered because the United States insisted on four features that the Soviet Union interpreted as perpetuating American arms superiority: (1) Disarmament was presented as a *package* of interconnected items of a symmetrical nature, a uniform percentage reduction in ground forces to be accompanied by a uniform reduction in uranium processing capacity or bomber strength. The right package to satisfy both sides was never found. (2) *Inspection* of remaining arms was demanded, and the United States proposed a large and well-equipped force of inspectors. The Soviets sometimes argued that the United States was more interested in inspection than in disarmament. (3) Disarmament was divided into fixed *stages* designed to perpetuate whatever technological advantages the United States enjoyed at the time a proposal was advanced, and the success of the inspection was specified as a precondition for advancing to the next stage. (4) The United States insisted on foolproof *control* over the results of inspections; punitive action without the possibility of a veto was to be taken forthwith against a violator of the rules. Invariably the United States insisted that arms were not so much a cause of tension and insecurity as a symptom of distrust and latent aggression. Once the Cold War abated and every nation abided by the rules of the Charter, meaningful arms limitation could be discussed.

Sometimes the proposals linked disarmament with intelligence-gathering or improving possibly unreliable weapons systems. Without an efficient radar warning system, the first generation of soft missiles, for example, were of dubious reliability. President Eisenhower proposed the "open sky" plan (1955) as a way to prevent surprise attacks and gather intelligence. He also advanced the "Atoms for Peace" plan (1953), the sole proposal that bore fruit at this time. That scheme resulted in the creation of the International

Atomic Energy Agency (IAEA) in 1957. It sought to combine the interests of underdeveloped countries in gaining nuclear lore and access to peaceful nuclear power with the interests of the major powers in preventing nuclear proliferation. Toward that end it was decided that fissionable materials made available for peaceful purposes should not be diverted to military use, and an international inspection service was set up under IAEA to control nondiversion. By appealing to an economic motive, therefore, the United States took a roundabout step in legitimating an international inspection service previously rejected by the Soviet Union.

Did the American public back the government's policy of putting national security ahead of collective security? By and large it did. Far from being compelled to change its policy as a result of public clamor or because of popular fear of nuclear fallout, opinion seemed to shift in response to autonomously determined changes in government policy. Between 1946 and 1953, approval of international control of atomic energy varied between 31 per cent and 63 per cent of the public, and this at a time when government policy favored such a scheme, subject to the conditions listed above. When, during the mid-Fifties, the government stressed the importance of nuclear weapons and the allegedly limited health hazard posed by atmospheric testing, most of the public went along; when the government reversed its arguments in 1958, however, most of the public fell into line again. The more highly educated tended to favor the suspension of tests and feared the hazards of fallout. Party became a salient predictor of attitudes only during the election of 1956, when the Democrats' Adlai Stevenson came out in favor of a test ban and President Eisenhower opposed it. When the government vacillated thereafter between unilateral cessations and resumptions of tests, the public once more followed, only to approve the limited test ban treaty, once it was concluded.

American scientists, the segment of the elite most emotionally and professionally involved with the issue, also divided into several groups. Their views were significant because the technical naïveté of many political leaders compelled attention to the scientific community's arguments and because most of the actual disarmament and arms control proposals advanced by the United States actually originated with scientists. Some scientists felt that international control, though desirable, was possible only with full world government. Since this was held unattainable, a continued national policy of nuclear superiority was strongly advocated. Others, while agreeing that containment was necessary, also argued that a danger point is reached in bipolar confrontations that has to be met with appropriate curbs on arms; and it is this school that ultimately gained control of the State Department's Arms Control Agency. Finally, the most vociferous and active group equates the arms race with vestigial human irrationality, as personified by political and military leaders, and holds out for unilateral disarmament as the only way to unwind the vicious spiral of arms, distrust, more arms, and more distrust, with nuclear war the inevitable outcome. The impact of this group of scientists on the peace movement has been overwhelming, merged as it is with arguments against war drawn from mental health, psychiatry, and pacifism, but its influence on the public and on policy remains marginal.

What, then, caused the government to alter its disarmament policy that sought to disarm the Soviet Union first? Certainly it was not any dramatic shift in public opinion among the mass of citizens. But there did develop in elite circles an awareness that the direct and total approach to disarmament had been utterly futile, while the dangers of nuclear war kept rising. Few would agree with astronomer Harlow Shapley when he contrasted the idealistic scientist with the do-nothing diplomat:

All goes smoothly. We in the International Geophysical Year [a major international cooperative venture in many branches of science] cooperate; in the UN they expostulate. . . . I pause here a second to exclaim, uselessly, "curses on the diplomats." Useless— but it gives me a bit of relief.[8]

But others, from 1958 on, began seriously to consider partial and separate steps toward arms limitation rather than massive package deals, in the hope of first steps leading to cumulative, later strides. An agreement to suspend the testing of nuclear weapons was high on the list of first steps. President Eisenhower's offer to the Soviet Union to negotiate a separate test ban treaty was suggested by Secretary of State Dulles, not by the scientists. What had caused the change in position?

[8] Quoted in Douglas Hurd, "A Case for the Diplomats," *Bulletin of the Atomic Scientists*, 16, No. 2 (February, 1960), 52. Scientists and administrators in the U.S. Atomic Energy Commission sided with the "pure containment" school and sought to sabotage disarmament suggestions by releasing dishonest statistics on the detectability of explosions. Scientists in the other two groups publicly exposed these figures, thus contributing to the loss of favor of the AEC group in the eyes of President Eisenhower, who increasingly relied on James Killian, the head of his Science Advisory Committee, rather than on scientific advice from the Pentagon and the AEC. (Robert Gilpin, *American Scientists and Nuclear Weapons Policy*. Princeton: Princeton University, 1962, pp. 165, 182.)

Two major developments in the international system itself, not at home, proved to be the causes. One was the pressure of small and nonaligned nations in the increasingly multipolar world of 1958. Previous negotiations had taken place in the Security Council, the General Assembly, and in special meetings convoked or sanctioned by the UN. After 1958, the pattern became one of separate negotiations *in secret* among the major powers, encouraged by the UN and conducted under its auspices. The most recent formula is that of the Eighteen-Nation Disarmament Committee (ENDC), made up of five Western, five Communist and eight nonaligned nations, with the nonaligned acting as mediators between the major blocs. The formula symbolizes the response of the international system to the threat of arms; it also illustrates the increasing responsiveness of the United States to this concern.

More important, however, is the threat of weapons itself. No longer a symptom of tensions, the hyperweapons of our era were increasingly perceived by policy-makers as a major cause of tensions, particularly as the Soviet Union matched every American technological advance. Secretary of State Herter clearly articulated the motivation behind this new mood:

> We approach these new negotiations with some hope that the Soviet leaders may be coming to realize that the arms race offers unacceptable risks. This realization could induce them to attach a higher priority to progress in arms control, as being in their own national interest.[9]

Herter went on to point out major dangers associated with an uncontrolled arms race. Proliferation could put nuclear weapons in the hands of irresponsible governments, and present strategic missile systems had such a short reaction time that a war by miscalculation was quite possible. These dangers should be met by agreements that would safeguard against surprise attack, allow exchange of information in times of crisis to assure an opponent that nuclear attack was not planned, and ban nuclear testing for the purpose of halting the increasing probability of proliferation.

President Eisenhower made clear that he feared catastrophe for both nations because of their weapons, and U.S. negotiator Wadsworth argued very cogently that, for the first time, it was the character of the weapons technology itself that caused the United States to change its policy:

[9] U.S. Department of State, *Documents on Disarmament, 1960*, p. 46.

The expanding pace of technological developments can result in unpredictable and erratic breakthroughs, and shifts in the precarious military balance could induce an aggressor to wage war when possessed of a temporary advantage.[10]

Ours is a world of growing dangers. There is a danger of surprise attack prepared in secret. There is the danger of nuclear attack from outer space. There is the menace of constantly mounting stockpiles of nuclear weapons and large armies. There is the peril of spreading capability for the production of modern weapons to greater numbers of Nations. There is the hazard of war by accident or miscalculation. We hold that these dangers must be dealt with now.[11]

This approach was accepted by President Kennedy, who shared his predecessor's belief in the possibility of limited arms control agreements as a slow curtain raiser for a comprehensive agreement. He also shared his predecessor's concern that it was the character of the arms race itself that produced the danger. Because both the United States and the Soviet Union had reached heights of invulnerability, they could both afford to cut back. The experience of the Cuban missile crisis must have contributed greatly to this mood. Pending the creation of a genuine collective security system with a UN Peace Force, then, the cumulative defusing of the nuclear world remained the American position in and out of the UN. "We believe that disarmament in balanced steps would increase the security of the whole world, including ourselves," said Dean Rusk.[12]

## 5. Arms Control and the Future of Collective Security

Since that time, the United States and the Soviet Union have installed the "hot line" communication link between Moscow and Washington (1963), and have agreed on four major arms control steps that also require implementation on the part of other countries. The partial test ban (1963) is one step, though France and China have failed to adhere to the treaty. The outlawry of nuclear weapons in space and the non-annexation of celestial bodies, an agreement concluded under UN auspices (1966), is another major step. A similar agreement was concluded in 1959 for Antarctica, at the same time throwing it open to the inspection

---

[10] *Ibid.*, p. 312.    [11] *Ibid.*, p. 324.
[12] "Disarmament and Arms Control," *Department of State Bulletin* (July 2, 1962), 7.

of any party to the treaty. Finally, the superpowers achieved agreement on a nuclear nonproliferation treaty (1968) that prevents them from aiding non-nuclear nations in the development of nuclear weapons and "other nuclear explosive devices." The IAEA was given new inspection powers under the pact to assure that the non-nuclears divert none of the fissionable materials to such purposes. But since some key countries have so far declined to adhere to the text, the scope of IAEA inspections remains unclear.

Significantly, these negotiations have pitted the nuclear powers against non-nuclear ones, quite irrespective of alliance and ideological links. Some non-nuclears increasingly fear that a nonproliferation pact would deprive them of access to nuclear technology and hinder their industrial development; therefore the draft treaty assures them that the nuclear powers will support a special aid program to avoid this possibility and guarantee the sharing of all in peaceful nuclear experiments. Others feel that unless the nuclear powers also considerably cut back their level of arms, foregoing the acquisition of nuclear weapons would condemn nations such as Japan, India, and West Germany to indefinite inferiority. And in the absence of nuclear arms, how would they protect themselves against possible nuclear blackmail by states not party to the treaty?

Concurrently with the acceptance of the treaty draft, the General Assembly demanded that immediate progress be made toward complete nuclear and general disarmament, a demand to which the superpowers began to accede in 1968. Discussions were also launched, aiming at completing the Partial Test Ban Treaty by including underground explosions. But while Britain and the United States continued to argue for the need of international on-site inspection, the Soviet Union reiterated that the ban could be self-enforcing because of adequate detection equipment in the possession of each superpower. To reassure non-nuclear nations against the possibility of blackmail before all these developments are culminated in new agreements and institutions, the Security Council adopted a resolution recognizing that nuclear aggression would have to be met with an immediate response from the superpowers. Acting under the Charter's article authorizing unilateral acts of self-defense, the major powers have a free hand to extend their protective nuclear umbrella over fearful non-nuclear nations. The UN therefore endorsed the Soviet-American declaration of aid to victims of nuclear threats from nonsignatories. This endorsement, however, contributes little to making the guarantee very credible, since the superpowers retain full freedom of action; conversely, each could veto an explicit Security Council resolution ordering the execution of nuclear guarantees.

Arms control, however, did not mean that efforts at comprehensive disarmament were given up. Like the Soviet Union, the United States committed itself to this goal and, like the Russians, submitted a comprehensive scheme to ENDC. Table 4.2 (pp. 88-89) contrasts the schemes and shows how much closer to a consensus the international system has propelled the superpowers since the earlier days, when disarmament negotiations were little more than Cold War propaganda battles. Note particularly the American insistence on the creation of a UN Peace Force as the crucial step in Stage 3.

Public opinion did not speak with any uniform voice during this period either. In 1960 and in 1963 the public, in almost equal proportions, supported and opposed UN-supervised multilateral arms reduction. Sixty-three per cent of the public supported ratification of the test ban treaty in 1963; 79 per cent thought in 1961 that Khrushchev was bluffing when he supported the same treaty.[13] Nor did elites present a uniform position. Study groups and task forces in both political parties supported the continuation of arms control steps. While fearful that disarmament, and to a lesser extent even arms control, would mean a decline in business, some segments of American industry nevertheless began to study the kind of changeover that a reduction in the arms budget would imply. In cooperation with the Arms Control Agency, studies were made to find out how the electronic industry could contribute to the manufacture of new detection systems. A few labor unions took the same adaptive position, but many ignored the issue. While some spokesmen for the military and for business deplored the outlawry of space weapons and of testing, the bulk of the American elite once more responded to the policy initiatives of Washington. Many business leaders welcomed the cut in taxes and the promise of greater stability and predictability of world conditions if disarmament were to progress.

The major challenge to this line of thought came from the peace groups dedicated to unilateral steps toward disarmament. They actually feared the progress of arms control measures because these tend to stabilize, not abolish, the balance of terror and the deterrent system. To the unilateralist, only schemes that would clearly lead to the abolition of arms through some graduated program of mutual reduction initiated by the United States were morally acceptable. Hence the efforts of the Arms Control Agency were attacked by this segment of the public because they did not go far enough but confirmed the *status quo*.

Controlling arms in one part of the globe need not be a reason

13 Gallup Polls, November 23, 1960; November 26, 1961; November 29, 1961; September 1, 1963; September 18, 1963.

to curtail waging war elsewhere. Unilateralists feared this, and President Johnson demonstrated it as he escalated hostile measures in Vietnam while unilaterally reducing the production of enriched uranium and shutting down some plutonium piles. At the same time, he called for more cession of peaceful fissionable material to the IAEA and voluntarily strengthened the inspection power of that UN agency by placing certain national American installations, as well as bilateral reactor programs, under its jurisdiction. Yet, simultaneously, he also intensified the arms race by committing the United States to the creation of a Manned Orbital Laboratory, to more surveillance satellites overflying enemy countries, and to an Anti-Ballistic Missile System. In the summer of 1968, these steps were countered with joint American-Soviet proposals to ENDC to forbid the placement of weapons on the ocean floor and the seabed. Further, the two governments informed ENDC that they expect to begin bilateral negotiations aiming at the reciprocal limitation of offensive strategic nuclear weapons delivery systems, as well as defenses against ballistic missiles. Yet these negotiations might be delayed by the Soviet invasion of Czechoslovakia. In short, it is unclear how enmeshed is the United States in arms control arrangements. Nor is it clear how seriously one can take the official policy of trusting a UN Peace Force as the sole agency for maintaining collective security after the advent of complete disarmament.

American enmeshment into the frail web of UN organs, agencies, and committees is minimal. Arms control arrangements are mostly self-enforcing, and the inspection powers of the IAEA remain to be tested. UN influence manifests itself primarily in the verbal and moral pressure exercised by the smaller nonaligned nations. For example, the World Health Organization continues to pass resolutions demanding that resources made available by cutting defense budgets be transferred to development aid projects. Very similar resolutions have been adopted by other UN agencies. When the UN Conference on Trade and Development did so, the United States was the sole nation to vote "no" while the Soviet Union abstained. Yet the United States began to bow to this pressure in 1968 when it announced that strong measures must soon be taken under the new Non-Proliferation Treaty, to assure the non-nuclear nations of the benefits of the peaceful use of atomic energy; toward that end it was proposed that IAEA be used to conduct peaceful nuclear explosions and intensify its nuclear technical aid.

The General Assembly is often used as a forum for the discussion of nuclear-free zones, world agreements banning the introduction of nuclear weapons into areas such as Africa and Latin America. After some hesitation, the United States came to favor the arrangement

TABLE 4 · 2

Disarmament Proposals (as of 1966) USSR-USA

| Topics | Stage 1 | Stage 2 | Stage 3 |
|---|---|---|---|
| *Duration* | | | |
| USSR | 18 months | 24 months | 12 months |
| USA | 36 months | 36 months | "as promptly as possible" |
| *Nuclear weapons* | | | |
| USSR | Cease testing and outlaw transfers of weapons. | Eliminate all weapons of mass destruction. | |
| USA | Ceace testing under international control and outlaw transfers of weapons. | Reduce nuclear weapons to minimum levels. | Eliminate all weapons of mass destruction. |
| *Delivery systems* | | | |
| USSR | Eliminate all delivery systems (except small number of homebased ICBM's). | Reduce delivery systems by additional 50 per cent. | Eliminate all delivery systems. |
| USA | Reduce delivery systems by 30 per cent. | | Eliminate all delivery systems. |
| *Outer space* | | | |
| USSR | Prohibit all military uses of space. | | |
| USA | Refrain from orbiting nuclear weapons and limit production, stockpiling, and boosters for space vehicles. | | |
| *Conventional arms* | | | |
| USSR | Reduce by 30 per cent. | Reduce by an additional 35 per cent. | Eliminate except as required for internal peacekeeping. |
| USA | Reduce by 30 per cent. | Reduce by an additional 50 per cent. | Eliminate except as required for internal peacekeeping. |
| *Military manpower* | | | |
| USSR | Reduce American and Soviet armies to 1.9 million men each. | Reduce both armies to 1 million men. | Reduce to number necessary to maintain domestic order and provide contingents for UN police force. |
| USA | Reduce Soviet and American armies to | Reduce both armies by 50 per cent. | |

| | | | |
|---|---|---|---|
| USSR | Reduce military budgets proportionately to arms and manpower reductions. | | Limit military expenditures to maintaining international and national police forces. |
| USA | Submit reports on military budgets and seek agreement on verifiable reductions. | | |

### Military bases

| | | | |
|---|---|---|---|
| USSR | Eliminate foreign bases and withdraw all troops. | | |
| USA | | Eliminate specific foreign bases through agreement. | Eliminate foreign bases and withdraw all troops. |

### Transitional measures

| | | | |
|---|---|---|---|
| USSR | Prohibit joint, and require advance notice of national, military movements and maneuvers; exchange military missions; establish communication systems. | | |
| USA | Give advance notice of major military movements; exchange military missions; establish observation posts and communications systems. | | |

### Inspection and Peace-Keeping

| | | | |
|---|---|---|---|
| USSR | Establish IDO * to supervise destruction of arms. IDO to function under Security Council. | IDO supervision of arms destruction. | Place national militia contingents under Security Council direction; command of troop units vested in body composed of "three principal groups of states" and each must agree to peacekeeping actions. |
| USA | Establish IDO to inspect and control destroyed and remaining arms. IDO to function under Security Council. | IDO inspection and control over disarmament steps and remaining arms. | UN Peace Force to function under Security Council; veto power not applicable to peacekeeping actions. |

* International Disarmament Organization.

Source: Jack C. Plano and Robert E. Riggs, *Forging World Order* (New York: Macmillan, 1967), pp. 333-34.

for Latin America. A text banning the testing, use, manufacture, production, acquisition, and possession of any nuclear weapon on the territory of any signatory was adopted in 1967 and ratified by some Latin-American nations during 1968. Its effectiveness, however, also remains in doubt because, of the nuclear nations, only the United States has given the guarantees of compliance that the treaty expects of all. Furthermore, European nations with territories in the Western Hemisphere have so far declined to give assurances that they will observe the ban in their Caribbean possessions. Finally, the treaty does not ban "peaceful" nuclear explosions, a situation creating uneasiness among the nuclear powers because of their certainty that there is little technical difference between "peaceful" and "weapons-related" blasts.

On the other hand, NATO powers rejected numerous proposals for the creation of inspected, nuclear-free zones in Central Europe, because they would tend to strengthen the Warsaw Pact forces disproportionately. Suggestions for regional arms control arrangements of other kinds continue to be made, and many may become attractive to groups of states as they reach a military equilibrium that satisfies everyone so that armaments can be cut back without disproportionate losses of national security. Agreements among industrial nations not to sell arms to Africa or the Middle East rank high among such suggestions. Others involve bilateral agreements on mutual inspection, such as a Soviet-American mutual surveillance pact for the Arctic. The pursuit of such steps, of course, would doom further the already marginal position of the advocates of dramatic unilateral disarmament.

The future relationship between disarmament and collective security is ambiguous. Consider this argument: the possession of nuclear weapons enables a nation to play a role far beyond the limits imposed by size, population, and tradition. Nuclear weapons may be the great equalizer of world politics. This lesson was learned first by the possessors of these weapons, the superpowers. Test bans and nonproliferation agreements, apart from making the globe a safer place for us all, also tend to perpetuate the extraordinary power of the United States and the Soviet Union. And this fact may doom them if nations such as India, Israel, Egypt, or Indonesia prove unwilling in the future to accept collective security arrangements imposed on them by a concert in the Security Council and seek the possibility of independent action by way of national nuclear weapons. As the Middle Eastern war of 1967 showed, superpowers that successfully deter each other are immobilized if they also fear escalation from conventional war, thus giving a determined small nation considerable room for independent warlike maneuver. The

UN has been unable to prevent this trend, and the proliferation of nuclear weapons would exacerbate it.

But now consider the opposite argument: escalating mutual fear will increasingly predispose the nations to accept the General and Complete Disarmament plans now in the hands of ENDC. The success of these plans, however, implies world government, because the agency that controls the UN Peace Force would, in effect, have to be responsible for world law and order. Complete disarmament implies world government, whether by the UN or some successor body, much as the implementation of the Baruch Plan for the internationalization of atomic energy would have spawned it in 1946. But do the nations want world government? There is not the slightest evidence that preponderant elites *anywhere* desire such a system, and many actively oppose it. Hence the failure of arms control to change the system could lead either indirectly and unwittingly to world government, or directly to the confirmation of the present system of imperfect collective security.

And this is perhaps the strongest argument outlining the future. In 1965 a special White House Conference on International Cooperation advised President Johnson to intensify his search for peace by way of various efforts to achieve disarmament. But the list of suggestions contains merely separate arms control items making up "further steps" leading—perhaps—toward general disarmament. Certainly the unilateralist flavor and passion is lacking.[14] In the meantime, the task of preserving world peace, however imperfectly, has once again become the primary responsibility of the UN Security Council, the forum par excellence of the major powers. Two decades were spent in efforts to outflank this system by means of regional alliances, by the forum of mankind represented in the General Assembly, through unilateral policies, propagandistic and grandiose disarmament schemes, and limited arms control measures that reaffirm the thermonuclear balance. But the inferences that the major powers unwillingly drew from their own outflanking maneuvers persuaded them to reaffirm their enmeshment in the imperfections of the concert and the balancing process in the Security Council. And so it will be as long as there is no massive nuclear proliferation or general and complete disarmament. But what if there is proliferation without the caution born from fear and knowledge of thermonuclear missilery, and what if this proliferation goes hand in hand with a greater multiplicity of blocs, each seeking its own nuclear umbrella? No known formula of national or collective security will be of much comfort then.

[14] Richard N. Gardner, ed., *Blueprint for Peace* (New York: McGraw-Hill, 1966), pp. 48-51.

# CHAPTER FIVE

# ALLIANCES AND REGIONAL SECURITY

## 1. Why Alliances and Treaty Organizations?

Regional military arrangements, with and without standing organizations, grow in direct proportion to disappointment with the efficiency of the UN collective security system. If the United Nations had performed as the United States hoped in 1945 (had promptly restrained and punished those who violated the frontiers and understandings that existed at the end of World War II), there would have been no need for extra-UN security arrangements. This, however, is but another way of saying that if there had been no Cold War and no anticolonial revolt, world peace would have prevailed spontaneously. The fact of the matter, of course, is that in a system of mutually antagonistic definitions of security—when one country's security is another's insecurity—there can be no satisfaction with a collective security system that is accessible to the influence of one's enemy.

And so the United States devoted much effort and thought to the construction of alliances, confusingly labeled by Secretary of State John Foster Dulles as "collective security" arrangements. Collective security properly refers to a global or regional system in which *all* member countries insure each other against *every* member; no state is singled out in advance as the enemy, and each might be an aggressor in the future. Alliances, however, usually come into existence when the members are agreed on the identity of the enemy and wish to insure each other against him. Confusion arises here, too, when the members identify divergent enemies, as they tended to do in the OAS and in SEATO. Properly, regional arrangements and alliances are devices for "collective self-defense," authorized by the UN Charter's Article 51, in the absence of effective UN efforts to repel an armed attack. All regional arrangements, whether initiated by the United States or by other nations, invoke Article 51 in the absence of effective UN efforts to repel an armed attack, even though that text also demands that regional action cease after the UN takes over. Moreover, few regional arrangements avail themselves of the Charter's Articles 52 and 53, which subordinate regional security efforts to UN authorization and control. If the aim is achieving military security not furnished to one's satisfaction by the UN, it is idle to expect conformance with the legal requirements of the UN Charter. But what happens when one's perception of the international system changes, as it did after 1956, with the introduction of multipolarity and multifunctional concerns? Do alliances retain their value, and do regional arrangements continue to restrain national and UN action?

A brief summary of American experience with three major regional alliances will provide an answer. The United States took the lead in NATO, SEATO, and the OAS, in an effort to insure western and central Europe against the Soviet Union, to insure Southeast Asia against China, and to insure the Western Hemisphere against Communist influence, in general, when grave doubts arose that the UN could do those jobs and when it was felt that unilateral action was either impossible or undesirable. What were the specific considerations that led to the weaving of these three overlapping webs?

The military aspects of Western Hemisphere defense originated in 1947 (after intense military cooperation during World War II), and they were incorporated in the multipurpose Organization of American States that took formal shape in 1948. The signatories agree to consider an armed attack upon one as an attack against all American states, and to come to one another's assistance in such an event. Methods for peaceful settlement are to be applied; but if they fail, the OAS, by a binding two-thirds vote, can order enforcement measures against the aggressor. In addition, the members must consult and seek to agree on joint measures "if the inviolability or the integrity of the territory or the sovereignty or political independence of any American State should be affected by an aggression which is not an armed attack, or by any other fact or situation that might endanger the peace of America. . . ." [1] The first obligation is a regional collective security formula: the members insure each other against any armed attack; the second suggests collective self-defense against communism. It was the second objective that was uppermost in Washington's mind in 1947 and 1948, while many Latin-American governments were more interested in the first. The consensus that gave rise to the system was thus diffuse.

The North Atlantic Treaty and the organization that eventually fleshed it out originated in 1948 and went into effect in 1949 as a result of western European desires to insure the fruit of economic recovery with military protection against the Soviet Union. The joint concern with an armed attack is the same as in the Rio Pact, but the obligation to act on it is worded more peremptorily:

. . . if such an armed attack occurs, each [member state] . . . will assist the Party or Parties so attacked by taking forthwith, individually and in concert with the other Parties, such action as it deems necessary, including the use of armed force. . . . [2]

The reasons why a quite unparalleled, joint military organization soon developed from this commitment are obvious once we throw

[1] Article 6, Inter-American Treaty of Reciprocal Assistance (Rio Pact), Sept. 2, 1947. All independent American states (except Canada) comprised the original membership of twenty-one states. Cuba was later expelled; Barbados and Trinidad were admitted. All independent American states are eligible to apply for membership. The "treaty area" is the Western Hemisphere only, including sections of the adjacent oceans.

[2] Article 5, Northern Atlantic Treaty, April 4, 1949. The subsequent discussion rests heavily on William T. R. and Annette Baker Fox, *NATO and the Range of American Choice* (New York: Columbia University, 1967), Chap. 3. The original members of NATO were: United States, Britain, France, Canada, Netherlands, Belgium, Luxembourg, Iceland, Italy, Portugal, Denmark, and Norway. Greece and Turkey were admitted in 1951 and West Germany in 1954. France withdrew from the Organization—but not from the Treaty—in 1965. The "treaty area" includes the territory of all the member states and the section of the Atlantic Ocean connecting Europe and North America, thus overlapping with the OAS treaty area. If an armed attack were begun on U.S. forces in Europe and extended to U.S. bases in the Caribbean, it could trigger the Rio Pact; an armed attack on Uruguay, for instance, could trigger NATO into action. Some NATO members also maintain close military ties with Spain and Malta.

into relief the specific objectives of the United States in underwriting the European concern. Washington expected, by way of American military aid, to spur the Europeans to rebuild and modernize their own armies and prepare their own defense. This, however, required the presence of very substantial American forces and American nuclear guarantee while the military self-help program took shape. Further, NATO was to raise European self-confidence and morale and furnish the institutions for more effective coordinated action, as in World War II. The common effort was to deter Soviet aggression by being prepared to meet it in central Europe and through massive nuclear retaliation (though the exact relationship between the two was to cause NATO great problems later). Built into this military emphasis, moreover, was concern for economic cooperation, liberalization of trade, and the building of a European and Atlantic economic infrastructure (that was also to cause problems later). The total effort was to facilitate political consultations of permanence and depth among the allies, including their respective policies toward the Soviet Union, the UN, and arms control suggestions. Central to the political concern was the desire to use NATO as a means for rehabilitating and controlling Germany. In doing all this, the United States was also extending the geographic space and the resources needed for fending off Soviet pressure. And this ambitious pyramid of interweaving objectives tended to be capped with suggestions for the maintenance (or creation) of an "Atlantic Community" of culturally kindred nations.

SEATO grew up in 1954, in the aftermath of the French defeat in Indochina and the American desire to minimize Communist influence in Southeast Asia. Each member agreed, however, merely to recognize

> that aggression by means of armed attack in the Treaty Area against any of the Parties or against any State or territory which the Parties by unanimous agreement may hereafter designate [i.e., Laos, Cambodia, and South Vietnam] would endanger its own peace and safety, and agrees that it will in that event act to meet the common danger in accordance with its constitutional processes.[3]

In addition, other kinds of threats would call for speedy interallied consultation. United States objectives were clearly spelled out, more-

---

[3] Article 4, Southeast Asia Collective Defense Treaty, signed at Manila, and Understanding of the United States and Protocol (Sept. 8, 1954). The members of SEATO have been the same since 1954: United States, Britain, France, Australia, New Zealand, Pakistan, Thailand, Philippines. France and Pakistan became inactive after 1964.

over, when Washington specified that "aggression" and "armed attack" referred to "Communist" action exclusively, though the United States agreed to consult in the event of other kinds of armed attack. Pakistan, by contrast, considered India its prime threat, Thailand feared as much from Cambodia as from China, and Australia was concerned mostly with Indonesia. Who, then, was the common enemy? The United States regarded SEATO as the device for legitimating a *national* military buildup in the area and for fostering military efforts on the part of the Asian allies, rather than as a vehicle for the ambitious collective tasks implicit in NATO.

Alliances are an adaptation to disappointed hopes for collective security. Americans learned to build alliances and to channel their policy through them. How did the public learn? Did it approve? Did major elites approve? Did world events after 1956 induce a change in the mood of the mass public or in the minds of American elites?

The American mass public has always approved of NATO in unstinting terms and has usually preferred it even to the UN. Although only 32 per cent of Americans approved of separate alliances—as opposed to the UN and national military efforts—in 1949, support grew rapidly thereafter. While all regional military pacts drew public approval, NATO was by far the best known and the most popular. In fact, Ronald Steel's summary is to the point:

> Ever since its creation in 1949 the Atlantic pact has been the object of a remarkable veneration. Our entire diplomacy revolves around it; it is the one constant in a sea of shifting values and allegiances. NATO has been more than simply one military alliance among many; it has entered our popular mythology, enshrined in the hagiography of the cold war. It has become a kind of passion, the one subject on which liberals and conservatives, management and labor, one-worlders and the radical right are able to agree. As the Crusades were to medieval Christianity, so NATO has been to American diplomacy under three administrations: the instrument by which all incongruities would be subsumed in the quest for a higher moral order.[4]

The mood of the mass public has remained broadly permissive of government initiatives regarding regional pacts, but the picture is more complex at the elite level. Opinion and local leaders have tended to consider NATO much more important than SEATO and lesser pacts, perhaps because there is a conviction that the Western

[4] Ronald Steel, *The End of Alliance: America and the Future of Europe* (New York: Viking, 1964), pp. 10-11.

alliance represents spontaneous cultural and political uniformities. On the other hand, there has been widespread feeling, at least since 1956, that military alliances, economic aid, and political friendship need not go hand in hand and that political-military alliances with nondemocratic nations are not desirable. While notions of "Atlantic Community" elicited a mixed response, there remained a clear commitment to American support for European unification, even after 1963 and despite implications of less support for anti-Communist policies. Ambiguity exists also with respect to sharing control over nuclear strategy with NATO allies. There is much uncertainty whenever questions of priorities, specific policy choices, and organizational questions arise. Certainly, while a broadly permissive consensus favoring regional pacts continues, doubts have become stronger as the world has become more multipolar and as broad cracks within existing alliances have become visible.

Disappointment and an appreciation of changed international conditions can trigger two kinds of responses to previously accepted strands in the web of alliances: a desire to withdraw from the entangling alliance or a commitment to improve it by strengthening the web. American elites, at the beginning of the Kennedy Administration, opted in favor of a new commitment and of upgrading common interests—and organizational ties—with their allies, above all in NATO and the OAS. As the international system developed more and more blocs without clear poles or leaders, and as functions and tasks grew more and more diffused, less and less certainty and self-assurance about the future of alliances were manifest. Doubt has not yet reached proportions suggesting a return to military isolationism. But technology and politics combine to make that option a credible one.

A broad military commitment was the common basis for all three pacts. Each survived repeated major changes in the international system, repeated reassessments of national policy, many changes in the destructiveness and effectiveness of weapons. Did each survive by sacrificing earlier objectives or by upgrading them, by weakening or by strengthening the web of American entanglement with other nations? Our survey of opinion merely suggested uneasiness within a permissive mood. The definitive answers are provided by the policy and the changing aims of the government. But first we must establish how, in principle, an initial military objective can trigger additional and expansive tasks.

Disappointment with the attainment of military objectives, clearly, can easily spill over into the realm of economics. When the resource base, the industrial infrastructure, and the soundness of the monetary and fiscal system influence the kind and amount of weapons produced, economic planning and defense planning can readily merge. Strategic planning may come to depend on economic planning and on regional decisions governing defense production. Similarly, when narrow geographic space confronts the invention of ever-speedier and more accurate planes and missiles, "national" military strategy becomes a farce. Technological breakthroughs, in short, may trigger adjustments in strategic planning that make a mockery of nation-states. Similarly, inequalities in scientific and technical knowledge among members of an alliance may create the demand for more scientific "sharing," for joint investments in educational and training institutions with little direct relation to defense. All these thrusts have, in fact, been felt in NATO.

Alliances made up largely of nations in the early stages of industrial and social development face very different problems of expectation and disappointment. The Communist military threat—in Southeast Asia and parts of Latin America—is often indirect. The challenge is the control of subversive activity, national and international, before the proportions of a civil war have been reached. Since subversion is linked to underdevelopment and the violation of human rights, in many cases, alliances may acquire the additional task of seeking actively to contribute to economic and social modernization, to technical education, and to the protection of basic human rights. This has occurred in the OAS to an increasing degree since 1960.

Finally, all alliances depend on a certain inevitable interdependence between basic political and diplomatic choices and military techniques. If war is the continuation of politics by other means, then the original political objective can never be far from the minds of the actors. Hence a vital clue to judging the adaptive capacity of an alliance is the evolving nature of its organs of political consultation. Do they meet increasingly often, do they discuss and decide on vital issues, do the votes carry a commitment to act? Are regional parliamentary assemblies linked to the councils of ministers and instructed diplomats? Are international staffs important in shaping decisions? These are the crucial questions for dealing with the growth and decline of regional commitments.

## 2. The Organization of American States

Latin Americans are hypnotized by the simple fact that the United States is overwhelmingly the most powerful and most efficient nation in the Western Hemisphere. Many believe that the United States is in a position to dictate the trade and investment—and hence the economic development—terms to Latin Americans; many also believe that the weakness of democracy and its frequent overthrow by domestic forces is caused by American diplomatic connivance or economic hegemony; and many are convinced that American military might, represented by the threat or promise of American forces on their soil, is the key to preventing change in the hemisphere. This perception is shared by the left and the right of the political spectrum: those on the left deplore it, and the right tends to find comfort in it. The attitude of both is the result of a long history of economic and military dependence, a tradition of internal instability and forceful overthrows of governments. From the Latin-American viewpoint, then, the purpose of the regional pact was as much to enmesh the United States in a network of legal and institutional restraints as it was to gain security from the exiled revolutionary groups based in neighboring nations. Hence it should come as no surprise that the norms of the inter-American system that took shape in 1948 were the principles of absolute nonintervention and the devotion to democracy. Both principles were invoked loudly and repeatedly, perhaps because they were violated in fact so much of the time.

The United States, like its southern associates, adopted a stance of formal and often empty declaration in lieu of consistent action, in conformance with the style of the "special relationship" that had grown up in the diplomacy of the hemisphere since the initiation of the Good Neighbor Policy in 1933. After 1948, cumbersome intergovernmental machinery was erected atop earlier *ad hoc* understandings and formal declarations. It was designed to facilitate peaceful solution of inter-American disputes as well as to provide regional security against extra-hemisphere enemies. Washington, however, was interested in using the machinery primarily for the maintenance of the *status quo*. Many minor disputes between Caribbean countries were successfully resolved through the pact's Council, Peace Commission, and *ad hoc* diplomatic committees. Washington sought to make of the OAS a miniature UN, obviating unilateral American intervention for the maintenance of domestic and international peace. Toward that end the United States successfully prevented inter-American disputes from being aired in the UN; having learned to use the permissive language of the UN Charter, it maintained stability by taking the path of gentle control over OAS institutions. No wonder that President Eisenhower could greet the OAS as "the most successful sustained adventure in international community living that the world has seen." [5]

The attraction of the OAS increased after 1954 when Communist subversion supported from East Europe, became an active issue. While extracting from its reluctant Latin associates a generalized condemnation of Communist-inspired subversion in the hemisphere, the United States succeeded in heading off UN and OAS discussion of the CIA-managed overthrow of the leftist government in Guatemala. Cuba, however, posed a much more serious problem. Again, the United States sought to use the OAS to legitimate half-hearted anti-Castro steps—with indifferent success. Washingon supported a number of condemnations of the Castro regime and the expulsion of Cuba from the OAS. Cuba's expulsion was the symbolic step that turned the OAS from a quasi-collective security grouping into an alliance. In 1964 the OAS went so far as to authorize economic sanctions against Cuba for having instigated subversive terroristic activities in Venezuela. Still, these steps were largely declaratory and rhetorical, and they were not consistently implemented. In fact, the Kennedy and Johnson administrations were eager at times to head off stronger and more consistent anti-Communist initiatives favored by right-wing Latin American regimes, and "the value of the OAS to the United States depended on its continuing to do *something* about Cuba, but not much." [6] On the other hand, certain Latin-American governments are still determined to uphold the nonintervention principle, even if an outcast nation benefits from it; and domestic sympathy for Castro in many countries prevents meaningful collective action. Paradoxically, as the United States became more attracted to the OAS as a legitimator of American policy, some Latin Americans considered it less legitimate to use OAS for that purpose. The consensus that had prevailed until the end of the Fifties became illusory as inter-American politics were increasingly polarized between stability and commitment to drastic change. "Whether the symbolic legitimacy the OAS has added to United States anti-Communist policies is worth these costs is indeed dubious," [7] comments one careful observer.

But Washington did not remain unaware of the hiatus as the Latin governments grew more restive and less cohesive among themselves. By 1960 the American government, uninfluenced by any

[5] Quoted in Fox and Fox, *NATO and the Range of American Choice*, p. 61.
[6] Jerome Slater, *The OAS and United States Foreign Policy* (Columbus: Ohio State University, 1967), p. 172. Emphasis in original. Slater's account is exhaustive.
[7] *Ibid.*, p. 174.

major shift in domestic public opinion, sought to bolster the effectiveness of the Western Hemisphere anti-Communist alliance by giving the OAS additional responsibilities. The upgrading of the organization's powers involved economic development aid, the protection of human rights and of democracy, a more interventionist policy involving OAS military forces in maintaining peaceful inter-American relations, efforts at closer political coordination among the governments, and eventually, Washington's encouragement of a separate Latin-American economic regional sentiment. Cuba (and the American failure to predict and control the radicalization of that island) was the chief element in this painfully learned lesson.

The Alliance for Progress is the visible symbol of the new economic task of the OAS. Basically a massive bilateral aid program with the United States as the donor, the Alliance also involves a number of multilateral ties. In the first place, the initial planning for such a massive program took place in OAS institutions and meetings. It was here that the initial Latin commitment was made to link drastic domestic social change—including tax and land reforms—with external economic assistance. A new and vital inter-American institution, the Inter-American Development Bank, was set up to advance hard as well as soft loans and outright grants to finance economic and social modernization. Even though half the bank's capital derives from the United States, its policy has been made largely by a dynamic Chilean, Felipe Herrera, who has created the impression that the institution is the Latins' own. The OAS Inter-American Economic and Social Council was made the vehicle for collectively reviewing the progress made by the Alliance for Progress year by year and to offer each country criticism and advice to better its performance. Finally, a standing committee of politically influential economists, whose Latin-American members each represent groups of countries, must review and approve the national development plans of each nation before the United States is to make Alliance aid available.[8] Despite this multilateralization of aid, however, the United States remains the most potent single force in the effort; moreover, the Alliance has failed to produce startling improvements in most countries and, in this sense, seems destined to fail. Therefore, the doctrine of seeking economic better-

---

[8] The committee is called CIAP, *Comité Inter-Americano de la Alianza para el Progreso*. Under the terms of amendments to the OAS Charter to be implemented in 1968, it is to become the permanent executive organ of the Inter-American Economic and Social Council. The committee took the place of an earlier unsuccessful organ of nine "wise men" (economists serving as individuals without political influence) charged with examining and approving national development plans.

ment through more rational industrialization policies by way of a Latin-American common market—able to discriminate against the industrial world—has gained much ground in Latin America. The United States, after being opposed or indifferent to it for many years, endorsed this approach in 1967. Its success would in large measure obviate the continuation of the OAS economic task.

Quite clearly, neither Washington nor Latin America expected the OAS to become an alliance having standing and coordinated military forces similar to NATO's. However, the snowballing of the Cold War and its entrance into the Western Hemisphere did bring with it intensified military activity that, for the most part, manifested itself in purely bilateral American military aid and training programs. Some limited joint planning was done in the Inter-American Defense Board, but the OAS as a formal alliance was not pressed into this service. Instead, the United States successfully used the political machinery of the OAS to legitimate its national measures against Communist threats—most notably in the Cuban missile crisis (1962) when the OAS, acting under the Rio Pact, endorsed the American blockade of Cuba.

But this manifestation of unity was perhaps the high point of inter-allied agreement, because it could be interpreted as opposing Soviet "intervention." More and more resistance to using the OAS as an anti-Communist device has since developed, while a desire for nonalignment in world affairs has grown in such nations as Mexico, Chile, pre-1964 Brazil, and Uruguay. This desire has taken the form of requesting that South America be made a nuclear-free zone, for example, a desire eventually recognized and endorsed by the United States. Again, then, Washington learned to scale down and rearrange its expectations when allies balked at the direction the grouping was given by the dominant member.

But what happens when sparks from embers of the Cold War become a local subversive movement? Two types of situations have arisen and continue to arise. In the first, a right-wing regime is overthrown by "progressive forces"; a civil war ensues, ends in a Communist victory, and results in efforts at subverting more conservative neighboring nations; this is the case of Cuba. The second involves the violent overthrow of a democratic-progressive regime by a conservative military group or a radical revolutionary one, with possible external subversive results. American policy-makers condemn both situations as undermining stability; both are combated through various economic, human rights, and bilateral military measures initiated by Washington. "Selective intervention" is used to deal with such events. But what if these measures fail?

The OAS has shown a marked reluctance to engage in any kind of "collective intervention" to protect an existing regime in the event of either kind of challenge. When the Castroites in Cuba overthrew the military dictatorship, the OAS did nothing; it engaged in very mild collective anti-Cuban measures only after Cuban complicity in subversive movements elsewhere was established. When the United States in 1963 wanted to use the OAS for collective intervention on behalf of democracy in Haiti, the plan had to be given up because most Latin-American governments were unwilling to join in. The tangled history of the Dominican Republic dramatically illustrates this reluctance to intervene. The OAS did condemn the Trujillo military dictatorship in 1960 and authorized economic sanctions against it (executed by the United States alone) when the Generalissimo's complicity in the attempt on the life of Venezuela's President Betancourt was proven. After Trujillo's own assassination, the United States wished to protect the fledgling democratic forces in the Dominican Republic against a military take-over; but all the OAS was willing to do was to endorse United States naval demonstrations and economic measures favoring the democratic regime. Apart from very effective missions of investigating committees, no other permanent involvement was then desired by the bulk of the OAS members. Nor did demands for collective action come forth when the military, in 1962, did succeed in overthrowing the democratic regime. No immediate response was mounted by the OAS when, in 1964, left-wing revolutionaries and parts of the armed forces rebelled against the ruling conservative military regime and sought to bring back the exiled President Juan Bosch, whose elected regime had been overthrown in 1962.

Thus in 1964, the United States intervened alone, to the accompaniment of loud and bitter protests from most of its Latin allies. Only as the purpose of the American military effort grew less and less clear and the opposition to the intervention increased, did the United States call for the creation of an OAS Peace Force to relieve American troops and restore tranquility in the country. As the Dominican crowds chanted, "UN, sí! OAS, no!" the appeal met with very indifferent response and resulted in the participation of only a handful of allied nations; but their participation sufficed to permit the gradual disengagement of American troops as the OAS negotiated an end to the civil war and supervised democratic elections. When Washington sought to perpetuate the principle of an OAS Peace Force to deal with similar situations in the future, however, the suggestion was opposed by the bulk of the other governments as an affront to the principle of nonintervention. Concerted and effective military planning, whether for local or extrahemisphere security, remains alien to the policies of the OAS. Stable Latin governments fear any kind of intervention; unstable governments have good reason to fear it even more, since their credentials to democracy are so often shaky. Conversely, the countries most hospitable to American suggestions for a stronger OAS, such as Guatemala and Venezuela, are also the ones most indebted to bilateral American support. And the inconsistent, if not opportunistic, manner in which the United States has sought to use the principle of collective intervention hardly contributes to the growth of a collective response.

Political consultation and planning have never gone beyond the clamor of an immediate crisis. Contrary to many suggestions, the OAS has not been used to plan the future of the Panama Canal or the possibility of a heterogeneous and multibloc Western Hemisphere system. Nor have proposals for the collective recognition—or condemnation—of revolutionary regimes got off the ground. Senator Fulbright, in arguing for American acceptance of Castro's Cuba as "a distasteful nuisance but not an intolerable danger," also urged that the OAS be developed further into the supreme agency for preventing subversion and confirming each nation's right to rule itself without intervention.[9] There is little in the record of the alliance to support optimism on this score. The alliance will not act collectively unless spurred by unilateral United States action, yet such actions discredit the United States and cast a pall of doubt over the OAS. If the United States has done little to upgrade the regional system as a repository of many policies, her Latin partners have done even less. What has been learned, then, is that collective action is possible only if interests are expanded and tasks upgraded. But the additional lesson must be that except in the field of development economics, even such expansion has not very much thickened the strands of the inter-American web. The OAS has not enmeshed United States policy toward global communism or toward the Soviet Union; nor has it done more than legitimate United States preferences for maintenance of stability in the hemisphere when the quarreling regimes are not part of the left-right confrontation. On the other hand, that very radical–conservative polarization in Latin America prevents the United States from following a consistent line of intervening on behalf of democracy, or against military or Communist regimes. At best, then, our marginal enmeshment keeps any kind of consistent policy from being enacted in the OAS.

[9] J. William Fulbright, *Old Myths and New Realities* (New York: Random House, 1964), pp. 32-35. In May of 1961, 70 per cent of the American public thought it was good to "work with" the OAS to deal with Cuba (Gallup Poll, May 10, 1961).

### 3. North Atlantic Treaty Organization

Before 1956, the "shield" of European and American ground forces was to hold back, delay, or trip up the Soviet armies while the nuclear "sword" of the United States Strategic Air Command would deal with the Soviet heartland; since 1956, the roles have been reversed: the American nuclear "shield" will deter its Soviet counterpart while the European "sword" will thrust its armored columns and tactical nuclear missiles into the Warsaw Pact forces. No metaphor, not even one with an inverted meaning, can disguise the fact that the alliance enshrines the inequalities of size and technological sophistication.

Until 1956 this seemed to pose no great problem. American military superiority over its European allies went unquestioned; their economic recovery from World War II was not yet completed, and the Cold War was a real and live threat in Europe. Furthermore, the American role in actually shaping NATO became crucial after the outbreak of the war in Korea. Briefly, the allies set up, within a few years after 1950, three major "integrated commands" with full powers to deploy and order the forces of the allied powers in case of war. The commands covered Continental Europe, Scandinavia, the Mediterranean, the northern Atlantic Ocean, and the English Channel. The most powerful of the commands was "Allied Forces Europe" headed by its supreme commander (called SACEUR) and his large permanent inter-allied staff (called SHAPE). In peacetime, these commands had the power to recommend training and equipment programs to their forces, to participate in planning the American and Canadian military aid programs, suggest and lobby for specific military and conscription legislation in all national capitals, and to conduct joint military maneuvers. A central military planning staff, covering all commands, was set up in Washington. Let it be understood immediately that the American military was crucial in all commands, headed the major ones, and dominated SHAPE both in terms of ideas and personnel. And as long as the fate of the member nations rested largely on the quality of the American nuclear force this state of affairs received no major challenge.

Further, it became clear by 1950 that military planning was not enough. Economic recovery and investment policies in Europe had to be geared to the military buildup in order to achieve independence from America. A civilian staff for NATO was soon set up to participate in this and to administer the construction of supporting facilities, such as airfields, pipelines, and later the ambitious ground environment for an automated air defense system. A military alliance had acquired an economic and an engineering staff, as well as the power to let international contracts to private firms. Moreover, the desire to economize in defense production led the member nations to entrust the NATO staff with designing and standardizing military equipment, negotiating multinational production contracts, and assuming central responsibility for supplying spare parts.

Since politics could not be banished from NATO, the allies had to "concert" politically and diplomatically in order to provide the policy consensus for the joint military activity. It is here that the difficulties arose even before inequality grew to be a major burden. While military and economic activities were delegated to permanent international staffs headed by the civilian Secretary-General or the military SACEUR, the major decisions were in the hands of the North Atlantic Council and its Permanent Representatives committee. Here all nations participate through their instructed delegates, and unanimity is required to make decisions; inequality is compensated for through voting and representation.

And agreement proved much harder to reach. The allies have never agreed on the basic purpose of NATO. Was it merely the military defense of Europe against Russia, or did it include global economic aid and counterinsurgency programs? Should it perpetuate the division of Europe in general and of Germany in particular, or was its task to reunify Germany and build bridges to the East? NATO diplomacy, even before the French withdrawal, could settle down only on some minimum common denominator. Thus political concerting in the Council was used to encourage the European nations to rearm energetically—without spectacular and immediate results. Economic measures of boycott against the Soviet bloc were discussed and advocated—but not implemented consistently. Diplomatic and military crises *outside* the treaty area were frequently discussed, sometimes because Washington wished to restrain European initiatives (as in the Middle East) and sometimes to draw Europe into the American policy pattern (as in the Far East). Colonial unrest and measures of decolonization proved to be topics of consultation that tended to disrupt the allied consensus. Only when all the allies perceived a crisis as threatening them all equally —as in the repeated difficulties in Berlin—did the consultation process effectively link politics and military strategy. The nadir of ineffectiveness was reached in the open interallied quarrel during the Suez war of 1956. In a way, the French withdrawal and the expulsion of SHAPE from Paris in 1966 merely underscored the erosion of consensus on basic political objectives as world events were interpreted very differently in Europe and in Washington and as Moscow appeared more and more benign.

Despite the leverage available to American political leaders and NATO military commanders of American nationality, the exercise of American leadership in the alliance did not produce consistent and effective results. Why? The answers apply to the periods before and after 1956. "Depending upon one's point of view," write William and Annette Fox, "one can classify American official manners as 'confusing, dictatorial, ruthless, insensitive' or 'courteous, tactful, diplomatic.'"[10] Manners and action proved sometimes contradictory and ineffective because the United States was seeking to please rival domestic and foreign groups simultaneously. Further, the very mixture of military, economic, and political tasks in NATO, far from necessarily complementing one another, confused and obstructed clear action in which one ally would stress diplomatic, and another military, measures. Finally, the leadership of the most powerful increasingly produced its own difficulties: the resentment of the led who decline to be manipulated by the mere invocation of the legal formula of sovereign equality. "'Partnership,' 'sharing,' 'consultation,' 'balanced,' 'mutual' and 'cooperation' help to make endurable those relationships which are not wholly symmetrical or reciprocal and which are better not publicly described by American officials in the harsher language of power differentials if the alliance is to hold together."[11]

The test of the healing magic of words came after 1958, when the economic recovery of Europe and the fading of the Cold War gave increasing credence to claims for absolute equality, symbolized by de Gaulle's stance toward NATO. By that time the special inducement once provided by the American military aid and mutual weapons development programs had faded because of Europe's own industrial and economic prowess. Europe was increasingly concerned with being able to produce its own sophisticated equipment, and the French decision to acquire a national nuclear deterrent force was welcomed in many quarters, as European ability to master nuclear technology grew apace at the national and the regional levels. But these sentiments did not go so far that they eliminated a minimum sense of common purpose. Despite restiveness, NATO agreed by 1968 on a new multinational air defense system, a refurbished Continental strategy, and on a NATO satellite communications system. As the Czech crisis unfolded, NATO characteristi-

[10] Fox and Fox, *NATO and the Range of American Choice,* p. 75.
[11] *Ibid.*

cally urged members to bring their forces up to previously determined numbers and effectiveness. Moreover, intensified air and naval surveillance of Soviet ships in the Mediterranean was initiated.

Nuclear weapons and the question of who would control their use are central and symptomatic of NATO's fate. The European allies were increasingly dissatisfied with a strategy that retained an unrestrained American capacity to use—or not to use—the ultimate weapon. Some feared American recklessness in targeting and command; others feared American timidity that cast doubt on the credibility of the deterrent. After all, the United States might not wish to risk its cities for the ground defense of the Elbe River line. Progressive American gestures aimed at distributing tactical nuclear weapons and knowledge regarding their use, while retaining control over the warheads, failed to resolve the issue. The assignment of European liaison officers to Strategic Air Command headquarters did little more. The stationing of American-manned missiles in Britain, Turkey, and Italy produced bipartite control but did nothing for NATO. As France sought to resolve matters by undertaking its own nuclear program, voices were raised in Germany that Bonn had better do the same, perhaps, alone or in concert with France or Britain.

American policy sought to adapt to this new NATO mood, but the learning that took place proved inadequate to the challenge. The American formula for retaining nuclear leadership while seeming to "share" it with Europe—and thus head off separate German nuclear rearmament—took various forms: the assignment of Polaris submarines to SACEUR, the creation of a NATO Polaris force, the setting up of a mixed-manned NATO fleet of surface missile ships. Britain contributed a plan that would have placed national nuclear forces under partial SACEUR control. None of these formulas satisfied European restiveness, and they were abandoned by 1965 in favor of an effort to chart NATO's nuclear future by means of a Nuclear Planning Committee of countries especially concerned, functioning under the NATO Council. Little overt strife on nuclear strategy has been evident since.

Previously, a strong but inadequate attempt to rescue NATO's common task had been made in the area of scientific and technological knowledge. Secretary-General Spaak and many Americans advocated meeting the European desire for rapid progress in scientific education and development by creating an ambitious NATO science program that would "share" American superior knowledge with an eager Europe. The program, though launched, was so modest that it was not able to deal with the issue, and it failed to upgrade the NATO task. Learning, then, came too late to reverse the disintegrative course into which NATO had drifted.

The revival of self-confidence in Europe, in the sense of national and continental self-awareness among the Six of the Common Market, was not lost on the American public. After France's vote in 1963 to exclude Britain from the Common Market, only 32 per cent of the public thought France a dependable ally, while the figures for Germany and Britain were 58 per cent and 63 per cent, respectively.[12] American officials began to modify their support for European economic and political integration by stressing that it must neither interfere with NATO nor with American access to the European export market. And as the Soviet Union kept making clear its determination to foster a weakening of NATO as part of its détente with the United States, more and more American observers wondered out loud whether it was worth preserving a divided NATO that could agree neither politically nor militarily.

The terms "Atlantic partnership" and "Atlantic Community" appear increasingly in the mid-Sixties. What do they mean? Do they provide verbal and political magic to cover over the schisms of diverging interests? Did they serve as a "Grand Design" for unity representing an adaptive America's response to an international system very different from the one that prevailed in 1949? When President Kennedy first evoked these phrases, they seemed to suggest a readiness to create a North Atlantic confederation on the ruins of the alliance. He made clear that he did not advocate an Atlantic free trade area and saw no reason for the United States to join the Common Market. Nor did a constitutional prescription for more powerful central institutions make its appearance in government thinking, though many such ideas were strongly advocated by the unofficial Atlantic Treaty Association and Atlantic Council, often with the support of the "elder statesmen" of an earlier NATO: Dean Acheson, Will Clayton, Lauris Norstad, Alfred Gruenther, and others. "Partnership" was the phrase that recurred most often, and it seemed to imply the groping toward a future web of interdependence in which North America and a united Europe would be equal military partners in deterring the Soviet Union, and they would be close trading partners by virtue of the drastic tariff-cutting implied by the success of the Kennedy Round.

While there were small pockets of fear among business and labor, the overwhelming number of interest groups seemed to favor such an approach. President Johnson, on several occasions, lauded the

[12] Gallup Poll, March 13, 1963.

contributions of the alliance, the necessity for retaining and deepening the trans-Atlantic partnership, as well as the undeniable necessity to adapt NATO to changing circumstances. "Every advance in the technology of war makes more unacceptable the old and narrow concepts of sovereignty," said Mr. Johnson.[13] Is NATO therefore slated to be a Community in form as well as in rhetoric? The President gave no hint, other than to urge that NATO continue to work for peace, that the United States continue to work for a united and independent Europe, *and* that the détente with the Soviet Union continue![14] Vice-President Humphrey hardly clarified these objectives by arguing forcefully that an independent and united Europe is both inevitable and desirable, that NATO be adapted to this end by more joint nuclear planning and political consultation toward a coordinated détente with the East *and* by a nuclear nonproliferation treaty. It still looked ˋlike a made-in-Washington alliance policy that could be realized only at the expense of French and German conceptions of the future.

To Americans—the public, articulate elites, and officials—"NATO" remains an ambiguous symbol. It seems to mean an organization, an alliance, and a unilateral American guarantee given to Europe. It also provides a shorthand phrase to describe a "special relationship" with certain allies, notably Germany and Britain. No clear distinction between selective American choices and ties as opposed to total commitment to an organization is ever made; yet "NATO" is made to cover both extremes. Granting this ambiguity, we must still ask ourselves whether the NATO web has grown stronger or weaker over the years.

Has NATO's organized influence restrained and limited American initiatives? NATO exercised an important influence on American military aid policy, the deployment of ground forces, and the design of weapons in the days of the bipolar and tripolar international system; but it had a much smaller role in influencing American strategic planning during the multipolar and multibloc phases. Nuclear planning has been done unilaterally by the United States; current efforts to approach it multilaterally through a select com-

[13] L. B. Johnson, "Our View of NATO," *Atlantic Community Quarterly* (Summer, 1966), p. 157. Republicans went further toward implementing an Atlantic Community objective by suggesting a tolerant attitude toward France, more nuclear sharing, and high-level diplomatic planning by a small group of experts. "Republican Fact-Finding Mission on NATO," *Atlantic Community Quarterly* (Fall, 1965), pp. 400–402.

[14] L. B. Johnson, "Making Europe Whole: An Unfinished Task" (address on October 7, 1966), in *The Atlantic Alliance: Current Views*, U.S. Senate, Committee on Government Operations, Subcommittee on National Security and International Operations (Washington: USGPO, 1967), pp. 1-6.

mittee of NATO members willing to take joint action is the first real departure from that practice, learned at great cost to American leadership. NATO has had little influence on American policy on economic aid and arms control, and very little on political and diplomatic measures outside the European area. Joint planning was featured in Berlin; it was absent with respect to the Middle East and Southeast Asia; it cast Europe in the role of the follower, not the partner, in Cuba. Since 1960, there has been a growing *decline* of common tasks and ties regarding joint defense procurement and weapons-planning, force assignments, and a military division of labor between America and Europe and among Europeans.

As for the success of the United States in using NATO to enmesh Europe in firmer ties, the picture is equally blurred. NATO has been undeniably successful in deterring the Soviet Union as long as there was a Communist military threat, and it was quite useful for reintegrating Germany into Europe while restraining her yearnings for reunification. However, little came of oft-professed American hopes of using NATO as a means for persuading Europe to adopt American-preferred defensive postures and military policies, building a Community, deepening political consultation, or coordinating economic warfare measures.

Leadership toward these American objectives could be exercised only by stressing inequality, by asking Europe to make sacrifices in sovereignty that the United States was far from ready to match. American officials were unprepared to engage in the kind of give-and-take that makes "sovereignty" irrelevant because technically respected officials with flexible instructions manage, in private, to work out pragmatic measures that satisfy specific and variable groups of countries within the alliance. This was sometimes successfully done in the economic institutions of the Atlantic region (OECD) but less and less commonly in NATO. In military affairs, drift tended to become diffusion; the shield and the sword begin to look more like an ink-blot on wet paper.

The NATO governments have not been unaware of these difficulties. Their effort to resolve them took the form of yet another high-level interministerial committee dominated by the small nations, the Harmel Committee, which presented a scheme accepted by the NATO Council in December of 1967, with French and American support. As a result, NATO was to devote itself to *collective* negotiation with the Warsaw Pact, the object being a broad European security agreement, including provisions for dealing with the division of Germany. In addition, parallel disarmament and arms control agreements between the two opposing alliances were to be sought. While endorsing this package that seeks to rescue NATO by attempting to give it the task of negotiating its own demise, the United States also suggested that Washington would continue to conduct *separate* bilateral talks with Moscow on questions of relaxing tensions, even after the occupation of Czechoslovakia. While urging continued support for the unification of Europe, the United States also wanted a partnership with Europe in speaking to the Third World with one voice.

NATO's new dedication to arms control, *détente* negotiations, and political consultation suffered an apparent check in November of 1968 as the Council of Ministers reacted to the Soviet occupation of Czechoslovakia with a renewed emphasis on the continued reality of the Cold War. The allies declared that Austria and Yugoslavia—though nonmembers—were in effect to be considered under the NATO umbrella. Intensified military preparations were undertaken as well. But if the Soviets now respond by de-escalation and show the restraint apparent before 1968, clarity of purpose among the allies will again vanish. Emphasis will shift once more to the package of measures suggested by the Harmel Committee, and the alliance will stumble along formally unchanged beyond 1969. The sweeping renegotiation of the treaty, once considered likely in that year, is then unlikely to occur.[15]

## 4. The Southeast Asia Treaty Organization

If the "voice of the United States was too loud, too peremptory, too confused, too disunified and heard too often and too soon" in NATO, the Atlantic alliance nevertheless did the job for which it was originally designed.[16] SEATO did not. The consensus on which it was based in 1954 was, at best, a convergence of very different national objectives. Time has done much to make them diverge and thus doom any tightening of the web of military interdependence with political and economic implications in Southeast Asia.

The legal obligation to come to the assistance of a nation threat-

---

15 See Eugene V. Rostow, "Concert and Conciliation: The Next Stage of the Atlantic Alliance," *Department of State Bulletin* (October 2, 1967); also Harlan Cleveland, "How to Make Peace with the Russians," address delivered on March 13, 1968. Dept. of State. Undated reprint. For a different interpretation see Alastair Buchan, "The Future of NATO," *International Conciliation* (November, 1967).
16 Fox and Fox, *NATO and the Range of American Choice,* p. 296.

ened by China or her allies was far from airtight. Further, American spokesmen have stressed that the obligation is an individual one, not dependent on a collective finding of the allied powers or the organization. Not unnaturally, therefore, they have also admitted that the weight of the American military commitment in Southeast Asia rests less on SEATO's multilateral machinery than on bilateral understandings between the United States and countries in the region, such as the Philippines, Thailand, and South Vietnam. SEATO was supposed to keep the Chinese out of these nations, as well as the North Vietnamese and the Laotian Communists; but it was supposed to do this by legitimating direct American military assistance and presence rather than by virtue of unified commands, joint defense production policies, or centrally determined strategies. Military assistance programs, the exchange of intelligence, training programs in counterinsurgency, and joint military and naval maneuvers made up the curriculum of SEATO, all of which could have been, and was partly, achieved by bilateral means. The commitment of Australia, New Zealand, Thailand, Malaysia, and the Philippines to American objectives did not require SEATO. Yet SEATO did not suffice to commit Pakistan or France to those objectives as the war in Vietnam dragged on, as both made their opposition to SEATO's endorsement of the American intervention very clear. Finally, Britain by no means shared all of America's objectives, particularly regarding the policy of isolating Peking.

On balance, as the presence of the United States in the area penetrated more and more deeply, Britain and France sought to use SEATO—unsuccessfully—to restrain American policy. Thailand, however, had unsuccessfully attempted to use the alliance to bring about a deeper commitment in Laos. The United States, on the other hand, was able to profit from SEATO in persuading Australia and New Zealand to contribute actively in the Vietnam war. Some mutual enmeshment thus took place, but not enough to give SEATO the degree of authority and legitimacy that NATO still enjoyed after its decline and after the French withdrawal.

## 5. Alliances and the Multibloc System

If the mutual restraints and multifunctional proliferation of activity implicit in the global multibloc system are considered either inevitable or desirable, these alliances have outlived their utility. This is as true of the lessons the actors themselves have learned from modern international politics as it is of the observer's meditations on those lessons and their meaning for the future.

American policy during all of the phases and periods that have unrolled since 1945 has been implemented by seeking to organize and transform the external environment through bilateral, regional, and universal groupings. The three overlap; they converge and they conflict; they are combined in one thrust only to be disassembled into separate and ill-matched components on the next major issue or the next crisis. But all three remain part of the picture, if only in providing the ingredients for a puzzle.

Alliances arose because of dissatisfaction with the global level of action, the United Nations. Regional pacts had most viability and demanded most of the security inputs of their members, certainly of the United States, at the time when the UN was considered of little use in dealing with the Cold War. Moreover, as the colonial revolution spread, Europeans began to think of NATO as a great family, while they perceived the UN more and more as a hostile tribunal. America's espousal of the UN at the expense of NATO during the Suez crisis of 1956 did nothing to dispel this impression.

But time passes, and the most recent period in world history has seen a cautious revaluing of global collective security, a use of the UN to defuse local conflicts and keep them out of the reach of the superpowers. As the colonial era recedes into history, the frustrations of the Fifties and early Sixties are forgotten, and the UN becomes once more an accepted means for seeking peace and security. The actors in regional alliances have learned to make use of the UN while also retaining their regional ties. The United States especially has learned how to play each instrument and not necessarily to sacrifice the universal orchestra for the regional solo. As regional organizations have helped the UN maintain peace on occasion, in Africa as in Latin America, some members of regional systems dominated by the United States have come to prefer UN to regional action. Since the chief actor—the United States—wishes to play on the regional as well as on the global stage, manipulate the UN as well as the three major alliances, he must pick and choose by keeping allies allied and neutrals neutral. As the United States sought, in the Third World, to build and maintain majorities favoring its global policies, the emphasis on regionalism was the loser. The lesson of 1951 had been: sidestep the UN and build a community of like-minded states; the lesson of 1968 seems to be: like-mindedness is a fickle quality; a successful global policy of relative peace demands a larger coalition, though not necessarily a stable or reliable one, than can be offered by SEATO, NATO, or the OAS.

This much the actors have seen and assimilated. But as observers, we may draw out even larger—as yet unseen—inferences. America's alliances are disintegrating. It may be that "America has no monopoly on New Frontiers, and as the nations of Western Europe pass into the hands of a new generation of leaders, they are likely to be more tempted by the prospect of a Europe united in neutrality than a Europe divided between two nuclear colossi." [17] The pursuit of a *détente* with the Soviet Union and the simultaneous support for West European unification are today compatible policies for the United States. But to seek to combine the preservation of NATO with both is to add apples and pears and pretend to have an orange-flavored fruit salad. More and more Latin-American states are veering toward their own kind of nonalignment as they assert their national identity, a trend likely to gain speed as Latin-American regional economic integration proceeds. If, at the same time, more and more Americans come to believe, as I believe, that alliances with underdeveloped and uncommitted nations benefit neither them nor the United States, the disintegrative process must win.

Increased dependence on unstructured collective security processes and rules in the UN will be accompanied by the proliferation of regional arrangements in the Third World, not dominated or even joined by the western nations. We will see new alliances and economic groupings, but each will be relatively noncohesive internally. Proliferation combined with the loss of regional cohesion will introduce a very large area of indeterminacy into the operations of the UN, moderated so far by the reluctance of both Washington and Moscow to take full advantage of each other's failures and discomforts. Coalitions that dominate in the field of trade rules live side by side with very different coalitions in the field of collective security or human rights or technology. Rewards and punishments in one issue area can no longer easily be offered in another by the dominant states of the system—the United States and the Soviet Union—because each issue area will become legitimate in its own right and because the diffusion of wealth and influence that defines a multibloc system naturally implies lessened influence for the superpowers.

As the observer interprets and puzzles over the blocks of action and thought of nations that make up the learning pattern, he must come to the conclusion that impulses originating in the global system are considered more important by the actors than inputs originating either at the regional or national level. American leaders

17 Steel, *The End of Alliance*, p. 97.

have always argued that the bilateral, regional, and global levels of action should, and do, complement one another in the attainment of American objectives and the maintenance of peace. Our Cook's tour through UN collective security and the role of alliances in American policy suggests that the coordination has been less than perfect and that disappointment at one level tends to trigger actor learning, resulting in emphasis on the others. To orchestrate harmoniously and effectively at all three levels presupposes unity of outlook and planning in Washington and in American politics, a supposition that is simply at variance with the facts of pluralism. It also assumes a capacity for rational calculation and prediction that American officials have not so far displayed. Regionalism has not consistently enmeshed the bilateral level of action so that it seriously restrains national American initiatives in world affairs. But interaction, negative criticism, the options provided by coalitions of supporters from the Third World at the level of the United Nations —all have had restraining influence on national action. This has not been planned or anticipated by American officials. Because American leaders are unable to orchestrate the three levels of policy into a powerful symphony of action, the global level of action has taught them lessons that condition national action more often than do the regional pacts and symbols, even if these do speak of "special ties" and "lasting communities." And so the wheel of consciousness and learning, given another twist, reaffirms reliance on the UN in conflicts that do not involve direct confrontations of the superpowers—not because this is welcomed or desired by America, but because there is no other way of safeguarding a national interest in a global web of interdependence.

# CHAPTER SIX

# WORLD TRADE AND FINANCE

Cotton marketing agreements, the flow of gold, and haggling over tariffs make less spectacular news than nuclear bomb tests, truce violations, or the disintegration of alliances; but they cause no less controversy, and they may entail human suffering and deprivation on a massive scale if not handled with care and solicitude. If the practice of collective and selective security is tied to the ideological passions and fears of peoples and their leaders, the practices of world trade and finance are no less rooted in convictions and commitments on what constitutes the good life and the good society—nationally as well as internationally. Mutually opposing values in the international trade and monetary arena, in and out of the United Nations, engender conflicts and patterns of accommodation that, in catering to the physical welfare of peoples and nations, may enmesh the nation-state in its pursuit of welfare. The United States is a giant among world traders and investors. It believes in free private enterprise, private capital, and competitive trading based on the liberal economist's doctrine of comparative advantage.[1] Can it prevail in a world that does not share these values very consistently? More than twenty years of experience in the web of international organizational discussion suggests that it cannot.

## 1. The Free Enterprise Vision of the International Economy

American policy-makers emerged from the cataclysm of World War II with well-articulated beliefs concerning the kind of economy they wanted for the peaceful and prosperous world that was to emerge from the fighting. They wanted a world in which the economic cutthroat practices of the Great Depression of the 1930's would not be repeated. They also wanted a world that would give scope to American private industry and agriculture, to sell abroad without suffering from tariff and quota discrimination or be victimized by unstable exchange rates and arbitrary currency devaluation. Finally, they wanted the needs of capital-importing nations to be served by American private investors rather than by government loans. In short, what they desired was a self-regulating and stable world economy that would give scope to American enterprise and that would require a minimum of institutional control. The economic development of the less wealthy nations and those devastated by the war would be advanced primarily through expanding world trade and private investment—not through government-to-government assistance.

These beliefs were widely shared among the business elite and the government. Economic issues are predominantly the preserve of the elites who are able to identify their interests in a global setting. There is no articulate public opinion in the realm of trade and finance, as shown by the unvarying pattern of equally divided positive, negative, and "don't know" answers in public opinion polls on world economic questions. In this chapter, therefore, we will be concerned exclusively with interest group and governmental opinion and its evolution. It is therefore of the greatest importance to note

[1] See Robert L. Heilbroner, The Economic Problem (Englewood Cliffs, N.J.: Prentice-Hall, Inc., 1968), pp. 534-37.

the special ties that exist between certain interest groups and the agencies in Washington that relate directly to their demands and needs. Economic policy-making is less consistently dominated by the President than are military and security matters. Congress has made its voice heard persistently and forcefully. The large departments of the government speak with many and often conflicting voices and thus reflect the aspirations of the elite groups that enjoy their confidence.

This was as true in 1945 as it is today. The Treasury Department and the banking world identify with the essentially conservative attitudes outlined above and attempt their implementation through the International Monetary Fund (IMF) and the International Bank for Reconstruction and Development (IBRD), institutions set up largely in response to desires of the financial community after World War II. American farmers, always eager to sell their surpluses and maintain high agricultural prices, channel their demands into the Department of Agriculture, which in turn seeks to shape international policy by turning to the Food and Agriculture Organization (FAO) of the UN. American labor approaches world economic problems partly by preaching the need for free unions everywhere, higher skills, manpower training, and productivity programs; it does so through the Department of Labor and the International Labor Organization (ILO). The social welfare profession, charitable groups, women's organizations, teachers, and communications specialists channel their demands for international welfare services and relief organizations through the Department of Health, Education, and Welfare, an important participant in the United Nations Educational, Scientific and Cultural Organization (UNESCO), the World Health Organization (WHO), and in special UN aid bodies such as the UN Children's Fund. Most business groups channel their demands through the Department of Commerce; this agency, in turn, is an important shaper of American foreign trade policy in the General Agreement on Tariffs and Trade (GATT) and in some regional organizations. And the Department of State? State is involved in all of these; but American representation in this tangle of international organizations is shared with the other departments, leaving State unable clearly and unambiguously to "plan" American economic policy. That policy, then, is the result of clashing and conflicting group interests and values reflected in equally discordant champions in Congress and in the Executive. Yet they all "make policy" when the President makes no effort to pre-empt the field.

The postwar governmental approach to world economic problems was thus shaped largely by business and banking interests.

Neither of these groups, however, is internally homogeneous. One segment is "fundamentalist" in belief; it stands for the universal validity of the American Way of Life in free private enterprise, and it distrusts government regulation at the national as well as the international level. Another, and generally more powerful, segment accepts these tenets but is ready in practice to adjust them to meet external obstacles. Further, and more importantly, this segment— usually found in the banks and big corporations on the northeastern and Pacific seaboards—is ready often to subordinate economic ideology to political imperatives. Thus, while spokesmen for this group advocated and endorsed the free enterprise approach to world economic entanglements in 1945, they were also prepared to sacrifice aspects of their ideological purity when Europe's failure to recover immediately called for the extraordinary *public* aid program we know as the Marshall Plan. Thinking in the Treasury Department differed from the business ethic only in that it added one Keynesian consideration: domestic prosperity was thought to depend on the international economy's taking up the slack of a recession at home without at the same time reintroducing the beggar-my-neighbor policies that had flourished during earlier depressions. Hence modest international pump priming through the IMF and the IBRD was seen as an ancillary device for assuring American prosperity.

The American master plan for a better world was made up of three interdependent parts, each the subject of prolonged international negotiations between 1944 and 1947. The UN had no prominent place in the plan. UN agencies were to be used essentially for immediate emergency services, such as feeding and resettling refugees, dealing with epidemics and famines, and regulating the technical aspects of telecommunications and air services. The basic ground rules of world trade were laid down in the Havana Charter and were to be administered by an autonomous International Trade Organization (ITO), a specialized agency-to-be of the UN. These rules governed permissible restrictions on private investment, dumping, trade in agricultural commodities and the prices to be fixed therefor, the permissibility of exchange controls, and quotas on imports. Further, the charter laid down the basic rule that tariffs that discriminate by giving preferential treatment to certain countries— the British Commonwealth system was in everybody's mind—were to be eliminated by the consistent application of the most-favored-nation clause in international tariff bargaining. State trading was permitted but subject to special rules. The United States insisted on ITO rules and powers of regulation that would combat the economic nationalism of others, thus permitting American exports and investments to penetrate their protected and discriminatory trading systems. America had come of age and felt able to compete successfully with all comers.

The second component of the master plan was the world monetary system, as institutionalized in the IMF. The essence of the system was stable exchange rates set authoritatively by an international agency in order to bar unilateral and arbitrary national devaluation of currencies, and the abolition of exchange controls, to free international capital movements. These objectives were to be accomplished by creating a world reserve of hard currencies— essentially dollars and sterling—and gold held by the IMF. When a country was tempted to change the value of its currency to cope with balance-of-payments difficulties, the IMF would give short-term assistance with hard currencies. About $9 billion in reserves was available. All member states retaining exchange controls pledged themselves to remove them. Changes in par values of currency beyond a fixed limit and not authorized by the IMF were illegal and could deprive the violating state of the right to draw on the IMF reserve in case of need.

On paper at least, the IMF was a powerful supranational organization. But since voting was weighted in accordance with the contributions of hard currency made by its members, the American share, coupled with the actual role of the dollar as the dominant world currency, sufficed to make the IMF a peculiarly American institution. Entanglement in an institutional web, in reality, masked American predominance in a world of soft currencies and IMF quotas very much smaller than the American. Yet, it was only because of monetary conservatism and the belief in private enterprise and economic market forces that a stronger IMF did not come into existence in 1945. One prominent Treasury official had thought in terms of a world monetary authority that would have powers similar to an international central bank. The British plan for a monetary authority had granted far larger pump-priming powers to the fund and more automatic drawing rights to the member governments. But free enterprise preferences carried the day over extensive regulatory powers to which the United States itself might be exposed.

The third part of the master plan was a world bank, capitalized at $10 billion, with the task of making loans to governments to rebuild war damage and engage in basic economic development in circumstances in which private capital was not forthcoming for the job. Again, the IBRD was not to compete with private investments and was not to make "soft" loans that might run counter to the American business ethic. Voting power was again made proportional to the contributions of the members, with over half of the power going to five major industrial nations; the United States acquired approximately 25 per cent of the votes in the IMF and 32 per cent in the IBRD. Since the work of the IBRD relates to economic development rather than to trade, we shall discuss its role in the next chapter.

And so the scene was set for American ingenuity to make its way in the world, to demonstrate the virtues of private enterprise and advanced industrialism in a world united in a single system of trade and finance through rules of nondiscrimination and exchange stability, to the combined benefit of people everywhere—industrial and underdeveloped, modern and traditional, capitalist and not so capitalist. The awakening was as rude as the adaptation of the American elite was rapid.

### 2. The World Economy and the Tarnished Vision

America's economic ideology encountered three obstacles that prevented its victory; two of them resulted from events and attitudes outside the United States, but one was the result of internal pressures. Economic liberalism is rarely espoused with passion by economic groups that consider themselves high-cost producers unable to compete with rival imports, and American businessmen and farmers are no exception. The internal political environment, therefore, militated against a consistent policy of cutting tariffs for items produced at high cost in the United States. Further, it militated against a managed international commodity policy that would keep American farmers from selling their huge output at nationally subsidized prices; nor would it permit American importers of primary commodities to pay higher prices than the world market created.

The outside world posed a series of purely economic obstacles. The countries of Western Europe were not prepared to establish free trade, forego exchange controls or quotas, as long as they thought a planned economy was required for postwar reconstruction. While the underdeveloped countries were not yet in a position to make their views prevail, several of them nevertheless took issue with the American preference for free trade over massive aid as a means for spurring development. They evinced no great enthusiasm for non-discriminatory tariff rules that would have the effect of subordinating their infant industries to the powerful industrial exporters or for currency convertibility that would soon strain their balance of payments and limit their ability to devalue. Further, they wanted the power to resort to state trading and to regulate international commodity trade in order to stabilize the prices of primary products. The Soviet bloc, finally, branded the world trade system favored by the United States as the global version of exploitive capitalist imperialism and insisted on the central role of state trading and national protection *against* private investment; the Soviets therefore declined to join the IMF and the IBRD.

Perhaps the sharpest challenge to the free enterprise vision came from the external political force posed by the evolving Cold War. It is surely one of the major paradoxes of our time that the defender of capitalism should employ an inverted Marxist argument in favor of a new economic policy running counter to liberalism. As the advance of communism in Europe came to be perceived as the major threat to the United States, Washington reacted by creating the largest—and most successful—foreign aid program ever devised. The program, among other things, also substituted grants for loans, soft loans for hard ones, permitted exchange controls and tariff discrimination against dollar imports, encouraged "socialist" planning, and subsidized in Europe the monetary support and clearing mechanism that had been rejected for the world when the IMF was set up! Why? Because of the conviction—shared by the majority of the business elite, labor, and the government—that systematic efforts to raise living standards and further industrial democracy must be made to head off the appeal of communism.

In short, between 1947 and 1958 the United States learned not only to live with, but to shape a web of economic interdependence that ran counter to much of the original intent and commitment. The dominant economic state in the world progressively gave up ideological purity in its effort to gear economic policy to the political objective of fighting communism, to seek a free world economy for its exports, and to retain a protected national economy for those segments that claimed inability to compete with imports. I shall illustrate this lesson in learned inconsistency by discussing international tariff policy in GATT, monetary policy in the IMF, commodity regulation, and the growing acceptance of economic regionalism.

Congress never consented to the ratification of the Havana Charter and the ITO never came into existence. The charter had been a compromise between the rival views summarized above and therefore satisfied few people in the United States. The Senate declined to act, essentially for these reasons stated by the U.S. Council of the International Chamber of Commerce:

> It is a dangerous document because it accepts practically all of the policies of economic nationalism; because it jeopardizes the free enterprise system by giving priority to centralized national governmental planning of foreign trade; because it leaves a wide scope to discrimination, accepts the principle of economic insulation and in effect commits all members of the ITO to state planning for full employment. From the point of view of the U.S.,˙ it has the further very grave defect of placing this country in a position where it must accept discrimination against itself while extending the Most-Favored-Nation treatment to all members of the Organization.[2]

Instead, the United States took the lead in an improvised substitute for the defunct ITO–GATT. This agreement never had to face the Senate because the State Department obtain American participation by means of executive agreement; in fact, congressional jealousy in the field of tariff and trade negotiation persuaded the Executive to minimize formal American obligations. Further, GATT came very close to being cast perfectly in the American liberal image. The agreement provides that import quotas must be eliminated, that tariffs cannot be raised and must instead be lowered by means of periodic multilateral negotiating encounters. While these negotiations were conducted by pairs of countries on an item-by-item basis, GATT rules stipulate that reductions must be passed on *without discrimination* by means of the most-favored-nation clause, thus making the process multilateral. The United States insisted that concessions must be *reciprocal;* i.e., of equal value to both parties. A code of fair trade rules was appended as well. Complaints that tariffs were raised despite agreement or that quotas

---

[2] Quoted in William Diebold, Jr., "The End of the ITO," *Essays in International Finance*, No. 16, October, 1952 (Princeton, N.J.: Princeton University), pp. 20-21.

were reimposed by a member were dealt with by means of a conciliation and arbitration procedure that could make adjustments in trade rules binding on the members. Because the procedures were close to the liberal vision, the Communist countries and many of the underdeveloped nations declined to join. GATT succeeded in appreciably lowering tariff barriers among industrial countries and in adjudicating some major trade disputes.

If GATT sidestepped the UN by creating a system favorable to the industrial West, so did the monetary system set up under the IMF. Further, this system, during the first decade of its life, satisfied the needs of nobody. Contrary to American expectations, the IMF did not succeed in persuading all nations to stabilize their par values and to refrain from unilateral devaluation of their currencies. Its dollar reserves proved inadequate to support all balances of payments under pressure. The institutionalized gold-exchange standard intended by the fund soon gave way, *de facto*, to a global dollar-exchange standard that owed its success to policies made outside the IMF. Indeed, the IMF decision-making style stresses the avoidance of sharp basic ideological and theoretical debate. Formal decisions are preceded by private negotiations between staff and national representatives and monetary experts. While formal votes are not necessary, the United States has never been "defeated" and usually had its way during the 1950's.

If GATT facilitated, and the IMF did not restrain, the increasingly mixed American approach to world trade, a number of other institutions and practices enabled the United States to reject and sidetrack economic demands not congruent with the remains of the liberal doctrine. The underdeveloped nations and some European ones attempted to use the UN Economic and Social Council, in 1950 and 1951, as a forum for discussing a global approach to employment stability, industrial production, commodity prices, and economic growth—suggesting a modest international economic plan. The United States succeeded in halting these discussions in ECOSOC. The Director-General of the FAO, in alliance with many underdeveloped and food-importing countries, suggested a World Food Board, a buffer stock arrangement under which the FAO would buy up surpluses at minimum prices and sell them at fixed ceilings when shortages occur, thus stabilizing prices and controlling stocks, while having a reserve available for famine relief. This world food plan was killed by the United States and Britain because of the preference for private trading in agricultural commodities.

This attitude has slowed down the conclusion of a series of comprehensive commodity agreements. American economists generally dispute the value of international agreements setting minimum and maximum prices, fixing production and import quotas, and allocating markets as an efficient means of increasing the export earnings of developing countries. Exporting nations expecting to be able to sell their primary products at prices exceeding the margin contained in the agreement prefer to remain outside the arrangement. The difficulty of accurately forecasting supply and demand interferes with the legitimacy of the quota assignments and the fairness of the price margins. Finally, the general trend in recent years has been a gradual decline of the value of primary commodities in relation to the exports of manufactured goods, thus confirming the industrial countries' reluctance to enter into commodity agreements. The United States became a party to agreements for wheat and sugar. Neither agreement worked well. The world wheat market was controlled in fact by unilateral export and price policies followed by the leading exporters—the United States and Canada—and the sugar agreement proved incapable of surviving the elimination of the world's largest sugar producer—Cuba—from the quota system.

Similarly, the United States opposed the creation of all regional trading and economic development arrangements that seemed to interfere with a global division of labor based on nondiscrimination and reciprocity. In Europe, it opposed the formation of customs unions with purely economic objectives. Elsewhere, it accepted with reluctance the establishment of the UN Economic Commission for Latin America and the more diffuse UN Economic Commission for Asia and the Far East. Both bodies were deprived of decision-making powers and independent sources of finance; both were simply to discuss regional issues and engage in technical assistance. It took a sharp change in the international system before the United States consented to participate in the creation and funding of regional development banks.

But in line with the lesson in inconsistency, there was one major exception to economic purity which was to gather volume and speed later: the encouragement of *politically justified* regionalism and discrimination in Europe. The noncapitalist elements implicit in the Marshall Plan were accepted easily because it was thought necessary to depart from free enterprise to combat communism! American industrialists associated with the Committee for Economic Development and the National Planning Association made their peace with this arrangement, on condition that a separate agency headed by an experienced industrialist be put in charge of European recovery, rather than the State Department, which was suspected of merely administering a global give-away program. And thus Paul Hoffman became the czar of European economic cooperation and the legitimator of regional economic discrimination that was to lead gradually to an American-endorsed West European federation, while the business fundamentalists who objected to subsidized socialism abroad went unheeded.

The institutional order in which all this took place was the Organization for European Economic Cooperation (OEEC), in which the United States was a *very* active observer represented by the autonomous American aid agency, the Economic Cooperation Administration. OEEC pioneered a method of intergovernmental discussion and confrontation in which frank criticism and collective pressure were systematically used to persuade member nations to adjust their economic policies to suit the program of the collectivity. The United States, at this time the supplier of the system, took the initiative in enmeshing the Europeans in this web of mutual aid and consultation. With the UN effectively cut out, this period then featured a United States-led world economy institutionalized in GATT, the OEEC, and the NATO-affiliated system for the economic boycott of the Soviet bloc.

America's success in enmeshing others in the rules of liberalism or the boycott policies of the Cold War was far from complete. As Europe recovered, American leadership became less effective in economic dealings with the Communist countries. Further, while GATT forced many countries to discontinue their discrimination against American exports, the same rules also tended to force the United States to relax quota restrictions against agricultural imports from Europe. There were also cases when the United States resisted this pressure, however, and made use of GATT to sidestep direct demands from her trading partners for a more import-minded policy.

As if sensing the inconsistency of doctrine and policy, as though the world's giant should have a guilty conscience about the tailoring of economic policy to international political forces and domestic protectionists, some elite groups began to urge revaluation of the UN as an appropriate global forum for making economic arrangements of importance to all, and to advocate a more positive attitude toward regionalism among underdeveloped and neutralist countries. These suggestions, however, bore fruit only when economic policy was examined in the context of foreign aid and development under the pressure of the rising Third World.

### 3. The Passing of American Economic Dominance

Since 1958 the enmeshment of the United States in the world economy has become more real, almost in proportion to a *lack of deliberate will* to be enmeshed. Certainly a lesson has been learned by the elites who take a consistent interest in world trade and finance. But it was not a lesson that grew logically out of the postwar commitment to pure international liberalism. Rather, the lesson learned was that a change in economic and political conditions may beget an unintended involvement in the policies and good will of others, an unwilled dependence on their views, an unplanned subservience to institutions and pressures built for different initial purposes. And to the extent that this lesson has been learned, unwanted and unplanned enmeshment in the web of international economic institutions has increased. What are the changes in conditions that triggered all this?

One major change was the direct result of American foreign aid, loans abroad, and the stationing of large numbers of American troops in Europe and Asia: the balance-of-payments crisis that has plagued American foreign economic relations since 1958. As the outflow of dollars—private and governmental—continued, the claims of a burgeoning world-trading community for dollars as the major means of settling accounts began to put a strain on the monetary resources of even the world's giant. Gold left the United States in large amounts in settlement of accounts, and not sufficient new gold was mined or imported to fill the gap. "Euro-dollars" was the term bestowed in Europe on dollars used as a standard means of moving capital while the pound sterling continued its decline from its former position of a major world currency. Given this condition, Washington lost the special power it had previously enjoyed as the major supplier of hard currency that aided in the balance-of-payments crises of others; the United States now needed the help of its former clients.

Another change was that those former clients now constituted the single largest bloc of world traders. The six European continental industrial nations united in the European Economic Community (EEC), recovered from the war, re-equipped, freed from colonial responsibilities, were now determined to export their sophisticated manufactures and protect their high-cost agriculture by discriminating against American exports. They were joined by Japan as a new and major industrial competitor of the United States. Europe's new economic independence and prowess also triggered a certain fear of American direct investments as interference with European planning; yet Europeans also feared being deprived of superior American technological and scientific skills if they excluded American capital, and they feared being victimized further by the brain drain of their technicians to America. In short, Europe's prowess also implied ambivalence and soul-searching about the proper relations between the Atlantic nations—attitudes that had their counterparts in a drifting policy in NATO.

Finally, the revolt of the Third World, aided verbally by the Soviet bloc, changed dramatically the former hegemonial position of the United States in the world economy. The Third World used the UN as the chief forum for denouncing the economic policies of the West. As it gained victory after victory in the General Assembly and the specialized agencies, American elite opinion began to question the continued utility of the UN as a vehicle of American policy; it seemed to become the forum for demonstrating American economic isolation instead. Yet the malaise of the business community with respect to the anticapitalist demands of the Third World in the UN stopped short of downgrading the UN completely. European elites by contrast experienced no such tolerance and frankly preferred to sidestep UN procedures and institutions. The centerpiece of the Third World's revolt was the claim that the GATT–IMF world economic rules hide a fundamental discrimination *de facto* against the export earnings of developing nations by allowing all sorts of indirect and covert financial burdens on the sale of their primary and manufactured goods, refusing to make capital available on any but sound banking principles, and by declining to stabilize the prices of primary commodities.

What, then, have Americans learned from this triple onslaught? The general trend of American foreign trade policy, notwithstanding the inconsistencies sketched, was toward lower barriers on trade. Yet the shallowness of the public opinion permitting this trend was demonstrated to President Kennedy when he sought new authority to lower tariffs further and negotiate with the EEC. Only 22 per cent of all Americans had heard of the EEC, and only 13 per cent had a generally correct idea of what it is; but among those, two out of three favored tariff cuts.[3] Indeed, it is far from easy to define the objectives of American foreign trade policy except as an inchoate collection of slogans, partly derived from economic liberalism and partly inferred from the politics of the Cold War, summed up as this "basic sextet of goals," by Michael Brower: "peace, security, freedom (or liberty), justice, well-being and prosperity."[4] The major aim of policy after the mid-Fifties became the acceleration of economic growth in developing nations, because poverty was viewed as a threat to the sextet of goals. Such acceleration was expected somehow to further the attainment of democratic institutions abroad and assure sufficient economic stability to permit security, peace, and freedom to prevail. This collection of slogans lacks internal consistency and rests on very superficial thinking. Yet there can be little doubt that government and private elites accepted it as a fair statement of the new American vision after American hegemony began to wane.

Thus, the doubling of the IMF's reserves in 1959 was not opposed by a single interest group, and it was supported by all the chief associations of labor, bankers, farmers, and business, even though ten years earlier such unanimity would hardly have existed. President Kennedy sought to equate peace, prosperity, and freedom with the military strength of the Atlantic countries in proposing a 50 per cent cut in tariffs between the United States and the EEC (by virtue of the Trade Expansion Act of 1962 and the subsequent Kennedy Round at GATT). His initiative was supported by every major economic interest group and many humanitarian and public service associations; opposition came chiefly from associations of specialized manufacturers that would lose their tariff protection (piano makers, the watch industry, bicycle manufacturers) and from the labor unions affiliated with these industries. The AFL-CIO, however, equated the world and the national interest with expanded trade (provided trade adjustment assistance was given to those hurt by lowered tariffs) and increased foreign aid. Labor also wanted the UN to negotiate a code for the protection of private foreign investments abroad. Farmers were quite content with the Kennedy approach as long as some surplus food stocks were removed from the world market by means of grants of food to needy nations (financed by the government under Public Law 480 and the World

---

[3] Gallup Poll, December 17, 1961.
[4] Quoted and developed in Benjamin Higgins, *The United Nations and U.S. Foreign Economic Policy* (Homewood, Illinois: Irwin, 1962), pp. 3–4.

Food Program), and provided that foreign food be kept out of the United States while export markets in Western Europe remained open. No party and no major group challenged the notion that increased trade, lower tariffs, a stronger world monetary system would all conduce to peace, American and world prosperity, Atlantic unity, free enterprise, weakened Communist appeals in the Third World, democracy, and stability. If the approach was less orthodox and less doctrinaire than in 1945, it was also less consistent and more indebted to liberal wishful thinking. It did rest, however, on a clear—if sloppy—consensus of the American elites.

If there was something of a plan in 1945, by the end of the Fifties its traces had been well obscured. Learning took the form of step-by-step, issue-by-issue adjustment. No new central institution was set up, though new tasks were added to the disparate collections of separate forums. No sweeping and rational review of trade and monetary policy took place. Incremental accommodations to a changing international environment occurred with respect to monetary policy, revision of the GATT rules, acceptance of the legitimacy of regional trade blocs and regulations, and the trade demands of the Third World, which called for and received its own forum for action in the UN Conference on Trade and Development (UNCTAD). Whether these accommodations have resulted in further enmeshments must now be determined.

The development of a dollar-exchange standard had condemned the IMF to a peripheral role in monetary affairs until, in 1958, the United States reversed policy and began a campaign of solving its payments problems with a reinvigorated world monetary system in the IMF. In effect, the United States wished to resign the role of being the world's central banker and bequeath it to the very IMF which had been denied that role because of American fears in 1944. This decision was made as a result of several developments. As the outflow of gold and dollars continued, the major European currencies, strong once more, all became convertible. As world trade was growing by leaps and bounds, it was in fact being financed with the American dollar and gold outflow despite the comeback of EEC currencies, thus linking American problems with a worldwide shortage of money; this is the so-called liquidity problem. Further, the EEC countries now told the United States to combat its gold and dollar losses with a policy of domestic deflation and retrenchment, a policy not acceptable to the United States because of the increased unemployment that would result.

How to rescue the dollar and provide liquidity? No permanent solution has been found, though the United States in 1965 proposed a radical plan for a greatly strengthened IMF that would provide automatic checking account privileges to the world's trading nations. The accounts would operate with a new international currency backed by all strong currencies, in addition to gold and dollars to be called Special Drawing Rights or SDR's.

General agreement on this major reform was achieved in 1968 when all the major trading nations of the world accepted the issuing of SDR's by the IMF in allotments proportional to the present national subscriptions of funds. The IMF is to distribute the new international currency equitably to developed and developing nations. The fund determines the basic timing, amount, and rate of allocation of SDR's. Important decisions will require a majority of 85 per cent, a figure that can be met by the collective vote of the European Economic Community nations and the United States; less important decisions will be made by simple majority. The staff of the IMF, however, will have important new powers of initiating steps and advising the Board of Governors. Clearly, the scheme moves the world considerably in the direction of a global central banking system and thereby makes American monetary policy much more dependent than ever before on the policies of other nations and international organizations. The trauma suffered by the flood of gold leaving the United States in 1967 and 1968 drove home this dependence and made the remedy more acceptable. But the United States had to pay a price: just when we were prepared to seek our salvation through enmeshment, the major trading partners in OECD's Group of Ten (seven European nations, Canada, Japan, and the United States) were inclined to support the new American policy only if taxes were raised, consumption curbed, and the payments deficit controlled. Because the Group of Ten had agreed to a series of measures that involved supporting the dollar and strengthening the IMF, the success of the new system would depend on continued harmony of views and policies in the Group. The renewed crisis of the French economy and continued weakness of the British pound and French franc contrasted to the German mark illustrate that this harmony cannot be taken for granted.

American desire to reform world institutions is much less in evidence when we turn to trade policy and to the accommodation of the Third World's demands. The developing nations, backed by the Soviet bloc, mounted nothing less than a revolt against the dominant GATT rules at UNCTAD I in 1964, an encounter described by a high American official as "the first major international conference in recent history in which the East-West confrontation was submerged by the North-South confrontation." Over the bitter dissent of the United States, the cohesive and well-organized bloc of 77 developing nations succeeded in bringing about the adoption of these major resolutions: commodity agreements should be drafted to stabilize prices; the developed countries should give discriminatory, preferential tariff concessions to the Third World countries by allowing the importation of their manufactures; the principle of reciprocity should be abandoned in tariff bargaining to allow the developing nations greater export earnings; the right of Third World nations to dispose of their natural resources is absolute, thus exposing foreign investors to the threat of nationalization. While these resolutions have not become part of the world trading rules, the effort to enforce them has now been given to a permanent UN Trade Development Board which, unlike GATT, is not under the control of the developed nations. The new forum is a watershed in American trade policy in international organizations even though at UNCTAD II in 1968 the United States conceded far less than demanded of it. The extent of the American adjustment can be illustrated by the policies urged and adopted in GATT, that "soulless forum of the rich" in the rhetoric of the Third World.

A Presidential Report in 1957 reiterated the importance of GATT to U.S. foreign policy:

> Experience through the years has demonstrated clearly the superiority of multilateral discussions and negotiations over bilateral in achieving the objectives of U.S. policy in these fields.[5]

Multilateral commercial diplomacy for the U.S. meant strictly reciprocal trade concessions negotiated for selective items, administered nondiscriminatorily among nations. The U.S. rejected across-the-board tariff negotiations at GATT, partly because the President was empowered by Congress to reduce tariffs only up to a limit of 15 per cent over a three-year period. Congress was also hostile to the idea of linear tariff cuts, because they would reduce its influence over tariff schedules on particular items. "The U.S. was a prisoner of its domestic legislation."[6] The emergence of the EEC as a major economic force plus America's increasing balance of payments deficit forced U.S. policy-makers to change their position on linear tariff reductions. Across-the-board reductions were at the heart of the 1962 Trade Expansion Act. Linear reduction as

[5] *Department of State Bulletin* (November 4, 1957), p. 725.
[6] Gerald Curzon, *Multilateral Commercial Diplomacy* (London: Michael Joseph, 1966), p. 95, also see pp. 74 ff.

a method of commercial policy is not a blessing to states interested in limited tariff cuts. It is positively discriminatory against developing nations, still dependent on exports of primary commodities, but anxious to find a new market for their still high-priced infant manufactures. Hence the American conversion to the linear reduction method in GATT in relation to other industrial nations did nothing to reassure the Third World.

The success of the Kennedy Round at GATT, then, merely confirms the part of the American approach that stresses nondiscriminatory trade liberalization and reciprocal benefits. Johnson Administration negotiators stress that one major utility of GATT for the United States lies in its availability as a forum for nondiscriminatory tariff reduction, "nondiscriminatory" for the Third World too. Others make clear that GATT keeps the preferential trading systems of Europe and Latin America under control by surveying their policies and giving third countries the opportunity to protest and retaliate if regional preferences pass the bounds of permissibility. When, in anticipation of UNCTAD, the GATT membership adopted an Action Program in 1963 that seemed to give some satisfaction to the complaints of the Third World, the United States made few and halting adjustments in its trade policy in line with the recommendations. It then refused to sanction the principle of preferential duties for developing nations' manufactures and made minimal tariff reductions to accommodate more imports of primary products. It continued, along with the EEC, to practice outright quota protectionism for agricultural imports. And it declined to generalize to other products the agreement on cotton textiles, concluded in GATT with the countries of East Asia. During the Kennedy Round itself, American negotiators insisted that these talks assured benefits for developing nations merely by virtue of their insistence on most-favored-nation treatment. As it turned out, the Kennedy Round resulted in a 37 per cent average reduction of tariffs of industrial countries, reducing them to a level of 9 per cent!

The textile agreement provides an interesting case study on the ability of the U.S. to carry out its free trade persuasions over considerable protectionist sentiments in an area which would definitely benefit developing countries. In 1961 the Kennedy Administration was under serious domestic pressure from the textile industry to apply import quotas on goods from Asia. Since 1962, however, under U.S. leadership, commodity agreements were concluded, providing for the orderly long-term expansion of new textile industries in Asia by virtue of phased reduction in import barriers in the West, if importing countries could insist on "voluntary export restraint" whenever cotton textile purchases introduced adjustment hardship for domestic producers. Some argue that the restraints have been more pronounced than the inducement to increase imports.

But UNCTAD did take its toll: in 1965 the United States agreed to an amendment of the GATT Charter that relaxed the principle of reciprocity as a condition of negotiating tariff reductions. It also cautiously endorsed commodity price stabilization and enhanced export earnings for developing countries. Still, the United States insisted that nonreciprocal concessions would have to be granted multilaterally; i.e., by the EEC as well as by the United States. By the time UNCTAD II met in 1968, the chink in the armor of pure free trade was growing visibly as the United States further changed its policy on preferences to developing nations: Washington conceded that it now favored tariff preferences for the export of goods manufactured by developing nations, provided the preferences were "generalized," i.e., offered by *all* industrial nations to *all* developing nations without discrimination, thus maintaining some export competition and preventing the creation of new uneconomic preferences.

UNCTAD took an even greater toll in the field of commodity regulation and regional trading preferences in the Third World. The United States, after taking much criticism from Latin America, agreed to the legitimacy of preferential trading arrangements *among developing nations* in order to permit manufacturing interests to benefit from the economies of scale. Moreover, and again in response to Latin-American prodding, the United States advanced from a cautious regional endorsement of commodity price stabilization to active participation in the International Coffee Agreement. By 1968, the United States told UNCTAD II that commodity agreements for sugar, cocoa, and wheat were also appropriate and that the principle of commodity regulation should be followed more energetically, insuring against loss of export earning in the event of growth of synthetics. Therefore, commodity agreements should be tied to schemes for giving exporting countries incentives for the diversification of monocultural practices. The icy facade of free trade doctrine seemed to be melting as UNCTAD II was told that development "requires an international harmonization of economic policies, the discipline of development plans, changes in structure and attitude both in the developed and developing countries. . . ." [7]

[7] Eugene V. Rostow, "From Aid to Cooperation," *Department of State Bulletin* (March 11, 1968), p. 360.

Perhaps the most telling lesson learned by the United States was the inevitability of regionalism in a world in which trade and politics simply would not remain in tight and separate compartments. Free trade areas and common markets in Latin America were accepted by Washington, it must be stressed, as proper and legitimate —though discriminatory and preferential—methods of industrialization. The endorsement of, and financial participation in, development banks in Asia, Africa, and Latin America was a milestone in American adjustment to a world bent on limiting free trade and private capital movements. But all these steps involved no serious enmeshment of the United States, since the institutions concerned were under the control of others and only marginally related to American interests—and GATT remained to criticize them. In the Atlantic region, however, the story is different. Here enmeshment may play a much larger role.

## 4. The United States and Atlantic Regionalism

"Like Pirandello's six characters in search of an author, the policy-makers sometimes appear to be casting about for more topical settings of such stereotyped subjects as 'trade blocs,' 'Atlantic community,' even—alas—the western alliance itself." [8] The slogans have been with us since the Marshall Plan; the new topical setting is the OECD. Is it more than a slogan with a headquarters? All-European integration of the most federalist type was the preferred American objective, and until the Sixties everything was subordinated to it. Few people in Washington stopped to inquire whether an *independently* strong and united Europe was a desirable development. Until de Gaulle made the point for America, little thought had been given to which of two rival European trade blocs should be supported. As late as 1962, President Kennedy believed that the partnership formula would paper things over nicely when joined to dramatic increases in Atlantic trade.

What was the United States after, in founding OECD? It was *not* interested in general trade policy and wanted no part of the OEEC

[8] Henry G. Aubrey, *Atlantic Economic Cooperation* (New York: Praeger, 1967), pp. 3-4.

Code of Liberalization. Congress in 1960 was so hostile to any fixed trade rules that it made the Administration demand the scrapping of the Code. Congress was used to GATT and therefore tolerated its item-by-item approach; in 1961 it did not want to give the Administration increased blanket powers over trade of the kind that Kennedy did get in 1962. The OECD voting formula, further, assured that no blanket trade obligations would be assumed by the U.S. The United States was interested in burden-sharing for foreign aid as well as in the discussion of growth rates and harmonized growth, because of the balance-of-payments troubles and the desire to cut back the dollar outflow to Europe. Officially, at least, Washington was not interested in the little-known technique of intergovernmental scrutiny, discussion, confrontation, and harmonization invented by OEEC. Consequently, the powers given to the OECD were vague and general compared to the predecessor OEEC's. The Senate Foreign Relations Committee, in its report favoring ratification of the OECD Charter, stressed only the sharing of aid and the joint Atlantic promotion of economic growth. Nondiscriminatory world trade development as an American objective was played down in order to leave this task with GATT. A high official defined the job intended for OECD in these terms:

> Cooperation in the OECD is not usually aimed at the development of uniform national policies. The consultative process leaves ample room for differences in policies stemming from varying emphasis of national objectives and multiplicity of national circumstances. The primary aim of policy coordination in the OECD is to ensure that national policies develop in step with each other.[9]

The advent of UNCTAD and the transformation of GATT have nevertheless enmeshed the United States in general trade discussions in OECD, as an unanticipated consequence of the Third World's revolt and the growing interest of some European nations in granting preferential tariff treatment. Although no startling Atlantic trade policy has emerged from the intensive discussion in OECD, there is some evidence that the organization is being converted into an "antechamber" in which the industrial nations concert their approach for the global encounters elsewhere in the web of international organizations. What is more striking is the entirely

[9] William R. Tyler, Assistant Secretary of State for European Affairs, quoted in *ibid.*, pp. 103-4.

unintended enmeshment of the United States in OECD discussions of economic growth and domestic economic policies needed for growth. The OEEC confrontation technique was carried over bodily into OECD—and the United States was made one of the victims as the payments deficit created a stronger need to harmonize economic policies with the European consumers of dollars. It was in OECD discussions that the Group of Ten negotiated its reserve currency standby agreement and OECD studies and talks were used to launch tax cuts and investment controls in the United States, as well as take up the matter of policies to guarantee minimum incomes. Europe came to understand—even if it could not change—certain inconsistencies in American policy, and American policy-makers whose ideas for change were blocked in Washington found collective allies and supporters for the alterations they wished to introduce at home. "In fact, as practitioners of multilateral diplomacy in the OECD and elsewhere have found on many occasions, an acquired habit of viewing problems from angles other than one's own does promote a search for acceptable solutions, and at the same time makes conflicting interests seem less divergent than they appeared initially." [10]

And so the world's giant has found it useful to engage itself in the regional machinery much more intensively than it had planned to do. At the same time it has been persuaded by the clamor of the Third World to take seriously UNCTAD and a new set of world trading rules departing far and deeply from free trade. GATT, with the admission of some of these claims and with the completion of the dramatic Kennedy Round cuts in tariffs, will have little left to do. At home, the authority given the Executive under the Trade Expansion Act sharply limits the role Congress and specific trade associations can play in the politics of foreign trade and finance, thus centralizing power at home as it shifts toward Atlantic and UN bodies abroad. At the same time, these unplanned developments have "practically obliterated the traditional distinctions in the economic and social fields between 'domestic' and 'international' jurisdictions." [11] Still, no new set of trade and money rules has emerged. While a shift in institutional enmeshment can be gleaned from the welter of activity, no consensus on substance can be seen as the Third World continues its demands for dramatic global income and resource redistribution, and Europe is prepared to meet the demand

[10] Aubrey, *Atlantic Economic Cooperation*, p. 148.
[11] Ruth Russell, "Changing Patterns of Constitutional Development," *International Organization* (Summer, 1965), p. 419.

in ways very different from America's. And the United States may yet find it necessary and desirable to grant developing nations extensive compensatory financial assistance for commodity price instability, in the IMF and in other types of commodity agreements. The curtain has just begun to lift on the retreat from free trade and private investment; before the retreat becomes a chaotic rout, the United States may come to prefer more overlapping between domestic and international economic issues and may quietly bequeath the resulting task of reconciliation to an international organization.

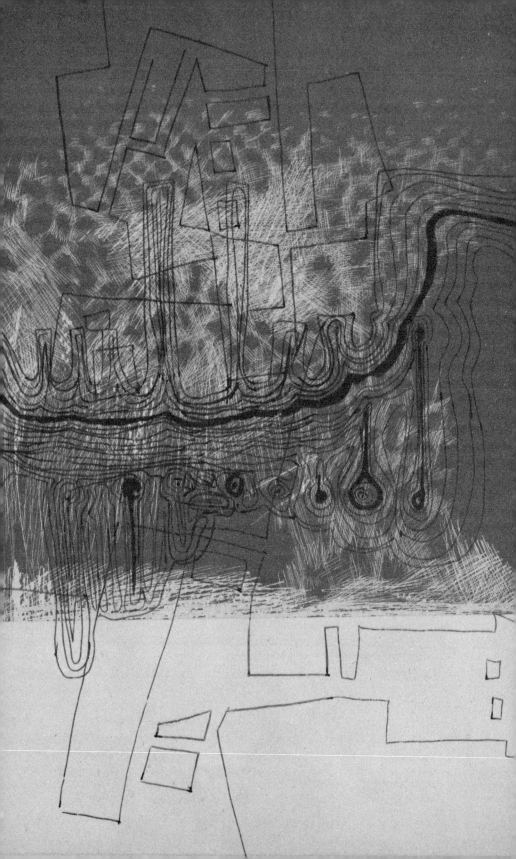

CHAPTER SEVEN

# ECONOMIC AND SOCIAL
# DEVELOPMENT

The lesson of America's encounter with the world's demands for economic change is very similar to the enmeshment process we sketched in the field of foreign trade and investment. Peaks of expectation were met with disappointment. Difficult processes of adjustment ensued, only to be confronted with additional disappointment, resulting in an unending incremental process of adaptation devoid of a central plan. One major difference emerges in comparison with the domestic setting within which foreign trade policy is made: the mass public *does* have vague and unstructured opinions about foreign aid, and that opinion often conflicts with government policy. America's major elites, particularly the business elite, once more separate into (1) fundamentalists critical of the economic involvement implied by a hit-and-miss foreign aid policy and (2) innovators willing to forego the purity of doctrine in order to use foreign aid as a tool of political influence. What expectations are attached to the use of this tool, how plausible these expectations are, and how much of the task should be done by international organizations rather than by the national government are the chief uncertainties to which this chapter addresses itself.

## 1. The Free Trade Vision,
## Foreign Aid and the Cold War

America did not have to face self-consciously the issue of "why should we extend foreign aid?" until 1947. Relief supplies were shipped to other countries before; private and public loans of huge scope were previously made to foreign governments, particularly during World War I; military equipment, food, and social services were donated to allies during World War II, directly and through an international organization, UNRRA. No serious question or challenge arose concerning the purpose and legitimacy of these aid measures, because there was a general consensus that all this was part of a war effort or a humanitarian relief operation. With the end of World War II and the onset of the Cold War, however, an aura of permanency and surprise was given to the foreign aid activities in which the United States had been engaged: permanency because the end of the war and concurrent acceptance of a vision of world prosperity based on private enterprise simply evaporated in the face of poverty, devastation, and the Communist challenge; surprise because the postwar American ideology had not allowed for this contingency.

The Marshall Plan of massive aid to Europe was the first major foreign aid program—the foreign trade and finance aspects of which we have already discussed—to shatter these dreams. What were its objectives and what can these objectives tell us about a learning process?

All foreign aid can be classified in terms of the aims the donor has in mind. We can identify aid intended merely to demonstrate the power and "presence" of the donor in a specific situation. Sometimes aid is given to influence, once or twice, specific decisions by a foreign government. Both kinds of aid can take the form of grants, loans, demonstrations, military equipment, or cultural missions. Whatever the form, the purpose is confined to the achievement of an immediate and short-run objective. Since such aid is always bilateral, it is of no concern to our problem. A third type of aid, called "strategic aid" by Montgomery, is our major concern. The purpose of the donor here is to contribute to the shaping of a certain world order, an over-all environment favorable to the values held dear by the donor.[1] The forms can again be all-inclusive; the purpose is sweeping, long-range, independent of local crises. It is identical with most multilateral programs entrusted to international organizations.

What then were American "strategic" objectives in 1947? The government, the innovative business elite, and labor were one in believing that there was a Soviet military threat to Western Europe, that it was made worse by the desperation of the European workingman who sought a better life in the face of war-shattered economies and timid European industrialists who could not rebuild, modernize, and produce enough at prices low enough to satisfy the population. The purpose of American aid was to correct these conditions; its underlying ideology was that economic power could create conditions that would make communism unnecessary—the inverse Marxism we encountered before. In Europe this was relatively simple, since democracy, industry, modernity, and science already existed and nations had a long and often bloody identity. The inverse Marxist objective has remained; but does it imply, in the case of the Third World, that democracy must be established along with industrialism and education—before or after military stability? And must there be an identifiable nation before there can be stability or democracy? To these questions, the American groping for purpose has not yet found any consistent answers. The omnipotent solvent for nagging doubt about this list of priorities and uncertain causal connections is that American foreign aid policy, like foreign trade policy, is to assure conditions of peace, freedom, stability, and prosperity. Whether peace depends on prosperity or prosperity on peace, however, remains beclouded.

Nor was the leap into foreign aid in 1947 based solely on these notions. Specific interests in American society received satisfaction then, as they do now. Farmers were assured that the Marshall Plan would facilitate the sale of agricultural surpluses in Europe; innovative manufacturers were told that the economic revival of Europe would provide a better climate for foreign investments and permit the credo of production-oriented industrialism to take root; labor leaders were given the opportunity to spread the gospel of American-style trade unionism, and conservative businessmen were assured that all this would conduce to strengthening private property, free enterprise, and conservative fiscal policies in Europe. In short, the

[1] John D. Montgomery, *Foreign Aid in International Politics* (Englewood Cliffs: Prentice-Hall, 1967), pp. 18-23; of bilateral American aid, 90 per cent is spent in sixteen countries crucial also to the military "strategic" calculations of the United States.

$11 billion aid venture was based on a mixture of very general objectives and very specific material and moral payoffs to certain elite groups.

Nor should we ever forget that Congress remains a crucial actor in the foreign aid field, more crucial than in the context of tariff and trade policy, because the President *must* have congressional approval to finance his programs. Many congressmen are unwilling to spend heavily for the benefit of other countries, because they doubt the value of such programs in achieving American objectives; and in periods of rising taxes, conflicting domestic programs, and international monetary instability, many simply prefer to spend American resources for programs closer to home. Moreover, when crucial domestic groups clash and disagree on proper priorities at home and abroad and when specific payoffs to key domestic groups become of questionable value, congressional acquiescence in strong foreign aid programs wanes rapidly.

And so it has remained. In 1966, 86 per cent of American foreign aid funds were "tied"; i.e., they had to be spent on American goods and services; in 1960 the figure had been 42 per cent. The kind and volume of foreign aid, about .65 per cent of the gross national product, have remained closely tied to the demands and interests of increasingly numerous groups, firms, and associations with a direct interest in foreign aid, including universities and foundations with technical assistance contracts overseas. Food surplus disposal, use of American ships, protection of overseas investments, encouraging industrializing nations to purchase American equipment, the desire to proselytize for the American way of doing research, managing enterprises, framing laws, and teaching school—all these have become vested interests of articulate elites. At the same time the overwhelming bulk of people remain ignorant of these efforts. When President Truman in 1949 followed up the Marshall Plan with the first long-range American technical assistance program— then called "Point Four"—progressive elites supported it for the same reasons they adduced in favor of the Marshall Plan, while fundamentalists feared that even technical assistance would undermine free enterprise. Since then government policy has undergone great changes; but not the mood of the public, which remains polarized as before.

The precise types of strategic foreign aid have not changed greatly from this pioneering period during which the threat of communism triggered the permanent entry of the United States government into the aid scene. Between 1946 and 1965, the United States spent, of $116.1 billion for aid, $81.4 billion for economic assistance of all kinds; the rest for military aid. In rough figures, the world economic aid picture in 1966 was as follows. All donors contributed a total of $10 billion, of which the United States supplied about one-half; this half consisted of about $3 billion in financial assistance, mostly in the form of long-term, low-interest loans, and about $1.5 billion in agricultural commodities (the Food for Peace Program). The UN agencies disbursed $1 billion; the major regional agencies (Inter-American Development Bank and EEC), another half-billion. In other words, only 15 per cent of total world economic aid was channeled through international organizations; the share of American aid so handled was considerably less. Clearly, military assistance was always an important part of the American effort; and for obvious reasons, it was not channeled through UN agencies. Even its appearance in the regional defense pacts sponsored by the United States is not a permanent feature, because it declines with the reduction of American hegemonial influence over these groupings and is replaced with sales of arms. Liberals argued that military aid not be confused with economic and not be used instead of the more important economic assistance; conservatives argued the reverse and continue to do so. Since we are concerned with the tension and evolution of bilateral as opposed to multilateral aid, military assistance programs—though often "strategic" in objective—are irrelevant to our quest. The forms of aid that preoccupy us are, first, technical assistance for economic and social development and, more importantly, capital aid for development in the form of grants and loans.

The free enterprise vision that inspired the American approach to world economic problems had definite consequences with respect to the unwanted and as yet undigested acceptance of foreign aid. It implied a marked preference for private over public funds, "sound" finance over inflation, loans over gifts and outright grants, bilateral operations over UN-sponsored activities that would imply sharing control with the recipient nations *en bloc*. The favored UN instrument of American action was the IBRD, an institution at first designed not to compete with private lenders and instructed to follow a hardheaded banker's approach even in its relations with poor nations. The United States was both the major contributor to the bank's loan fund and the major purchaser of its bonds—and it also wielded the greatest voting power. No votes were ever taken, however, because successive presidents of the IBRD (all of American nationality) enjoyed the full confidence of the major member nations *and* of the U.S. Treasury. Paul G. Hoffman, the head of the UN Development Program and formerly the administrator of the Marshall Plan, innocently described the close ties between Washington and the IBRD:

we had no problem [in coordinating IBRD loan policy to the Marshall Plan] because we discussed all these loans they were thinking of making and they were always good enough to come to us and say "What about the impact of this loan to Turkey? Do you think we ought to go ahead with it?" That was informal and that is one of the best ways of control. . . .[2]

Eugene Black, the powerful president of the bank from 1949 to 1962, enjoyed the full confidence of successive high American officials and congressional leaders. He was relied upon by all to remain true to the more conservative aspects of the American approach to world economic problems; whether he actually did is part of the story of the major lesson learned by the United States.

A second favored instrument of multilateral action was the UN Expanded Program of Technical Assistance launched in 1950 with substantial American support. It made no capital funds available; instead, it sent experts to underdeveloped countries to train local specialists and help in setting up development projects. It also financed the training of local specialists abroad. Hand-in-hand with EPTA went American support for similar programs run by UN specialized agencies such as WHO, concerned with public health; FAO, relating to agricultural productivity; ILO, having to do with manpower training; and the UN Children's Fund for famine relief and malnutrition. None of these instruments involved grants as a long-term method of international development, and the loans remained closely tied to American interests. Multilateral capital contributions other than technical expert services were confined to humanitarian gestures and excluded long-range development aid.

The United States fought off, between 1948 and 1955, a number of bitter complaints from the Third World that all this was quite insufficient to enable the developing nations to "catch up," to bring about some measure of global income redistribution. Third World arguments in UN bodies, like those of the United States, insisted on some vague link between "peace" and "prosperity"—though they omitted any public suggestion of the supposedly stabilizing influence of anti-Communist development programs. Indeed, the Third World's emotional clamor for aid in industrialization was based on no more elaborate objectives and consistent purposes than the American approach. Yet the United States, asserting its free trade and enterprise vision, still prevailed against the clamor.

What were the components of this clamor? One was the demand for a large-scale UN development program based on outright grants

<hr />

[2] Quoted in I. L. Claude, *Swords into Plowshares*, 3rd ed. (New York: Random House, 1964), p. 364.

to developing nations, designed to underwrite national industrialization plans, rather than loans tied to specific improvement projects (such as rail lines, dams, or foreign-exchange-earning industries) as disbursed by the IBRD. The other was the insistence on special investment policies and trading rules for regions of underdeveloped nations, notably in Latin America, in order to have aid take the form of protecting the countries in the early stages of industrialization from the self-serving aid measures and aggressive sales practices of the industrial countries. The regionalist argument was the special province of the UN Economic Commission for Latin America in its search to protect the struggling countries at the "periphery" of world trade from the rapacious giants at the "center." It failed to arouse American interest in special regional development programs until Castro's Cuba triggered the reaction we now call the Alliance for Progress.

In every session of all appropriate UN organs from 1951 on, capital aid on easy terms was demanded as a function of "SUN-FED." As these resolutions were offered, the United States opposed them with a variety of arguments. They would feed irresponsible projects and hurt sound financial practices; they would aid socialist planning at the expense of private capital; the necessary funds were not available; world disarmament would have to precede the mobilization of adequate funds. Whatever the argument, the United States did not retreat from its position, shared as it was by most of the other industrial nations of the West; and yet the Third World did not give up its onslaught. As the Soviet Union turned more and more to UN agencies for its international programs and verbal overtures, as the Korean War ended and as the Third World made its massive entry into the international system during the mid-Fifties, things seemed to be stalemated.

The question therefore becomes: had seven or eight years of conservative foreign aid made an impact on American public opinion? Had foreign aid become a legitimate arm of foreign policy in the eyes of the American public? Had a consensus developed regarding the merits of bilaterally or regionally controlled aid as opposed to operations controlled by the entire UN membership? The answer is that the general public continued to distrust aid in general and UN aid in particular and that specific interest groups and regions actively opposed both. Selected segments of business opinion began to wonder also about the appropriateness of American policy as the Cold War was increasingly perceived to be an indirect encounter involving the souls and loyalties of the Third World. These businessmen were joined by a great variety of community leaders after 1956, even though the public's mass response did *not* change.

Thus, in 1954, 52 per cent of northerners and 57 per cent of southerners preferred to handle all aid bilaterally. Seventy-four per cent of southerners wanted to cut off aid from countries refusing to cooperate with the United States. Fear of Communist and neutralist influence was cited by opponents of a role for the UN, though those familiar with the role of Americans in UN agencies proved far more tolerant. In 1957, 28 per cent of the public favored the same or increased foreign aid; 61 per cent wished to reduce the American contribution to all kinds of programs, though military aid was much more acceptable than economic. In 1954, the prestigious Randall Commission reported to Congress that "underdeveloped areas are claiming a right to economic aid from the United States. . . . We recognize no such right." [3] Similar opinions were expressed by the National Association of Manufacturers, the Chamber of Commerce, and the National Foreign Trade Council. The IBRD fared well in business circles because of Eugene Black's image-making, but schemes like SUNFED were roundly condemned as give-aways. Southern elite circles had strongly favored foreign aid in its earliest years. By the mid-Fifties, southern members of Congress were the most consistent opponents of economic aid of all kinds as the changing world economy seemed to result in stronger competition for the South's traditional exports—cotton, tobacco, and textiles— and as the self-assertion of the Third World was increasingly perceived to be a racial challenge.

On the other hand, certain innovating industrialists had suggested as early as 1951 that the IBRD approach to economic development in the Third World was inadequate. Specifically, it was suggested that international lending agencies make generous loans to *private* firms abroad, in order to stimulate entrepreneurial initiative in traditional societies. Rather than rely merely and mainly on technical assistance in the UN, more public lending tied to technical aid should also be made available through the UN, in order to create an adequate infrastructure for later private American investment in such countries. Gradually, such opinions infected the thinking of local opinion leaders in the United States and of some leaders of national associations. Thus Rosenau reports that of his sample of 647 such leaders in 1958, 34 per cent wanted to increase foreign aid, 49 per cent wanted to keep it at current levels, while only 7 per

[3] Quoted in L. K. Hyde, *The United States and the United Nations: Promoting the Public Welfare* (New York: Manhattan, 1960), p. 144. See also the rest of Hyde's discussion.

cent wanted to decrease it! [4] When put into the context of continued mass skepticism toward foreign aid, the proposition that a "passionate minority" of informed and active leaders suffices to marshal support for governmental initiatives gains a good deal of strength. That minority proved to be the critical mass, translating post-1955 learning in Washington into a new approach to foreign aid, though hardly one based on a more coherent set of strategic objectives, or a more reasoned choice of bilateral as opposed to multilateral instruments.

## 2. The Third World Challenge and the Institutional Response

America's response was eventually to take the form of expanding foreign aid until the plateau of the mid-Sixties was reached *without* opting finally in favor of bilateral or multilateral assistance, but supporting both. If aid designed to impress, bribe, or cajole a foreign regime remained entirely bilateral, not all of the strategic foreign aid was given to UN agencies, either. Hence, although reasons militating in favor of multilateral strategic aid were adduced more commonly after 1956, the major response of the United States to the lessons of the early Fifties was merely to accede to the creation of new UN institutions in the foreign aid field, without endowing them with all the financial potency desired by the developing nations and without detracting from continued bilateral activity. Further, from 1962 on, the conditions attached to to bilateral aid became increasingly tied to the needs of the American economy.

Since the IBRD was the favored instrument of multilateral aid, it is not surprising that the United States sought to meet the Third World challenge simply by enlarging and legitimating a broader development task for the bank. The first sign that the Republican Administration might be willing to depart from its premises came in 1955. U.S. Treasury officials and leading bankers and businessmen professed to feel increasingly uneasy over the image they were creating abroad by unbroken American resistance to the SUNFED idea; this uneasiness was increased by persistent reports by Ameri-

[4] James N. Rosenau, *National Leadership and Foreign Policy* (Princeton: Princeton University, 1963), pp. 18, 208, 213. The same "innovative" reasoning eventually won out in the bilateral aid field, too, with the creation of the Development Loan Fund in the late Fifties.

TABLE 7 · 1

United States Foreign Aid: Bilateral vs. Multilateral
1956-1965 (dollars are in millions)

| | 1956 | 1960 | 1962 | 1963 | 1964 | 1965 |
|---|---|---|---|---|---|---|
| Total flow of public financial resources[a] | $2,006 | $2,834 | $3,671 | $3,755 | $3,462 | $3,730 |
| Total net bilateral flow | $1,440[b] | $2,540[c] | — | $3,557[d] | $3,188[d] | $3,462[d] |
| Total net multilateral flow | $ 566[b] | $ 294[c] | — | $ 198[d] | $ 274[d] | $ 267[d] |
| Multilateral flow as per cent of total | 28% | 10% | — | 5% | 8% | 7% |
| Total flow of public technical assistance | — | — | $ 454 | $ 452 | $ 515 | $ 490 |
| Total net bilateral technical assistance | — | — | $ 413[e] | $ 424[e] | $ 433[e] | $ 466[e] |
| Total net multilateral technical assistance[e] | 14[f] | — | $ 41[e] | $ 28[e] | $ 82[e] | $ 24[e] |
| Multilateral flow as per cent of total | — | — | 9% | 6% | 16% | 5% |

a OECD, *Development Assistance Efforts and Policies: 1966 Review*, Table 2, p. 148.
b U.S. Fiscal Year 1956-57, UN doc. E/3131, par. 86.
c *International Conciliation*, No. 534 (Sept., 1961), p. 140.
d OECD, *op. cit.*, Tables 5, 6, 7, pp. 152-57.
e OECD, *op. cit.*, Table 11, pp. 162-63.
f *International Conciliation*, No. 514 (Sept., 1957), p. 131.
— Not available.

can delegates to UN sessions reporting the bad image. Once this aura existed, Eugene Black took the initiative in persuading Administration leaders that a flexible IBRD policy of investing in private enterprise abroad, without insisting on government guarantees of soundness, would aid development, free enterprise, and America's international reputation. Thus was born the idea for an affiliate for the bank, the International Finance Corporation (IFC). American officials and conservative business leaders, however, accepted it only after its capital was limited to $100 million and after it was denied the power to acquire voting stock in private firms abroad. Once assured that IFC would be subordinate to the widely respected IRBD leadership, American elite and government opinion welcomed it.

But the creation of IFC did not stop the demand for SUNFED. And again it was the bank that used its prestige in American elite circles to espouse the idea of enlarging its loan activity by acquiring a new affiliate able to make soft loans: the International Development Association (IDA). Multipurpose, low-interest loans repayable in local currencies would be made to nations already so burdened with repayment and interest charges that they no longer constituted bankable risks for the IBRD. Although Black supported the idea, public initiative came from Senator Mike Monroney (D, Okla.). SUNFED agitation in the UN, via the quiet pressure of the IBRD in Washington, had influenced the senator to push for a new American approach to foreign aid. Monroney stressed that IDA would remove economic development from domestic American political debate and save the United States money by mobilizing soft foreign currencies more effectively. Internationally, Monroney stressed that IDA would remove the political stigma that attaches to nationally-administered loans, give the recipient nations a voice and an opportunity to learn the virtues of long-range financial planning, in which they could help each other through the use of local currencies. As for the IBRD, it seemed to welcome any initiative that would enable it to avoid a renegotiation of its mandate and charter, as a result of the SUNFED pressure, and give it an image other than that of the hard-nosed and calculating banker. The testimony of American aid notables such as Averell Harriman and Paul Hoffman made it clear that they shared this feeling and thought of IDA as a useful device to head off the dreaded SUNFED. Even then the Treasury remained cool, and conservative Republican leaders opposed, until a highly successful press campaign launched by Monroney showed that public support existed and until Eugene Black took it upon himself to "sell" the Republican opposition.

IDA, its acceptance in the United States, and its extension and renewal in 1962 illustrate a shift in elite attitudes. The idea of IDA was opposed only by the shipping industry because of the implied increase in UN powers. The Farm Bureau Federation objected to the constant enlargement of the foreign aid burden, but the AFL-CIO demanded that the American share of soft-loan funds of IDA be tripled! The shift in opinion is even more significant if we consider the policy actually followed by the new IDA. Because IBRD, the parent institution, felt that there was no demand for sound hard loans that could not be met from the existing resources of the bank, it permitted IDA to follow a lending policy much less restrictive than its own. IDA's generous policy involved it in difficult choices among the many poor nations seeking first attention. It therefore adopted a set of very unbank-like criteria: only the poorest countries that had exhausted earlier financial sources, were poor credit risks, and were unable to assume new debt burdens were aided, provided they made an honest effort to meet the performance criteria laid down in the loan agreement and sought to manage their economies to avoid inflation. On the other hand, IDA also reassured the United States by adopting the IBRD's policy of encouraging private enterprise and not lending to state-owned industries. When Black took the lead in demanding the expansion of the IDA task in 1962, he took pride in these unorthodox practices. The Democratic Administration supported his initiative and assured some congressional opponents of the extension that American balance-of-payments difficulties would not be exacerbated even though the IDA dollar loans were "untied" and not necessarily spent in the United States.

IFC and IDA do not exhaust the adaptability of the IBRD and its American friends. George Woods, Black's successor as president of the family of lending institutions, continued the subtle mixture of hard and soft banking policies but expressed more sympathy than Black felt for soft lending and support of state enterprises. Woods altered the bank's own policies by allowing very long-term loans, increasing IDA resources from the parent's earnings. He also veered toward the country approach to development assistance, away from the more limiting project approach. Further, he encouraged receiving countries to put their loan requests into the context of comprehensive economic planning and even talked about the need for a UN development plan in order to rationalize and improve allocation of the world's lending resources. The bank also began to support agricultural and education projects. This departure from the previous decade's development banking, oriented toward free enterprise and free trade, is as remarkable as it is dependent on the similar shift in American elite attitudes. IBRD even assumed delicate political tasks, such as the organization of international financial consortia to develop the Indus Valley, produce Iranian oil, and refinance the Suez Canal, contrary to American intentions in 1944 but eventually with Washington's blessings.

But the IBRD was still a long way from being a capital aid fund under the control of the Third World. Nor did these reforms and adaptations still the demand for SUNFED. Washington had attempted to use the specialized agencies to approximate Third World demands without actually creating an independent capital aid fund. Thus, in addition to the extensive technical assistance operations carried out by the specialized agencies, the United States enthusiastically supported operational programs such as WHO's malaria eradication campaigns, UNESCO's basic education programs in Latin America and Africa, ILO's manpower training programs, and —most important—the FAO-run World Food Program. As initiated in 1962 and extended in 1965, this program seeks to use food surpluses for development. Nations with surplus food donate it; others may donate cash or shipping services. These resources are then allotted to developing nations able to use food as a component in specific development projects or to stave off famine. During the first three years, $100 million were spent; for the second three-year period, $275 million are targeted. Why did the United States agree to this, despite its opposition to UN-run commodity programs? It endorsed the World Food Program as an alternative preferable to a rival scheme advocated by Canada, the Third World, and FAO: a comprehensive commodity plan that would have included price and marketing arrangements as well as aid to developing nations and that would have taken the place of the bilateral American Food-for-Peace Program. Because the rival plan was to reach proportions of $12 billion, it would effectively have removed from the world market vast quantities of food and thereby contributed to price stability while making free food available to the poorest nations.

Since none of these cautious concessions succeeded in reducing the clamor for SUNFED or in giving the United States a more benign image, more incremental adaptation was felt to be necessary, though no massive conversion to the SUNFED idea or the principle of radical income redistribution occurred. A major step was the idea launched by Paul Hoffman in 1958 to combine the rationalization of specialized agency technical assistance with increased investment in nonbankable enterprises. The term "pre-investment" was chosen in order not to offend opponents of the soft approach. Emphasis was to be placed on surveys of resources and educational facilities in relation to industrialization plans, the examination of such plans, and the intercession of the UN in obtaining public or private funding for them. This program took shape in the form of the United Nations Special Fund. Its operations considerably increased technical assistance pre-investment resources and extended control over the entire UN technical assistance program by making the specialized agencies dependent on central funding. In so doing, it met the American insistence on streamlining specialized agency operations and avoiding overlaps. In American eyes, the Special Fund was so successful that Washington advanced the idea of having it assume officially all UN development assistance other than IBRD–IFC–IDA operations, and direct the specialized agencies' assistance programs under the label UN Development Program. In 1965, UNDP, under Hoffman's direction, was set up even though the Third World regretted the centralization. Nor did it stop its clamor for SUNFED.

In fact, the clamor grew louder as the number of ex-colonies in the UN increased. The General Assembly formally voted a Capital

Development Fund into existence in 1966; this may have been an act of ritual defiance of the rich because, unhappily, the fund was not endowed with money. Over the negative votes of the Western *and* the Soviet blocs, the Third World decided to set up an autonomous agency directly subject to the Assembly—i.e., not a specialized agency or a bank based on weighted voting rights—to make no-interest loans to governments, groups of governments, or private entities. Aid "shall be of a kind and in a form consistent with the wishes of the recipients and shall not involve any unacceptable conditions for them, whether political, economic, military or other." [5] Thus the revolt against bilateral aid and the IBRD was ritually completed.

A few years earlier, the Third World had demanded the creation of a new, specialized agency to be devoted to making grants for the stimulation of industry, another version of SUNFED. The United States was opposed to this venture, too, but eventually supported a watered-down version of it when the UNCTAD came out strongly for an industrial development agency. A small Center for Industrial Development, with an ambiguous mandate and very small budget, was created in the UN Secretariat. The Soviet Union, knowing the extent of American opposition, urged the UN to enact the scheme anyway, predicting correctly that because of the pressure, the United States eventually would feel compelled to support a larger venture. Industrialization, Washington felt, was too important an issue to be left to the domination of others. And thus the logic of the enmeshment process rather than any distinct change of heart at home forced another incremental adaptation. In 1965 the General Assembly unanimously voted to create another autonomous agency under its control, the UN Industrial Development Organization (UNIDO), a compromise between the full-fledged specialized agency demanded by the developing nations and the small Center preferred by the West. UNIDO came formally into existence in 1966. It is ruled, like UNCTAD, by a 45-nation Industrial Development Board, the majority of which represents underdeveloped members. UNIDO has a very broad task. It aids all phases of industrialization, pre-investment, training and education, and the marketing of processed, primary, and manufactured goods; it contributes to national and regional planning and seeks to help in changing rules governing industrial property in order to accelerate the diffusion of technological knowledge. Its program thus may well compete directly with the UNDP and programs of spe-

[5] *United Nations Monthly Chronicle* (January, 1967), p. 109. A pledging conference in 1967 yielded a mere $1.3 million, almost none of it pledged by industrial nations.

cialized agencies, even though it was at first decided to finance UNIDO from UNDP funds. There is some poetic justice in the fact that in 1967 the Soviet bloc felt constrained to join the West in voting *against* a Third World resolution in UNIDO seeking to turn the new organization into a plain capital aid fund!

And so the United States, against its will and better judgment, found itself tied into two new aid organizations dominated by the recipients, devoted to soft loans or grants, and hostile to private enterprise. The liberalized policies of the IBRD and its affiliates and the UNDP, far from heading off this trend, seem merely to whet the appetite of the developing nations. The strategy of giving a little, to avoid having to concede the principle, failed utterly to stem the tide of enmeshment. Not even the grudging concession at UNCTAD II to earmark 1 per cent of GNP for foreign aid each year can change this conclusion. The logical corollary to this trend, equally dramatic and equally unintended in 1955, was the systematic effort on the part of the United States to use regionalism as a device to share the aid burden and coordinate aid policies among all major donors. The vehicle for this was the OECD.

In OECD, the United States felt it necessary to use and submit to the confrontation procedure, to explain its own aid policies and persuade the Europeans and Japan to contribute more as they grew richer. This step brought important results, as embarrassment compelled Canada and Britain, among others, to step up their aid. OECD became the forum in which the developed countries counseled on how to meet the cohesive pressure of the Third World. OECD was used by the United States to organize European aid consortia to shore up the economies of Greece and Turkey and incidentally prescribe strict rules for the economic conduct of the two recipients. Thus OECD became known as the "rich men's club" in the aid as well as in the trade field. Through its Development Assistance Committee, it "deals always with the line at which the edge of one donor's program is in contact with that of another, with problems that are common to nations which have increasingly made aid a part of their national long-range policy." [6] But it does not give multilateral aid itself or prescribe common rules for the bilateral assistance provided by its members. Nor does it coordinate important matters of differences in national approach; instead, it concentrates on minor items on which the donors can agree. The level of interest rates, amortization terms, and grace periods on loans provide such cases of successful coordination. If it is a rich men's club, it remains a reasonably ineffective one, because it has

[6] Seymour J. Rubin, *The Conscience of the Rich Nations* (New York: Harper & Row, for the Council on Foreign Relations, 1966), pp. 19–20. Paperback.

not been successful in influencing the basic political objectives and techniques underlying national donor efforts.

### 3. The Multipolar System
### and the American Consensus

The burgeoning of unwanted institutions and adaptive practices has not resulted in increased American contribution to the aid effort. In 1964-1965 the IBRD family and the UNDP disbursed $1.2 billion; American bilateral economic aid was worth $2.2 billion. In the same year, the UN technical aid personnel in the field numbered 5,000 persons, while the corresponding figure for the U.S. Agency for International Development was 5,300. At the same time, the United States was cutting back its contribution to the regular budgets of the specialized agencies that provide the bulk of the UN technical aid. Moreover, since 1966 the mounting domestic crisis in the United States and the fiscal conservatism of Congress combined to reduce the foreign aid requests of the administration, resulting in a mere $2.3 billion of new appropriations in 1968-1969, from a high of over $3.7 billion in 1963. During all these years there is little evidence of a mass public attitude more precise than before or more favorable toward foreign aid, especially multilateral aid. Is this true also at the elite levels?

Among academic specialists in foreign aid and development, there is some evidence of the acceptance of a new position for the United States. Most economists agree that more aid could easily be given by the United States if the OECD-endorsed target of annual contributions equal to 1 per cent of gross national product is to be met. American aid has not reached that target in recent years. If the principle of the progressive income tax were used to compute national contributions to IDA, the United States could be responsible for 65 per cent of the funds instead of the 43 per cent actually contributed. UNIDO and the Capital Development Fund could be generously supported without making them into giant give-aways if the distribution and evaluation of aid were made the collective responsibility of the recipients, as it was in the OEEC under the Marshall Plan. Furthermore, an increase in the multilateral aid component would reduce the uneconomic practice of tying aid funds, which continues to flourish. Economic aid intended to contribute to stability, prosperity, and peace in long-range terms is the shared objective of the United States and the UN. Why not increase the UN share of such aid, since there is no conflict of objectives? In addition, there is some evidence that specialists are increasingly claiming certain advantages for UN aid: they believe that it will restore the notion of a master plan for world betterment, a plan that was lost early in UN history, and the United States will be prominently associated with this revival; countries resisting the strings of bilateral Soviet or American aid would have a multi-lateral program large enough to suit them if America's professions in favor of nonalignment are to be believed; economic problems could be tackled on their merits and outside the special political aims usually implied in bilateral aid, and without fear of wounding sensibilities or seeming to intervene. UN intervention seems to be more legitimate and acceptable than national measures of this kind.

Yet the business community shows little inclination to accept these ideas. Instead, even the internationally-minded and innovative business elite is beginning to resent the tactics used by the Third World to circumvent the development ground rules of the IBRD family. Some regard the various versions of SUNFED now enacted as a kind of development blackmail. Such businessmen might accept the argument that support for public investment is necessary for the building of the transportation, education, and communication facilities that will eventually support private investment; but they are not yet prepared to accept full-fledged planning in the Third World under UN auspices, financed in large measure by the United States. Such sentiments have been expressed more and more in terms of pressures on government departments that deal with specialized agencies. The State Department encouraged expensive crash programs for large-scale education projects launched by UNESCO to foster nation-building in Africa, most notably in the Congo. At the same time it sought to head off politically-inspired human rights programs and UNESCO's vaguely drafted campaigns to combat illiteracy. The business elite, however, remained remarkably cool toward both approaches. The Department of Agriculture and the farmers' organizations stress the research role of FAO, as opposed to State's concern with the contribution to development that FAO could make. Businessmen grew more and more disenchanted with the ILO as that body increasingly politicized its deliberations with colonial questions instead of stressing productivity programs. The Department of Labor and the AFL-CIO were disappointed because the human rights program of the ILO seemed to support anticolonialism more than the drive to build up unions independent of the government. Even relations with WHO showed evidence of bifurcation of objectives and interests. The U.S. Public Health Service and the medical profession were content to carry on with WHO's sober but popular research and discussion facilities oriented toward specific diseases. But a French initiative to include in WHO a "world cancer research institute" caused the State Department to counter with suggestions for a "world health communication center" with ambiguous functions. Public relations and prestige dictated an approach that confused the issue, lines of responsibility, and elite identification.

So far we have no clear indication that congressional opinion in the United States had swung decisively behind the new objectives and methods of foreign aid implied in the actual institutional development in the UN—even in American-dominated UN institutions. The general congressional preference for "sound" international financial measures was of course deliberately catered to by including IDA in the bank and not identifying it with "unsound" SUNFED-like ideas. Yet the discussion of the Monroney Resolution suggested that many senators thought UN aid superior to bilateral aid for building stable and prosperous economies. The House of Representatives also approved the resolution, even though the Secretary of the Treasury admitted that purchases in the United States from dollars lent by the IBRD amount to less than the American contribution to the bank. But when the extension of IDA was debated in Congress in 1963-1964, the admission that its untied loans do not necessarily and always benefit the American economy resulted in a great hue and cry and the fear that this type of foreign aid would exacerbate the balance-of-payments crisis. The bill to replenish IDA coffers squeaked through the Senate by a vote of 38 to 31; it was, on first try, defeated in the House of Representatives by a vote of 208 to 188. It took the personal testimony of Secretary Rusk and Secretary Dillon to bring about a successful reconsideration, testimony that sought to prove IDA policies to be wholly consistent with the American national interest since "political upheavals, arising out of economic despair, inevitably must threaten us all." [7] There is some evidence that the eventual victory of the IDA replenishment bill was due less to the eloquence of the argument than to the fact that its passage was tied to a package of domestic bills of interest to some initial opponents. By 1967, IDA's coffers were empty again, and congressional willingness to replenish them was in doubt.

[7] Dean Rusk, during the IDA reconsideration hearings, as quoted in James H. Weaver, *The International Development Association* (New York: Frederick A. Praeger, Inc., 1965), p. 209.

Naturally, there was as little enthusiasm on Capitol Hill as else-where for the trend toward autonomous UN capital aid agencies, organs that are seen as politicizing economic development activity and detracting from the sober work of the specialized agencies. In all fairness, though, it ought to be mentioned that the opponents were the same people who, in the late Fifties, attacked specialized agency programs as useless, overlapping, inefficient, and bureau-cratic. Congress felt that American-initiated politicization, such as opposition to the admission of Communist China, was quite per-missible, while similar efforts by other nations were not. Develop-ment has been perceived by Congress as part of the fight against communism. The continuation of multilateral aid under declining American control, in the face of the East-West détente, makes little sense to many legislators. A new and broader justification for such aid has yet to be widely accepted.

Neither the elites nor Congress substituted consistency for the platitudes describing foreign aid objectives discussed in Chapter 6; but perhaps aid officials in the Executive department elaborated an operational doctrine that tied American policy to the changing web of interdependence. "The choice for the United States between giving aid bilaterally and giving aid through international organs is a pragmatic one," says Richard N. Gardner, a former State De-partment official. "The test is which route is more likely to achieve the purposes for which the particular kind of assistance is being granted."[8] This is the question. Gardner enumerates the reasons for multilateral aid that are increasingly gaining favor, provided the purpose of the aid is clear: the recognition of independence and neutrality of new nations, the wider choice of expert personnel and contributing funds, and the tendency to strengthen the autonomy of international organizations as "instruments of peace and welfare."[9]

Pragmatism indeed: American officials favor a doctrine that ex-plains strategic economic aid as furthering "political development" in recipient nations; but they cannot agree on whether "political development" means anti-communism, pro-Americanism, or attach-ment to peaceful change. Further, they cannot explain *how* eco-nomic aid is able to realize these political objectives as long as it is evaluated largely in economic terms; in practice, the objectives of a country's program come to mean "economic growth in the short run." The expectations of the professional aid bureaucrat and his political superiors are much more modest than those of Congress

---

[8] Gardner, *In Pursuit of World Order,* p. 116.
[9] *Ibid.,* p. 117.

and the major elites. Hence they prefer not to deal directly with the political objectives underlying foreign aid because they distrust their own ability to influence politics abroad decisively with foreign aid measures.[10] Sometimes a pragmatic consensus seems to be much the same as a lack of consensus among the very people most in need of clarity of purpose.

## 4. International Aid, American Objectives, and the Future

Clearly, American policy on foreign aid has sought to adjust to mounting international criticism by gradual concessions that had the cumulative but unintended consequence of ushering in a new UN-centered and Third World-dominated system of rules for, and institutions of, aid. It is not yet clear whether the same pressures will also force a reluctant United States to engage in massive international income redistribution by means of generous financial contributions to the new program. This process parallels that of new rules for world trade but has gone even further in terms of actual American enmeshment. We follow the tactic of identifying with the minimum common denominator of agreement in General Assembly debates on development, and these have grown increasingly political. On the other hand, the determined resistance of the West to the demands of the developing nations in UNCTAD has already resulted in the evolution of a new decision-making device: the technique of "conciliation" has been adopted in UN trade organs, compelling continuing negotiations among the three blocs until unanimous interbloc agreement is reached on a given issue. Third World nations have realized that their voting power alone will not make the developed nations pay or relax their control over world trade rules. The same evolution is almost certainly in store in the new UN aid organs. On these terms, then, the international system rather than domestic opinion has brought about a very major adjustment in American response to the desires of other nations.

Domestic opinion has been permissive, but it has not yet adjusted to the new forces. As in 1955, actual government policy is considerably more receptive to foreign challenges and UN pressure than is domestic opinion. Elite opinion eventually caught up with

[10] Robert A. Packenham, "Political Development Doctrines in the American Foreign Aid Program," *World Politics* (January, 1966), pp. 194-235.

government. But in the meantime, the system has changed some more, and the catching up must happen all over again if a new consensus is to come about. Americans have been assured that foreign aid—UN and bilateral—will stabilize volatile nations, establish democracy, help free private enterprise abroad, teach economic planning, defeat communism, help in nation-building, and aid the American farmer, educator, and industrialist. They see, however, that these objectives appear to conflict and are diluted in practice by Congress and the Executive. They see further that very little of this seems actually to be realized in aid operations. They do not always understand that short-run and long-run aims may well conflict, that democracy in a generation's time can be built—perhaps—on the basis of an aid-supported military dictatorship today. But since the objectives of the UN are hardly more explicit or consistent, the rational choices of means and instruments are not made easier by the mere fact that the balance of persuasive power has shifted in favor of the UN. We must conclude therefore that the very ambiguity surrounding the objectives and successes of foreign aid make it more difficult for a new cohesive American consensus to arise.

It may be that regional development programs, as in the Alliance for Progress, will command more support than UN measures are given in the United States. Regional programs demand of recipients specific social and economic reforms and provide, through the OAS, collective ways of evaluation and criticism. No wonder some people favor the strengthening of the regional machinery as a second line of defense in the event of a rupture between the United States and the Third World-controlled UN aid institutions. In the meantime, however, we are still unsure that prosperity brings peace along with it or if peace and security must exist before prosperity can be introduced in the nonindustrial world. American officials sometimes argue one theme and then the other. Economic aid is necessary to make communism unpopular; but communism must be contained and defeated before economic development can take place. And why democracy is expected to flower on the basis of anticommunism alone—whether preceded by economic development or followed by it—has never been made very clear. Indeed, the real challenge for American policy must be the recognition that with improvement of *some* living standards, silent frustrations will break out into open rebellion, thus making the revolution of rising expectations the archenemy of economic aid. And one may thus have to conclude that our growing enmeshment in these institutions will lead to the attainment of none of the many objectives of strategic foreign aid.

CHAPTER EIGHT

# COLONIALISM AND HUMAN RIGHTS

In an epochal resolution adopted in 1960, the General Assembly proclaimed the need for a "speedy and unconditional end to colonialism in all its forms and manifestations." Further, the Assembly found that all peoples have the right to self-determination and that "the subjection of peoples to alien subjugation, domination and exploitation constitutes a denial of fundamental human rights, is contrary to the Charter of the UN and is an impediment to the promotion of world peace and cooperation." [1] All the Charter actually said on the subject, however, was that the members had the obligation to contribute to the attainment of "self-government or independence" of colonial territories and to cooperate in the promotion of human rights. Moreover, in 1965 the

[1] General Assembly, Resolution 1514 (XV) on Granting of Independence to Colonial Countries and Peoples, Dec. 14, 1960, par. 1.

**165**

Assembly voted a treaty demanding the elimination of all forms of racial discrimination; in 1966 it adopted two covenants of human rights that establish, among others, the internationally protected right to national self-determination, work, leisure, founding a family, education, free speech, assembly, and voting in free elections. As early as 1948 the ILO had adopted treaties that created the internationally protected right to found, join, and maintain trade unions and bargain collectively with employers, all without government interference. In 1945, the founding UN members had assumed "that each colonial power should at its own discretion and in an unhurried way lead its dependent peoples to well-being and self-government"; in 1961 they were accommodating themselves to the proposition that colonialism is "an intolerable and illegitimate abuse to be done away with as speedily as possible by the international community." [2]

The United States abstained on many of these votes and opposed outright aspects of the human rights covenants. Yet the American public, if asked, would surely proclaim its endorsement of the principle of self-determination and even argue that the origin of the United States itself is related to that principle. Moreover, most Americans would surely support the proposition that the enjoyment of democracy, through protected human rights, is a cornerstone of world peace and should therefore be advanced through the UN. Why, then, the uncertainty and malaise?

## 1. Massive Social Change and the United Nations

Much of the uncertainty is due to the particular link between independence and human rights that is stressed with increasing vehemence by the majority of non-Western and economically underdeveloped UN members. What, substantively, is the issue as seen by the majority? The Third World argues that *colonialism* implies the direct or indirect control of one nation (or ethnic group) over another; usually the dominant group is assumed to be white and the dominated colored. Further, colonialism is equated with economic exploitation, foreign capital, large Western corporations, the capitalist system in general. To end colonialism, therefore, the exploited peoples (or nations?) must not only

[2] Rupert Emerson, "Colonialism, Political Development and the UN," *International Organization* (Summer, 1965), p. 486.

acquire political independence but also gain control over their economies, natural resources, and economic development policies. World peace is not possible, the argument continues, until all vestiges of colonialism have disappeared, thus making decolonization a central task of the UN.

What does this have to do with the enjoyment of human rights? The right to self-determination is held to be *the* basic human right. Further, since the anticolonial struggle necessitates freedom of expression, the political and civic rights associated with democracy are needed for the achievement of independence—though this implies little for their continued enjoyment after independence is secured. Since decolonization is equated with economic progress, the right to work, to enjoy minimal living standards, and to benefit from education can be seen as close corollaries of self-determination. And since racial discrimination is the form of oppression most often experienced by the Third World, the human right to be protected against discrimination emerges as the chief demand. Again, the maintenance of peace is then held to be dependent on the elimination of discrimination. The Third World, in effect, says to the West: "We will use violence to attain independence and the end of colonialism; if you wish for peace, use the United Nations to end colonialism; the colonialists are the aggressors, not we, because they deny us independence, economic betterment, and equality."

The United States itself contributed heavily to the evolution of the multipolar and multibloc system under which these arguments can be made with increasing forcefulness and effectiveness. So did the Soviet Union. By seeking to strengthen its own side during the bipolar phase of the international system, each superpower helped call into being the Third World as an autonomous force. Once born, the new force changed the character of the system and imposed new constraints—not anticipated earlier—on the main powers. These new constraints raise the issue of intervention by the UN on behalf of human rights, democracy, equality, and independence. They compel the major powers to ask themselves how far such powers should be permitted to develop. And they make the major powers cautious and uneasy about the genie they helped liberate from the bottle of colonialism and underdevelopment.

How, then, do the demands of the Third World affect the powers of the UN and thereby change the nature of the system to one of greater possible enmeshment? In the field of human rights, the extent of enmeshment depends on the institutional mechanisms actually adopted. Four approaches have been used. The least constraining is the technical assistance with, and advice on, protection of human rights; this is given in setting up international labor standards in member states. More constraining is the creation of voluntary norms by UN agencies, giving member states a standard toward which to aim, without binding them firmly; the International Covenant on Economic, Social, and Cultural Rights illustrates this mechanism. Third, the UN can, by virtue of specific conventions, create norms that are legally binding on member states once they ratify the texts; the convention dealing with genocide and the political rights of women illustrates this mechanism. Finally, legally binding norms can be accompanied by procedures compelling various degrees of actual implementation by member states, ranging from the obligation to submit annual reports to being questioned by an international investigating commission or even used before the International Court of Justice (ICJ). The malaise of the United States grew as the more powerful mechanisms were discussed.

Colonial issues featured another set of institutional constraints. Under the UN Charter, two procedures were set up, largely as a result of United States diplomacy in 1945. Certain territories could be placed voluntarily under the trusteeship system. The trustee nation assumed the obligation to prepare the trust for "self-government or independence" without being bound to a timetable, and to give the needs of the indigenous population priority in its administration of the economy and society of the trust. The trustee was obligated to report to the UN Trusteeship Council, permit inhabitants to petition the council, and to admit visiting UN missions instructed to inspect the implementation of the trust agreement. In fact, only twelve territories were placed under the system—all seized from enemy states in the two world wars—and by 1968 all but three island groups in the Pacific had achieved independence or had been merged with neighboring independent states. For all colonial territories not placed under the trusteeship system, the colonial powers bound themselves to give priority to the needs and well-being of the indigenous inhabitants and to take all measures to advance them toward "self-government," not independence. They agreed to report annually to the UN on their policies excepting political matters, in each territory under their sovereignty.

The obligation to report annually was soon escalated into a major measure of international control, ending in 1961 with the de facto merger of the two procedures: The Special Committee on the Situation with Regard to the Implementation of the Declaration on the Granting of Independence to Colonial Countries and Peoples (commonly known as the Committee of Twenty-Four) assumed the power to tell each colonial nation when to set a territory free, to whom the free government is to be turned over, and how the transfer is to be made. It also assumed the power to visit colonies, hear petitioners, negotiate with colonial administrators, conduct plebiscites, and recommend that the parent General Assembly condemn colonial powers. Clearly, the political and legal power of the UN in the field of decolonization had grown immensely in fifteen years. Could the United States be sure that its freedom of action would remain unimpaired?

The observer, as distinguished from the actor, may regard the tangled skein of colonial and human rights issues as a possible breakthrough area in the competence of international institutions to constrain their nation members. And to the extent that the actor comes to share the observer's conclusions, his resistance to further enmeshment may well grow apace. The issues of human rights and decolonization have added as many institutions to the UN as collective security activities, disarmament, and world trade regulation. Is the enmeshment permanent? Why did the United States first feed the fires of a UN human rights task and encourage UN-fostered decolonization and then have second thoughts? Will the second thoughts be the lessons the actor learns from institutional growth? With decolonization all but completed, will the alliance between anticolonialism and the international protection of human rights continue unabated? Will the continuation or the breakdown of that alliance serve American objectives of a peaceful and stable world that is resistant to antidemocratic forces?

## 2. From the Cold War to the North–South Confrontation

American policy in the UN with regard to the international protection of human rights was largely propagandistic in style and anticommunist in substance during the bipolar period. Like all other member nations, the United States voted for the Universal Declaration of Human Rights in 1948 and thus endorsed a set of norms with great moral resonance but no legal force. At the same time, the United States made great use of UN organs, to press home charges of violations of human rights by communist regimes and to demand UN censure of such acts. One result of these charges was the adoption by the ILO of the two comprehensive conventions dealing with freedom of association and the right to collective bargaining, texts the United States hoped to be able to use at Soviet expense. In this context the United States made no objection to the creation of a standing ILO conciliation commission with the power to investigate charges of violations of these conventions, not expecting that this enforcement mechanism might be used against the West as well as against the Soviet regime or Latin-American dictators. While the Soviet bloc was accused of resorting to forced labor and of denying the citizens of East European countries the right to vote and oppose the Communist party, the United States itself declined to ratify the conventions on freedom of association, claiming that a federal constitution made these matters subject to state regulation and that American workers already enjoyed these rights.

Nor was the United States very happy with the effort launched by the UN to translate the Universal Declaration into a legally binding covenant of human rights. One issue was the question of whether "human rights" are essentially the political rights associated with the practice of democracy—the American position—or whether they include substantive matters such as the right to a job, a family, education in one's own language, full employment, and social security—the position argued by the Soviet bloc and developing nations. The United States tended to regard these substantive economic and social policies as the product of the exercise of political rights rather than as fundamental legal norms. Further, the Soviet bloc wished to limit the enjoyment of all rights by subjecting them to the need for public order and state policy. Another issue involved the question of whether there is a "collective" right to self-determination and to the control over natural resources, a question answered negatively by the United States. Finally, the issue arose concerning how human rights, even if defined to everyone's satisfaction, could be implemented or enforced under UN control. As the debate in the General Assembly increasingly veered toward specific formulations opposed by the United States, the earlier enthusiasm for the covenant began to pale.

American fear of enmeshment was not alleviated by the decision of the Assembly to draft two covenants, one dealing with political and civil rights subject to regular reporting, investigation, and conciliation of complaints of violations, and one dealing with the more controversial economic, social, and cultural rights, which would merely set standards for future attainment by member states. The two texts were completed and adopted by a unanimous General Assembly in December of 1966. But the United States' affirmative vote contained no hint of a willingness to ratify the covenants.

The preference of the United States for anticommunist propaganda over concrete commitments was made plain in its position on the UN convention making genocide an international crime. The Genocide Convention of 1948 defined the acts considered criminal, whether committed by private individuals or public officials, and called for each member country to make laws that would enforce the International Court of Justice's judgments against violators. This requirement was enough to make the United States decline ratification, even though the principles of the convention were lauded by the public and the President, whose memories of Nazi exterminations of ethnic and religious groups were still fresh. Other texts prepared by the UN to deal with specific rights suffered the same fate. The United States was particularly reluctant to commit itself to any international obligations that were justiciable under the aegis of the ICJ. It became a party to the Court's Statute only with the reservation that the compulsory jurisdiction of the ICJ over the United States excluded "disputes with regard to matters which are essentially within the domestic jurisdiction of the United States of America as determined by the United States of America." [3]

Since, during the bipolar period, the force of the Third World in the UN was far from dominant, and anticolonial advocacy was one of the favorite themes of the Soviet Union, the United States followed a restrained policy on colonial questions. Its primary objectives were not to annoy the European allies, who were also the major colonial powers, and not to interfere with the gradual development of self-government, stressing social and economic methods that were then still in vogue. The anticolonial forces failed to commit the UN to the early colonial crises in North Africa and Indochina, and the United States supported the West in resisting their inclusion in the UN agenda. And as far as the institutional competence of UN organs was concerned, the United States joined other colonial nations in insisting on the parity principle of composing UN commissions and councils, granting equal representation to colonial and noncolonial nations, and limiting the UN's power to issue sweeping orders governing the political future of non-self-governing territories.

We sometimes forget that the United States is a colonial power too. By virtue of the UN Charter's provisions on non-self-governing territories, Washington assumed the obligation to report on the progress of the populations—other than their political development —of Puerto Rico, the Virgin Islands, and American Samoa. When does a territory cease to be non-self-governing? [4] Like other colonial nations, the United States claimed the sole right to make this de-

---

[3] This is the famous "Connally Reservation." U.N. Treaty Series, I, 9-13.
[4] When information ceased to be transmitted upon Hawaii's and Alaska's admission to statehood no controversy over whether they were then "self-governing" arose. Submission of information on the Panama Canal Zone stopped when Panama objected.

termination and to cease transmitting reports to the UN. When, in 1952, the new commonwealth relationship with Puerto Rico went into effect, the United States ceased to transmit information and asked the General Assembly to vote, by a two-thirds margin, to approve America's stewardship and thus ratify the unilateral decision. The attempt failed: while approving the commonwealth status, the General Assembly in 1953 also asserted its competence to make future determinations about the cessation of reports and the status of colonies, and the right to do so by simple majority. Washington had no choice but to go along.

Further, the United States is an active participant in the UN Trusteeship System by virtue of its trust over the Pacific Islands Territory. In fact, the United States is the major designer of that system. Its initiatives in 1945 were largely responsible for the principles of the system and the specific competences given the Trusteeship Council. The desire to strike a blow in favor of gradual progress toward colonial "independence or self-government" did not mean, however, that the U. S. Navy was willing to forego control over Pacific islands just wrested from Japan in a four-year war. Hence, the United States proposed—and insisted—that the Charter include provisions for "strategic trust territories." These are areas of military significance in which the inhabitants have the same rights as in ordinary trusts, and the trustee has the same obligations *except* that specific areas are closed to UN visiting missions and the supervision of the trustee's actions rests with the Security Council, where the trustee may exercise a veto. As Senator Tom Connally, a member of the U. S. delegation that drafted the Charter, put it:

> We signed the Charter on the theory that our interests in the Pacific and elsewhere were amply protected. . . . When we do agree that . . . [strategic areas] go under trusteeship, we have the right to stipulate the terms . . . we keep the control in our hands.[5]

American policy lived up to this attitude during the first years of the trust administration. Although actual supervision was turned over to the Trusteeship Council, the United States did close military bases to UN missions and used the islands extensively for naval and air bases. Furthermore, they provided one of the chief testing grounds for nuclear devices. Despite suggestions from the

---

[5] Hearings on the ratification of the UN Charter, 1945, as quoted in Daniel Cheever and H. Field Haviland, *Organizing for Peace* (Boston: Houghton Mifflin, 1954), p. 310.

UN that civilian control be substituted for the Navy's rule and that territorial self-government be encouraged, little was done along those lines. Some land was alienated, but war damage was removed, and the education of the islanders was greatly stressed. Self-government was introduced gradually at the village and district levels. But no great cordiality was shown the United Nations.

After 1955, the Third World's presence in the UN began to give a very different flavor to discussions of colonialism and human rights. The anticommunist stance of the United States hardly faltered, but the arguments now had to be adjusted to a differently composed General Assembly and a much more adaptive Soviet Union. The United States became clearly defensive and fearful of UN institutional prowess and intervention in the discussion of human rights. A high American official explained in 1956:

> They are not, in our opinion a proper subject for an international convention or treaty. We do not believe that you should try to legislate international morality when you lack enforcement power. And the United Nations does not have, *nor do we wish to see it acquire,* such powers in this field.[6]

Washington indicated that in UN discussions it would oppose aspects of the two Covenants on Human Rights, and it would decline to ratify the finished texts, in any event. The United States successfully stressed instead the need for technical assistance to nations wishing to improve the administration of human rights. It endorsed a system of triennial reports from UN member nations, describing their progress toward a higher level of human rights, and it succeeded in launching UN studies on how best to advance the cause of certain specific human rights. The opposition to more stringent measures, however, was shelved when the technique of a legally binding convention could be combined with Cold War propaganda. Hence, the United States supported the ILO's effort to outlaw forced labor and argued for a UN convention guaranteeing freedom of information, an enthusiasm that was considerably dampened when the communist and certain underdeveloped nations wanted to limit the unrestricted gathering of news. As a result of the deadlock, the convention of freedom of information was never completed.

The controversy over the meaning of the right to self-determination and its many substantive and procedural implications caused

---

[6] Assistant Secretary of State Francis O. Wilcox, *Department of State Bulletin* (Nov. 12, 1956), p. 907. Emphasis supplied.

the United States great difficulty. The inclusion of this right in the two covenants was one of the reasons for American coolness toward the texts; the subsidiary right for permanent national sovereignty over natural resources brought to the fore the tangled issues of foreign investment, the role of private enterprise in economic development, and the right of new nations to nationalize foreign-owned mines and oil wells. American spokesmen sought unsuccessfully to resolve the issue by having the UN define the right to self-determination in a general legal formula protecting the *individual,* rather than as a *collective* political right useful to the Third World in the general struggle for decolonization—territorial and economic. But the persuasive power of numbers asserted itself by 1958 and 1959: even though the United States opposed the highly emotional and politicized approach to the question of self-determination, she consented to serve on UN commissions charged with surveying alleged violations of that right.

Institutional conservatism also found it wise to bend to the winds of change in UN discussions of decolonization. By 1960, some headway was made in opposing the consistent Third-World and Soviet argument that the untrammeled exercise of the right to self-determination must mean the attainment of full independence of each colony, regardless of size, ethnic composition, and economic viability. In that year the General Assembly finally accepted the proposition that colonial territories, in exercising the right to self-determination, could opt for free association with the colonial power, provided the individuality of the territory was preserved and the population was free later to opt for full sovereign independence. Further, the Assembly agreed that voluntary and informed integration with another nation was a solution as acceptable as full independence. The United States supported the slowly increasing powers of the Trusteeship Council in negotiating and supervising such solutions, especially in cases in which the population was divided on the future of the trust territory, where UN-conducted plebiscites and General Assembly decisions became the method for solving the disputes.

The issue of Portugal's and South Africa's policies toward their African dependencies forced a further quiet accommodation on the Eisenhower administration. Until 1958, the United States had held out for the right of each member nation to determine whether it would submit information on its colonies, thus upholding Portugal's argument that her colonies were not non-self-governing, because they were constitutionally part of the mother country. Defeated in UN debates and votes, the United States abandoned the argument in 1959 and joined a committee that spelled out in detail the obligation of new members to report. This committee, incidentally, set the procedural precedent for the adoption of the sweeping UN declaration on the termination of colonialism, in 1960. Policy toward South-West Africa was not much different. The United States defended the proposition that South Africa inherited the obligations of the League Mandates System and must report to the UN on its stewardship; but at first it declined to support any suggestions that would have put serious pressure on South Africa to comply, just as the United States had resisted Third-World efforts to strengthen the power of the UN Committee on Information from Non-Self-Governing Territories. But by 1959, Washington gave way here, too, by joining those who favored more forceful steps to make South Africa live up to UN resolutions.

Most spectacularly, American responsiveness to the UN became much more marked in regard to policy in the Pacific Island Trust Territory. The nuclear tests of 1954 had resulted in massive fall-out damage to the health and food supply of islanders living close to the test site. They petitioned the UN for aid, inveighed against American use of the trust for military purposes, and demanded restitution. The United States not only forwarded and endorsed the petition but stopped using the trust area for further nuclear testing. By 1966, $1 million had been paid in damages to the islanders. Further, the United States acceded to Trusteeship Council requests by vesting the Department of Interior with responsibility for administering the islands and by moving the capital to the territory, away from Guam. But military sites continued to be excluded from UN supervision, economic development was very slow, and self-government remained confined to the local and district level, even though the UN urged the creation of all-territorial popular institutions.

And so the United States became the victim of systemic changes it had helped trigger. Strong domestic opposition to the legal subordination of American constitutional premises to international conventions—as symbolized by the Bricker Amendment movement —was largely responsible for the retreat on the human rights issue, except when it served the purposes of Cold War propaganda. The North–South confrontation that was ushered in by the tripolar system which took shape in 1955, however, forced a quiet reconsideration of earlier colonial practices—substantive and institutional. The accommodation was undoubtedly facilitated by the fact that American policy since 1945 had always vacillated between the decolonization preferences of sections of the Department of State and Congress as opposed to the pronounced procolonial attitudes of the Department of Defense and certain other congressional leaders. Because of the dissensus in Washington, American policy in the UN was able to mediate between the Third World and the West "as best it could, and in the process it has received a considerable amount of abuse from both sides." [7] But the dissensus also prevented the United States from adopting a doctrinaire position on these questions; it neither consistently endorsed nor denied the colonial origins of the nation itself.

### 3. Progressive Enmeshment, the Multipolar Setting and Human Rights

Even though the domestic attitudes toward the international protection of human rights had not markedly changed by 1961, the Kennedy administration nevertheless decided to adopt a more aggressively favorable position on advancing the cause. In thus deciding to project a pro-Third-World image to the international community, the Administration was actually bowing with good grace to the very same force to which the outgoing Eisenhower administration had adjusted more grudgingly. In addition, of course, the Kennedy administration was also pleasing American civil rights advocates who had been less successful in gaining President Eisenhower's attention. And since hatred of all forms of racial discrimination and colonialism had acquired the proportions of a typhoon, the Kennedy administration chose to throw in its lot wholeheartedly with the emerging world forces—up to a point. The limit to America's enthusiasm for a UN role in human rights protection turned out to be the matter of collective rights and the continued distrust of conventions; the fervent espousal of radical decolonization found its boundary in the political style chosen by the General Assembly's Committee of Twenty-Four.

Washington "embarked on a new policy of considering UN human rights conventions on their merits . . . [they] can play a vital role in defining standards, clarifying experiences, and exposing to the consciences of the world denial of what should be the heritage of all," [8] said a government spokesman. He explained that American

---

[7] Lincoln Palmer Bloomfield, *United Nations and U.S. Foreign Policy* (Boston: Little, Brown, 1960), p. 193.

[8] Richard N. Gardner, in *Department of State Bulletin* (August 26, 1963), pp. 320–21.

adoption of human rights conventions would stress the interdependence between the enjoyment of liberties and the maintenance of peace, and it would encourage other nations to ratify the conventions. Conversely, the United States would be able to criticize honestly states that violate norms they have accepted, and the American view of the conventions would be given more weight than heretofore. Even though the administration then asked Senate advice and consent for the ratification of the ILO Conventions on Slavery and Forced Labor and the UN Convention on Political Rights of Women (none of which would have had the effect of changing domestic law), the Senate took no action.

Nor did the Johnson administration's enthusiasm last very long. By 1964 its UN spokesman noted that with the completion of decolonization, new nations seemed to lose interest in the protection of human rights as they proceeded to suppress those of their own citizens who dissented. Economic development was given primacy over the right to speak, vote, or write freely; ethnic and national aggregates were considered the beneficiaries of UN-defined rights, not individual men. American disapproval of the trend in the UN was expressed by Arthur Goldberg when he urged that "the ultimate object of UN activities, the ultimate object of any organized society, domestically or internationally, is man—the individual." [9]

The single human right to which the UN majority has remained passionately devoted is freedom from racial discrimination. The UN in 1965 adopted a strongly worded convention outlawing all forms of racial discrimination. UNESCO in 1960 had adopted an equally sweeping convention outlawing discrimination in education, following the ILO's adoption in 1958 of a similar text with respect to employment. The American voice on this issue, however, had barely been audible—except in joining the global catharsis of castigating South Africa. It was only after 1961 that American delegates urged that South African policy violated Article 56 of the UN Charter in not promoting the advancement of human rights. At first anxious merely to have the UN go on record in opposing *government policies* that permit or decree discrimination, the United States eventually accepted stronger language that castigates discriminatory measures irrespective of government complicity. Clearly, it was no accident that the course of American race relations and tensions found its counterpart in a more forthright American policy in international councils.

But the fact remains that even after 1961, establishing interna-

[9] Arthur Goldberg, in *Department of State Bulletin* (Oct. 11, 1965), p. 586.

tional norms for human rights met with tepid enthusiasm in the United States. In supporting the UNESCO Convention, the United States delegate also announced that because of the federal government's limited powers over education, the United States would be unable to ratify the text. Efforts were made by the United States to weaken the UN Anti-Discrimination Convention by removing the provision that enjoins states to suppress groups and prosecute citizens advocating racial intolerance. American spokesmen argued that such suppression would be a violation of freedom of speech; upon failing to win their point, they—in praising the Convention—nevertheless declared that the article in question would not impose new obligations on the United States. However motivated, the impression was clearly created that these suggestions and the subdued participation of the United States in the debate betray a marked lack of enthusiasm.

Of all the global agencies to which the United States belongs, UNESCO has probably been most closely intertwined with human rights. UNESCO's initial purposes—before it, along with other specialized agencies, was swallowed by Cold War politics—included the prevention of future war by inculcating respect for individual human rights, by combating the evolution of the antihuman doctrines epitomized by Nazism. This was to be achieved by means of education and information campaigns in which the services of *individual* intellectuals, private groups of humanitarians, and professionals, rather than governments, would be central. Consistent politicization of UNESCO shattered this approach, and the organization's program in favor of human rights is now formulated by its Director-General only with the permission of the member governments and the budgets voted by them. American policy has been vacillating and inconsistent with respect to the general UNESCO program, including its human rights component.

UNESCO claimed the major role in the task of making known the Universal Declaration of Human Rights and all other human rights actions taken by the UN. It has published articles, prepared films, written teachers' manuals, and revised textbooks in order to publicize the rights, inculcate respect for them, and link them somehow to the preservation of peace. It has undertaken and published studies on prejudice, race tensions, the equality of women, and the rights of ethnic minorities. It conducts seminars and study groups on freedom of the press, broadcasting, and the formulation of national information programs. And it plans to supplement the appropriate rights defined in the Covenant on Economic, Social, and Cultural Rights with a more intensive and specific program of its own. In addition, UNESCO's current major effort—the improvement and planning of mass education in Africa—is said to be suffused with an emphasis on universal human rights.

These services are all in the realm of advice and technical assistance. To be effective, governments must permit the information to be circulated, and they must consent to the operations of UNESCO on their soil. Nevertheless, UNESCO has aroused more passionate opposition as an "unpatriotic" agency in the United States than it has anywhere else; conversely, it has also had more enthusiastic and emotional support from humanitarian and libertarian groups in the United States than it has had elsewhere—and these attitudes have remained constant for twenty years. Therefore, the State Department has made little use of UNESCO, preferring not to call attention to its existence. Before 1960, the United States generally opposed the program, counseled retrenchment and proved uninterested in generous financial support. After 1960, however, America discovered the utility of UNESCO teacher-training services for advancing the nation-building program in Africa—the same program that was to be served with foreign aid strategically placed to foster self-confident, anticommunist regimes in former colonial territories. From that point on, American financial support for UNESCO suddenly increased without, however, yielding a discernible spurt of legitimacy in the mind of the American public. Nor is such a feeling likely to grow if the Convention on Discrimination in Education, through its enforcement machinery, were to be turned against practices in the United States.

The key to the American malaise with the international protection of human rights, therefore, is the matter of enforcement and implementation. When a person's or group's rights are violated in a nation, remedial action requires that the law or practice of that nation respond to international criticism, advice, help, or punishment. Until 1961, the United States had stressed the purely voluntary techniques of education, study, and technical assistance as the most appropriate for inducing nations to respect rights defined by the UN. And indeed, the UN has considerably increased these activities. With the completion of the UN and UNESCO Conventions on Racial Discrimination, however, the mechanism for advancing implementation has become much more sophisticated and potentially enmeshing. The UN Convention provides for an 18-member Committee of Experts with the task of examining annual reports submitted by each party, describing efforts made to implement the convention; this committee submits its evaluations to the General Assembly. Governments may lodge complaints against each other, alleging violations of the convention, and the committee also has the task of examining and settling such complaints. Failing the agreement of the parties to these efforts, the committee can create a special conciliation commission to conduct additional inquiries and negotiate a solution. Should this solution be rejected, however, the committee is limited to using the power of publicity to bring about compliance. Finally, the convention creates a procedure whereby private individuals can lodge complaints against their own governments—provided the governments submit a special declaration accepting the jurisdiction of the committee to receive individual petitions.[10] Some nations wanted to include an unconditional right of petition, and some wanted none at all. The United States supported the compromise actually chosen. The UNESCO Convention created a Conciliation and Good Offices Committee with very similar competences regarding the receiving and hearing of complaints, and with enforcement powers limited to issuing publicity adverse to the defaulting state. This time, the United States, by abstention, declined to support the special protocol, thus confirming its malaise.

Very much the same procedure has been used by the ILO since 1951 in its implementation of freedom of association, a right much more firmly established in the United States than freedom from discrimination is—yet the United States prefers not to be enmeshed in it, perhaps because the ILO procedure makes it simpler for non-governmental groups and private citizens to file complaints against their own and foreign governments. The United States has no objection to another ILO-pioneered procedure: the submission of elaborate annual reports on the implementation of rights, and their critical scrutiny by international officials and delegates able to embarrass and expose publicly an uncooperative government. Perhaps because of the preference for publicity as a sanction over the quasi-judicial activities of international conciliation commissions, the United States endorsed the enlargement of the reporting obligation to the UN and expressed its support for the creation of a standing UN machinery for giving greater effect to the Universal Declaration of Human Rights, possibly through the creation of a UN High Commissioner for Human Rights.

A UN High Commissioner for Refugees has existed since 1952.

---

[10] The enforcement and supervision provisions included in the International Covenant on Civil and Political Rights are almost identical, though a bit weaker because the right of parties to allege violations on the part of other parties is made contingent on the prior deposit of a declaration of acceptance of this obligation. The right of individual petition is dealt with in a separate protocol.

His role illustrates the potential of such an officer in conciliating disputes over human rights when governments are determined to avoid the formal legal procedure. The High Commissioner hears complaints, reminds the parties of their obligations, suggests compromises, and uses his prestige to enable pairs of governments to extricate themselves honorably from stalemated positions, thus incidentally helping to cement and strengthen the rights of refugees. However, neither the United States nor the great majority of other countries have shown any interest in strengthening institutions capable of binding legal definition and enforcement: the ICJ or special human rights tribunals of the kind that exist in Western Europe. The Connally Reservation remains in force despite increasing suggestions for its repeal. And the trend toward a multibloc world with widely divergent political and social vaues is unikely to contribute to a growing willingness to submit disputes over the rights of one's own citizens to the compulsory adjudication of an international court. And so the United States prefers voluntary action; but she is accommodating herself to compulsory reporting and conciliation just the same, even though the bulk of the public hardly sympathizes. And circumstances may even propel her into a still more active role when larger foreign policy issues seem involved.

This possibility is illustrated by the unplanned and unwished evolution of the Inter-American Commission on Human Rights of the OAS. The United States did indeed favor policies strengthening democracy in the Western Hemisphere and opposing dictatorial regimes of the right and the left. These commitments, however, did not imply the desire to intervene, change policy, cut off aid, or withhold recognition every time an undemocratic change of government occurred; nor did they include a strong wish for a standing investigating body, able to pinpoint violations of rights that interfere with the practice of democracy. Yet, just such a body evolved after 1960, in indirect response to certain reformist Latin-American regimes' demands for collective intervention on behalf of democracy. At the same time, an Inter-American Court on Human Rights was to be created, but it died on the vine. The commission, composed of seven experts serving as private individuals, was to assist in "furthering respect" for human rights, thus providing a sop for the reformers, though not asserting itself otherwise. But it did assert itself, "despite early United States efforts to emasculate it." [11] Even though instructed to undertake only general studies and promotional activities, the commission nevertheless received and considered complaints addressed to it alleging specific violations of

[11] Slater, *The OAS and United States Foreign Policy*, p. 256 ff.

rights by Latin-American governments. Furthermore, the commission interpreted its restrictive official mandate to allow on-the-spot investigations of the complaints, with the permission of the government concerned. Investigations have been carried out in the Dominican Republic, and complaints from several other Caribbean nations have been scrutinized. Furthermore, the United States made its peace with the commission when it demonstrated its usefulness to American objectives in easing the transition to Trujillo's successors, supervising the Dominican elections of 1963, energetically and successfully advancing respect for human rights in the Dominican civil war of 1965, as well as castigating Castro's Cuba. At the same time, the commission had the restraint not to force its services on anyone and to avoid the race discrimination issue in the United States. But it merged as an autonomous body whose active role was legally recognized in 1966, an enmeshment resulting from an earlier vague commitment and an initial propagandistic motive. It could happen in the UN as well.

## 4. Progressive Enmeshment, the Multipolar Setting and Decolonization

"We should be eternally grateful to the UN," said an Undersecretary of State, "that the complex business of transforming half a hundred new states from dependence to sovereignty has, for the most part, been accompanied by speeches rather than by shooting." He thought this good for world peace because it hastened the end of colonialism, even though it also resulted in the "premature" addition to the UN of many "ill-prepared nations." [12] The desire to accelerate the demise of a practice that was bound to embitter future relations between the numerically growing Third World—enthusiastically supported by the Soviet bloc—caused the United States to abandon its mediating role and to join the anticolonial bloc. This policy, however, came to an end when the implications seemed to be nation-building at the expense of values cherished by the United States.

Thus, the Kennedy Administration joined the anticolonial majority

[12] George Ball, "The United Nations Today," *Department of State Bulletin* (Nov. 16, 1964), pp. 695, 698.

in insisting that South Africa must admit and cooperate with a UN committee dispatched to hasten the separation of South-West Africa from the Republic. It also supported the establishment of a UN presence in the territory. The Johnson Administration, in 1966, joined an overwhelming majority in the UN in terminating South Africa's rule over South-West Africa and in making that territory the direct responsibility of the UN; further, the United States joined in scathing denunciation of South Africa's repressive policies in the former mandate and scrupulously applied the UN-voted embargo on military equipment against South Africa. But Washington balked at voting for UN intervention while the South-West Africa case was pending in the ICJ, and it opposed resolutions that justify strong UN intervention as a means to combat alleged exploitation of South-West Africa by Western capitalists. Further, it opposed the majority's desire to label apartheid "aggression" under Chapter VII of the Charter. The persistent issue of Portugal's refusal to heed UN resolutions regarding self-determination of Angola and Mozambique highlights a similar tendency on the part of the United States. Washington, while joining in condemnations of the Portuguese attitude, nevertheless sought to restrain UN intervention, in order to give the parties more time to work out their own solutions. While assuring the UN that no NATO arms were used by Portuguese forces in Africa, the United States continued to insist that no coercive steps be taken. However, the United States also fully supported the activities of the Committee on Information, against Portugal's obduracy. In fact, the shift took place largely because of the embarrassment that Portugal created for the West. From an early position of severely limiting UN competence to decide questions of submission of information, the U.S. moved by 1961 to supporting: (1) the obligatory nature of Article 73(e); (2) the competence of the UN to decide which territories fall under the article; and (3) the expansion of the responsibilities of the Committee of Information. The shift was fundamental.

Much ambivalence was evident when the United States had to adjust to the Assembly's revolutionary declaration calling for immediate independence for all colonies, the celebrated Resolution 1514 (XV). In part because of American insistence that the admitted right to self-determination need not necessarily lead to full independence, the United States abstained on the crucial vote. Other reasons for such self-effacement were that the resolution did not recognize the need for a socio-economic base for political stability and the right of the administering power to maintain law and order. Nevertheless, after it was passed, the Special Committee created to implement the Resolution was endorsed by the U.S. delegate, who said:

We believe its main function should be to survey the situation and to present to the Assembly . . . guiding principles of action in the all-important area.[13]

Such adaptive powers proved to be insufficient, because the Committee of Twenty-Four promptly interpreted its mandate to be far more active and specific. The principle of parity of representation was abandoned because the committee was stacked with Third-World representatives. It heard petitioners, investigated complaints, visited most colonial territories, and gave the colonial powers instructions about which of several rival nationalist groups should be made the government when "immediate" independence arrived. The United States gradually joined the outvoted minority of Western nations on the committee in opposing the dramatic tactics of the majority that pressed for immediate withdrawal of the administering power and urged that the most radical nationalist group become the successor. In fact, the propensity of the majority to invest only neutralist or communist-leaning groups with UN legitimacy proved to be the feature that made the work of the committee unpalatable to Washington. As the Committee of Twenty-Four, for all practical purposes, became *the* organ to complete decolonization, the United States once more withdrew from the anticolonial consensus and rejoined the West.

How did the United States fare when its record as a colonial power was reviewed in the UN? Washington displayed increasing responsiveness to UN pressure as far as the administration of the Pacific Island Trust Territory is concerned. When several members of the Territory's medical staff petitioned the Trusteeship Council, complaining about inadequate medical facilities, the United States invited WHO to investigate it, and it promised to implement the report that resulted. As a consequence of UN prodding, land alienation stopped. The repeated demand for all-territorial political institutions led, in 1965, to the creation of a popularly elected Congress of Micronesia with limited legislative powers. Economic develop-

[13] Jonathan Bingham, *Department of State Bulletin* (Jan. 8, 1962), p. 72. Also see the optimistic expectation of Adlai Stevenson in *Department of State Bulletin* (Feb. 5, 1962), and of James J. Wadsworth in *Department of State Bulletin* (Jan. 2, 1961).

ment was spurred with the inauguration of a five-year plan, as previously demanded by the UN, though the U. S. Congress was slow to vote the necessary funds. The UN continued to press the United States to set a date for full independence. Washington responded in 1967 by creating a special commission to query the islanders about how they wished to exercise their right to self-determination; some local spokesmen suggested that independence was not their goal.

The Committee of Twenty-Four also had occasion to survey American policy in Puerto Rico and the other small islands. The tiny Puerto Rican Independence Party succeeded in interesting the UN Afro-Asian group in its claims of being denied self-determination, and the matter was referred to the committee in 1964. In 1967 the committee adjourned its investigation sine die, without making a report. Samoa and the Virgin Islands were the subject of a committee investigation in 1965. The committee recommended to the Assembly that the United States be reprimanded for not responding to requests to hasten their independence, dismantle military installations, and admit UN visiting missions. Even though the antimilitary portions of the resolution were not adopted, for lack of a two-thirds majority, the remainder was. Understandably, the embrace of the Third World initiated in 1961 soon led to a considerable cooling of ardor. Institutional enmeshment, however, had taken place in the meantime. Whether it will survive the multipolar system that spawned it, and outlive the end of the colonial system as a whole, is a matter that will concern us later.

## 5. Opinion, Policy, and the Future

It is one of the many paradoxes of international politics that the enmeshment of the United States into UN decolonization measures and procedures was at its height just when the issue itself was becoming obsolete. The commitment to the international protection of human rights gained much of its popularity as a result of being part of the decolonization syndrome: the rights most vociferously advocated and enshrined in UN texts are the guarantees of self-determination and freedom from racial discrimination. It is more than doubtful that the Third-World majority would have espoused the cause of individual human rights on its own merits, and one may wonder whether its enthusiasm will outlast the end of the colonial system. Did American public opinion support the UN's human rights program? Will it support such measures in the future?

Evidence of public sentiment on the human rights and decolonization questions, with a focus on UN authority and American adherence to it, is very scarce. When put in very general terms, of course, Americans feel constrained by their national ethos to espouse both programs. At the onset of the multipolar world system, around 65 per cent of the public expressed support for UN-conducted plebiscites to determine the wishes of colonial peoples.[14] Enthusiasm on that score seemed to decline during the Congo crisis, most dramatically in the South. After 1963, the Kennedy and Johnson administrations were reluctant to enmesh the United States further in the network of legal commitments to examine domestic legislation, report findings, and submit problems to UN conciliation agencies. Certainly there is some relation between this hesitancy and the fear that the public would repudiate such steps.

Certain elite groups, however, were persistently in favor of American commitment to a UN human rights program. Their concern has remained essentially unaltered since the adoption of the Universal Declaration in 1948. Between 1945 and 1955 "one or more civic, religious, business, child welfare, women's, technical, legal, medical, criminology, professional, informational, and labor groups pressed vigorously for machinery to handle human rights communications and petitions, for the right of complaint by individuals or organizations, a judicial review body for complaints—even a UN attorney-general to examine violations—and were met over and over again by the combined opposition of the British, Soviet and U.S. governments."[15] The same groups and their vigorous lobbying were largely responsible for the continued American commitment to UN-supported refugee and children's aid programs, even though the government had been eager to curtail them. Time has done nothing to diminish the enthusiasm of these groups. In 1964 they organized a nationwide committee grouping 35 citizens' organizations, overwhelmingly of a religious character, to lobby in favor of the ratification of UN human rights texts and for strong measures against South Africa. Although the Department of State had catered to these groups by appointing Mrs. Eleanor Roosevelt as the United States delegate to the UN Human Rights Commission (the body that

[14] Gallup Poll, March, 1956.
[15] Hyde, *The United States and the United Nations: Promoting the Public Welfare*, p. 190.

drafted many of the human rights texts), it cannot be said that Washington proved responsive in more substantive ways.

Nor are these elite groups unopposed by other groups. Conservatives generally and some business organizations in particular have opposed UN human rights treaties because they fear that an irresponsible President might "use the treaty-making power to effect internal social changes" and thus introduce socialism through the back door.[16] Business was not attracted to the UN program, for understandable reasons, when the UN Covenants acquired their articles dealing with the nationalization of natural resources. Groups that identify strongly with states' rights and private enterprise therefore had always opposed the UN program, and they continue to do so. Others, however, did not take this position until the advent of America's racial crisis in the late 1950's. It was only at that point that they began to relate attitudes toward domestic issues with international commitments.

Still others, moreover, seem to be making their peace with a gradually evolving global concern with human rights. A task force of the Republican National Committee, in 1960, advised that the United States support independence movements everywhere and support the right of foreign nations to choose *any* system of government that survives a free election. And many officials in Washington, by the early Sixties, felt that the American world image would be unnecessarily tarnished by standing aside from the human rights movement. Noting that UN scrutiny of American practices was unlikely to reveal anything to the world that the wire services and television networks had not already made very well-known, Harlan Cleveland urged that

> Americans need to consider whether, as the necessary price for shining the UN's searchlight on oppression elsewhere, they are prepared to have the UN turn its attention to the mote in our own eye.[17]

But by 1968, one suspects, as the size of the mote had grown, so had the price of mutual enmeshment.

The special conditions under which the UN human rights task has acquired whatever authority and legitimacy it possesses are about to be swallowed by time and history. As the trusteeship sys-

[16] John Foster Dulles, April 6, 1953, quoted in *ibid.*, p. 174.
[17] Harlan Cleveland, "The Evolution of Rising Responsibility," *International Organization* (Summer 1965), p. 832.

tem becomes a victim of its own success and as the Committee of Twenty-Four runs out of territories to free, it is unlikely that the new states still struggling to become nations will entertain with much fervor such things as internationally guaranteed rights of ethnic minorities or UN antidiscrimination measures from which their own dissenting citizens might benefit. In short, the success of decolonization spells the failure of a consistently applied UN human rights program. Why then should the United States continue to follow the cautiously and inconsistently positive policy it has adopted since 1961?

Harlan Cleveland suggested one reason. A growing world law of human rights, better than mere political invocation and propaganda speeches in the General Assembly, would aid the American policy of buttressing individual rights in new nations and thus launch them on the way to democratic stability and legitimacy. Further, such a policy would continue to serve the Cold-War strategy of embarrassing communist totalitarian nations. But to succeed, the policy must take the road already traveled by ILO's human rights machinery: propaganda must yield to law and standing institutions for conciliation and adjudication. The United States would have to commit itself to permanently legitimate and authoritative third-party intercession. Washington's complaint of violations of freedom of speech in Egypt, for example, may be answered by a Syrian complaint of racial discrimination in Alabama. There is little reason to suppose that this degree of legal enmeshment is desired simply in order to retain ideological leverage abroad.

Another reason, closely related, is the possibility of using the protection of human rights as a device to socialize new nations, to expose them to standards of tolerance and accommodation. Linked to this motive would be a commitment to set a good example. Upper Volta, the argument runs, is not likely to commit itself unless the United States also does. Yet the United States has much to gain in using the UN as a device for legitimating a democratic and responsive regime in Upper Volta, including some kind of UN "presence" to assure the observance of human rights.

The dedicated activities of pro-human-rights groups in the United States have yet to demonstrate their ability to overcome the stubborn divergences in national habits and aspirations exposed tellingly by Marcel Slusny:

The vocabulary used is the same but the words do not convey the same concepts. Using as an example only the concept of trade union freedom, we see that all the delegates at International Labor Conference meetings proclaim their adherence to this principle. But it is clear that we are . . . witnessing a dialogue among deaf men because the delegates of the western countries, above all the trade unionists, conceive of union as an organ to defend an occupation which must remain independent of the state and of the employers. However, the Spanish delegate, for example defends a corporatist conception, while the representatives of the Soviet bloc countries . . . consider unions as transmission belts between the state . . . and the producers.[18]

The superimposition of these major doctrinal and national differences over the related issue of whether collective or individual human rights should be the object of UN intervention is unlikely to facilitate a speedy end to the debate over whether human rights should be advanced through technical assistance, seminars, and discussions, or legal texts, conciliation commissions, and adverse international publicity. If the political will to carry out human rights commitments does not keep up with the legal possibilities of doing so, the growth of a luxurious jungle of resolutions, declarations, conventions, annual reports, and conciliation commissions is likely to make little difference. Neither the schizophrenia nor the malaise of the United States will receive therapy from this condition of the international system; at least in the short run, the system will reinforce the illness. American objectives regarding democracy at home and abroad are not likely to gain from discussion in the UN, particularly if they are laced with Cold-War and antineutralist arguments. But who is to say with certainty that in the longer run of a generation, the continued and passionate advocacy of human rights and the use of international publicity will not make themselves felt in Upper Volta as well as in the United States? The negative consequences of enmeshment in the short run may yet pay unintended dividends.

[18] Marcel Slusny, "Quelques Observations sur les systèmes de Protection Internationale des droits de l'homme," *Mélanges Offerts à Henri Rolin* (Paris: A. Pedone, 1964), pp. 393-94.

# CHAPTER NINE

# SCIENCE, TECHNOLOGY, AND PLANNING

Diverse scientists, engineers, theologians, and revolutionaries usually manage to agree to one proposition: the combined effect of scientific thought and its application in technology has been the transformation of the world. Within the last three centuries, man's increasing ability to manipulate the physical environment has made greater changes in life styles than have occurred in the previous million years of human evolution. Few believe that these changes have reached a plateau, since the sum of scientific knowledge seems to double every decade; all agree that the devotion to scientific and technological progress creates problems of adaptation, diffusion, and understanding.

The scientific revolution is here to stay. . . . Indeed, it is only beginning. What we have seen in the past is as nothing compared to the future. We shall be found wanting if we do not plan with that thought in mind. Our success in achieving the objectives of creative evolution requires both an ever more vigorous effort in science and technology and an enormous improvement in techniques for integrating the products of science and technology into society.[1]

A committee of the U. S. House of Representatives admitted that more and more science is indeed necessary to cope with the products of earlier discovery, but "our success in the development of such new knowledge must be accompanied by careful and improved methods of putting that knowledge to work. Otherwise we may strangle in the coils of an unplanned, unwanted but unstoppable technology." [2]

Our concern is not with science itself but with its political implications for the international system. When the social consequences of science are seen as discrete "problem areas," the matter seems clear enough: we can see around us the threat to the natural environment posed by pollution, the exhaustion of energy resources, the unsettling effect of cybernetics and automation, the unmanageability of the flood of new information, the decay of public transportation and of the cities. These questions seem almost straightforwardly "technical." But what happens when these technical and scientific "problems" are related to urban renewal, crime alleviation, upgrading the quality of education, and to the reduction of social tensions? What was amenable to scientific understanding and technical manipulation now becomes infused with passionately held values. The role of politics reasserts itself when decisions must be made on what technique is suitable for the solution of which social problem. Politics, as in Seaborg's statement, also reasserts its role when men must determine which scientific trend triggers or aggravates what social problem and confuses social values—and what to do about it.

Basic to the conundrum is the Janus-faced nature of science itself: it is both an agent for the improvement of man's lot and the author of some of his most urgent problems, including war. Nevertheless, men have stressed, by and large, only the progressive and even utopian aspects of science and technology. In international politics they have geared it to economic development, social advancement, and, *mirabile dictu,* peace. Put differently, men have

---

1 Glenn T. Seaborg, quoted in U.S. House of Representatives, Committee on Science and Astronautics (89th Cong., 2nd Sess.), *Inquiries, Legislation, Policy Studies re Science and Technology: Review and Forecast* (Washington: Government Printing Office, 1966), p. 20.
2 *Ibid.*

been content to seek the adaptation of societies and nations to the demands of science and technological innovation. It is only in the most recent decade that voices of fear and doubt have suggested that man cannot stand much more innovation and that science and technology should, perhaps, be tailored to man's measure. In international politics and in the halls of international organizations this has meant a simultaneous and confusing commitment to the reliance on science and to its banishment back into the genie's bottle. The conundrum is hardly resolved by the generous use of the term "international scientific cooperation" and by the facile assumption that such activities constitute milestones on the road to world peace.

Before we can deal with the place of international organizations and American policy in this welter of conflicting questions and trends, a few definitions must be introduced. What do we mean when we talk of *science?* Science, or basic science, is man's inquiry into the physical and biological nature of the universe (including man himself) using a systematic mode of thought based on the philosophy of science and employing primarily empirical tools of research. But what of *technology? Technology* will be used here as a synonym for *applied science,* or application of results or lessons of scientific inquiry to the control of man's physical and biological environment through fields such as engineering, medicine, meteorology, agronomy, anthropology, and psychology. Clearly, applied science includes social science insofar as the abstract lessons of social inquiry are self-consciously related to policies designed to alter or control the environment, thus giving a certain apolitical, or transpolitical, twist to the making of public policy. As for *planning,* the third element in our trinity of concerns in this chapter, it refers to systematic efforts to think through and choose among possible applications of science, to devise methods of social control.

The planner sometimes claims to be acting apolitically, despising ideology and specific values in the service of the truth as revealed by the scientific method. Many physical and biological scientists, as well as psychologists and sociologists, claim that their recipes for social action are based on "science" rather than prejudice or crude self-interest and are therefore much superior to the hit-or-miss solutions devised by politicians. Marxists and many non-Marxists devoted to "peace research" maintain that they possess a scientific basis for social decisions. The rigorous subordination of policy-making to such prescriptions is offered as the way to end international conflict and diplomacy described in preceding chapters: it would substitute a different kind of knowledge for the interest-tainted consciousness of political actors. Are these claims justified?

That scientism can become an ideology in the service of a few passionately held values in the mind of the planner is a proposition to be demonstrated later.

We must thus deal with these questions: (1) When and how does basic science pertain to international relations? Does the diffusion of scientific knowledge contribute to peace, thus making international scientific cooperation a natural part of UN activity? (2) When and how does applied science or technology relate to international politics? How do international organizations get involved in dealing with the dangers of applied science or in advancing its benefits? (3) How has applied social science impinged on international politics? Do international organizations make use of applied social science rather than interest-dominated policy inputs? (4) What is the extent of international planning? Who are the planners and how do they decide on priorities? How do they identify the problem areas of basic and applied science and seek to deal with them? (5) Irrespective of the conscious knowledge of political actors and planners and their efforts to deal with the promise and the dangers of science, what does the entry of international organizations into the field of science suggest for the maintenance or transformation of the international system? And at all times, of course, our concern remains the extent of American enmeshment in the web of scientific and technological interdependence, the witting or unwitting role of American policy in fashioning that web.

## 1. International Organization and the Community of Science

Immense prestige has been bestowed on basic science, on the cerebral feats of an Einstein arriving at basic laws of the universe, and on the giant installations manned by nuclear physicists who explore the laws' limits and ramifications. If less public acclaim is accorded to the efforts of biochemists probing the mysteries of the brain and to social psychologists studying the nature of aggressive drives, their efforts still represent parts of basic scientific inquiry with clear implications for international life—in the long run. Immediate links, however, are more elusive. For the scientist, it may be enough to note that "in much of our research the entire earth, its land, oceans, atmosphere and all its life becomes our laboratory and the source of our studies. Therefore, national boundaries must be overlooked—as they are by the object of our investigation, nature itself."[3] But for governments, this has not been enough to embark on massive common projects and vest them in international organizations. Basic scientific research, for all its prestige and for all the devotion of its practitioners, remains marginal to action at the intergovernmental level. UNESCO, the main agency with jurisdiction, admitted that it "has made but scant contribution to the development of the basic sciences—mathematics, physics, chemistry and biology—on which, nonetheless, all other progress eventually depends."[4] UNESCO efforts were confined to calling conferences and symposia designed to increase and accelerate the diffusion of basic scientific knowledge, to help in the formation of international associations of scientists, to call attention to problem areas in research subsequently dealt with by other means. Such efforts were helpful in creating the European Center for Nuclear Research and the International Center for Theoretical Physics. But UNESCO's major contributions were confined to the applied sciences.

Although nations continue to dominate international cooperation in basic scientific research, scientists strongly resemble a "community" of their own. Thus their crucial role in policy-making deserves emphasis. Scientific research and the application of science to man's life are politically unique in that there is almost no public or elite opinion to influence policy; there prevails a vague but benign attitude of somehow considering all science "good." Lay government officials, moreover, are usually unable to evaluate the nature and implications of scientific discoveries; they depend on science advisers and administrators in making decisions. In a very real sense, therefore, scientists working in or near government *are* the makers of national and international policy in their fields. What kind of people are they?

It is hardly surprising that scientists tend to transfer their characteristic mode of thought and analysis to social issues and public policy. Hence many of them think of national and international politics as straightforward problem-solving techniques, leading them to naïve utopianism—or to its opposite, naïve belligerency.[5] Instead of dealing with issues incrementally, they tend to "deal with the whole problem," usually conceived in politically naïve terms. Similarly, they prefer quantum jumps in knowledge to incremental

[3] Glenn T. Seaborg, "What's Ahead for International Science?" *Bulletin of the Atomic Scientists* (January, 1967), p. 27.

[4] UNESCO, *Appraisal of UNESCO's Programmes for the Economic and Social Council* (Paris, 1960), p. 91.

[5] These sets are developed more fully and illustrated by Warner R. Schilling, "Scientists, Foreign Policy and Politics," *American Political Science Review* (June, 1962), pp. 291 ff. The terms used here are Schilling's.

improvements, and they question the intelligence of political leaders unable to deal with the human environment in such total terms. While some scientists tend to assert the value of technology for its own sake—to build the machine just because it is possible and interesting—others see their profession as serving mankind positively, as no profession has served it before, *provided* science can be confined to acts with exclusively peaceful consequences! And these scientists, regretting the politicization of research and knowledge, yearn for the lost paradise of unhampered international scientific cooperation and sharing of results. When the obvious practice of international politics runs counter to these mental images, scientists are quick to portray themselves as peacemakers, as envoys of human understanding, as pure souls able to substitute the therapeutic powers of knowledge for the corrupting marsh of interest-dominated politics.

Hence the notion of a community of scientists, organized apart from government but in the service of international cooperation for peace, is a natural outgrowth of these ideas. The feeling gains strength from the mere numbers of scientists at annual international meetings: about 20,000 Americans met with 80,000 foreign colleagues at 2,000 conferences, colloquia, and seminars in the mid-Sixties. Some of the impulse for this burst of communication is inherent in the nature of basic research and reflects no political commitment. Equipment used in nuclear and high-energy physics research is beyond the capacity of most countries to acquire, therefore the pooling of resources is necessary. Radio astronomy, space research, meteorology, and the exploration of the ocean floor are transnational by definition and, to be feasible, require cooperative arrangements. But the explicit or implicit desire to use science to get "beyond politics" is also very pervasive.

Thus the prestigious Conference on Science and World Affairs, a private gathering of renowned scientists, for years dedicated itself to developing the use of science as a way of preventing war. At first the participants simply expressed their faith in peace and rationality; eventually they arrived at the conclusion that scientists have special needs and skills that give them the right and duty to work actively for peace. How? It is perhaps fortunate that successful basic research requires active sharing of knowledge—and hence cooperation across frontiers—and that the practice of this cooperation is thought to be a virtue in its own right because it creates common interests and mutual trust. Thus research that is of interest to scientists anyway is clothed in the garb of an unwitting servant of peace: the needs of the research must lead to stronger international organizations with regulatory powers and the ability to stimulate more meetings, new international research centers, the systematic use of scientists in aiding economic development, disarmament, and therefore peace. Science is thought to produce political spin-offs because it is supremely rational, unvictimized by tradition and prejudice. Scientists can thus aid in diffusing rational thinking to other fields and by their active participation in government, even infect politicians with the virus. Knowledge is good in itself *and* good because it is able to remove the causes of war by meeting human needs. If basic scientists are the apostles of this knowledge, they might be able to succeed in international politics where diplomats and generals are failing.[6]

The community of science, whether based on the needs of basic research or the transpolitical mission, is organized into a nongovernmental international organization, the International Council of Scientific Unions, with a membership of national scientific unions from 54 countries. ICSU is a peak organization of dozens of specific international professional associations. The ensemble is a powerful international lobby that has succeeded in inspiring, organizing, and carrying out some of the most impressive international cooperative research with the full financial support of governments, and with direct political results in some cases. Thus ICSU organized the International Geophysical Year and the exploration of the Antarctic Continent, leading directly to the Antarctic Treaty, neutralizing and demilitarizing that last body of land not yet annexed to some nation's sovereign impulse, preserving it for collaborative scientific exploration. A similar effort was the International Indian Ocean Expedition and the International Year of the Quiet Sun. Further joint forays into the natural sciences are planned. One is the continuous observation of the world's weather, in an effort to make total environmental forecasts; this aim has led to the establishment of the World Weather Watch under the auspices of World Meteorological Organization. The special radio communication systems required by the weather research satellites have resulted in increased

---

[6] For evidence of these self-images of scientists, see Seaborg, "What's Ahead for International Science?" *op. cit;* "Conference on Science and World Affairs," *Science* (October 6, 1961), pp. 984-90; Emmanuel G. Mesthene, "Can Only Scientists Make a Government Science Policy?" *Science* (July 17, 1964), pp. 237-40; and almost any issue of the *Bulletin of the Atomic Scientists.* Glenn T. Seaborg believes that only science and technology can solve the problems created internationally by science and technology—including the abolition of war and the growth of a more "rational" political order. ("Science in a World of Widening Horizons," *Department of State Bulletin,* Feb. 21, 1966, pp. 280-88.)

powers of wavelength allocation for the International Telecommunications Union. Rising interest in joint basic biological and medical research—with the cure of cancer the ultimate goal—has given WHO new funds and tasks.

Indeed, as biology and biochemistry displace physics as the field of major scientific breakthroughs, biologists are advocating the launching of a global Biological Decade to sensitize men and governments to the enormous dangers inherent in the permanent, unwanted alteration of human environment that could result from biological discoveries. To prevent possibilities such as mind control and sex selection, perhaps creating disequilibrium between numbers of males and females, a total ecological approach to biological research is being advocated. Even though UNESCO supports this new and critical thrust, the United States government has elicited very little interest.

All these activities, committed to the search of knowledge, are based on the implicit assumption that all mankind will benefit from the results. Hence none of this has been politically controversial. The accrual of new powers to international organizations and scientific associations was readily accepted by governments, even actually lauded by American policy-makers. Although not centrally concerned with international science and technology until John F. Kennedy launched the New Frontier in 1961, Washington at that point began to accept a doctrine not very different from that of the most optimistic scientists. The great promise held by science for the economic betterment of mankind was extolled; the challenge of preventing technology from destroying man's physical environment was thrown into relief; man was enjoined to be ready for constant adaptation and adjustment to be free to profit from the bounties of science; and all this was held to be good for international peace and security. Why? Cooperation among scientists and engineers under government auspices was thought to yield a dedication to common needs and shared technical tasks to which even ideologically opposing nations can subscribe, thus building bridges to Communist and Third-World nations and fostering new international law and institutions. These sentiments continue to be expressed by the highest American leadership today.[7]

But governments did not necessarily support international basic science for the pure and disinterested reasons that scientists like to stress. Governments expected to gain prestige, propaganda victories,

---

[7] See, for example, Harlan Cleveland, "The Future of International Politics" and "How to Make Peace with the Russians," reprints distributed by the Department of State, 1968. President Johnson made the same point in his Glassboro, N.J., address of June, 1968.

and influence over foreign scientists while helping to attain purely scientific objectives. Indeed, the fact that political and transpolitical objectives are rarely irreconcilable in actual operations has not yet been grasped by many scientists. When a government is convinced that it will lose by participating in such an enterprise it will withdraw, as Peking China withdrew from the International Geophysical Year. Communist scientists have frequently attempted to use scientific conferences as media for passing resolutions critical of American foreign and military policy; four professional meetings held on Soviet soil in 1966 were marred by the intrusion of Cold-War politics. Nor have American scientists shown much resistance to making use of their gatherings for political purposes in which the search for rationality and sober judgment was not always evident. In short, the flowering of noncontroversial international basic science ventures under the auspices of the community of researchers has yet to demonstrate a uniform, even growth of rational problem-solving behavior in the realm of politics.

Nor has there been marked evidence of the progressive enmeshment of nations in collective enterprises of basic science, despite the lip service of governments. Organizations like ITU, WMO, and WHO lack even the limited impact of the UN economic agencies. They simply regulate a well-defined area of undisputed and absolute interdependence of no significance to peace, or they collect and disseminate scientific knowledge discovered by national and private agencies. Under UNESCO auspices they sometimes take the initiative in first discussing a new area of concern and then organizing an international division of labor for tackling operational research. They very rarely *do* the actual research. Nor have they been given the power to evaluate ongoing or new basic research and to judge its relevance to the future of science or to potential international systems of interdependence. It is only in the field of applied science that this threshold is being approached.

## 2. Applied Science and International Organization

The scientific community, jolted by its mushrooming prestige in the dawning Nuclear Age, was moved to assert its peacemaking endowments. But the world took little notice of its proposed role, except to infuse basic research with a new, nationally-centered purpose. Neither basic nor applied research in its pure, knowledge-oriented form was given much recognition until the early 1950's; in fact, after 1953 the interest shown in the international implications of science and technology was directly related to military considerations and to the Cold War. UNESCO failed to launch cooperative global scientific ventures—primarily because scientists themselves distrusted all government and preferred to work out their own global ties. Growing involvement in scientific ventures at the UN level did *not* owe its birth to curiosity about the ocean floor, cosmic rays, quasars, or the earth's crust. It was conceived by fears of military insecurity.

The lead was assumed by the United States, who proposed that peaceful use of nuclear energy be linked with stopping the proliferation of national nuclear programs having warlike implications. The mechanism was the International Atomic Energy Agency (IAEA), with the combined task of encouraging peaceful use of nuclear energy and providing international safeguards against the diversion of fissionable materials to war production. IAEA did not come into existence until 1957. It did not acquire powers commensurate with the American objective until the United States itself changed its policy in 1962. Further, the Soviet Union apparently did not decide to upgrade IAEA powers until the Russian leaders also acquired a vested interest in preventing nuclear proliferation. In addition, continued nuclear testing by the superpowers in the mid-Fifties prompted the General Assembly to denounce the hazards of fallout and radiation and to appoint a panel of experts to publicize the dangers of testing. Even though the United States was far from pleased with this interest in matters scientific, the fear generated by these efforts provided a further motive for internationalizing the militarily and politically embarrassing aspects of the atom. How the fear of the atom and efforts at nuclear arms control are linked to American policy on disarmament was discussed in an earlier chapter. By 1967 the initial desire to slow down the acquisition of military nuclear lore by less developed nations had resulted in voluntary American submission to IAEA inspection of national and bilateral reactor programs.[8] Further, the superpowers want the IAEA to inspect compliance with the nuclear nonproliferation treaty. And in the process, a UN agency has become an important actor in the application of nuclear energy to national development programs.

Much the same impulse was at work in another field of applied

---

[8] Arnold Kramish, *The Peaceful Atom in Foreign Policy* (New York: Harper, 1963), Chap. 14; and Glenn T. Seaborg, "Existing Arrangements for International Control of Warlike Materials," *Disarmament and Arms Control* (Autumn, 1964), pp. 422-33. The change in policy was initially recommended by a panel of scientists.

science: the penetration of outer space. Characteristically, it is the technologically leading nation that first seeks to create international rules and procedures governing future research, in order to retain its lead and slow down the race. In the nuclear field, the United States was the leader; in the space race, it was the Soviet Union. Hence the Soviets took an early lead in seeking UN-sanctioned rules reserving space for peaceful purposes and barring its use for surveillance satellites. Furthermore, the Soviets wanted no private corporations engaged in space communications, whereas the United States insisted on the rights of private companies to participate in the creation of global communications systems. At the beginning of the Space Age, the United States was content to work for UN rules that would safeguard the right of all nations to launch probes and assure the security of astronauts and space vehicles. Hence agreement was reached on safety rules, on the permanent neutrality of celestial bodies, and on the rights of all nations to explore them. By the mid-Sixties the apparent stability of the balance of terror had led to a further agreement barring the placement of orbiting weapons in space. And all nations agreed to register their launchings with the UN, exchange scientific data, and to place a few of their scientific exploration efforts under the auspices of a UN launching site in India. But the United States persisted in its preference for unregulated national efforts using orbiting laboratories and satellites of military value and denied the UN a major role in space communications. "Where knowledge is, or could be power, the pursuit of knowledge is clearly a political activity. As a result, national investment in space science has turned out to be more sensitive and scientific cooperation has been less secure than other more mundane, more pressing, less mysterious forms of technical cooperation in space." [9] The United States has made a great effort to share its space research activities on a bilateral basis—in collaborative research and launching activities with countries such as Argentina and Brazil. But it has shown little interest in multilateral activities.

This American policy is being challenged by some scientists and other specialists, though it is not questioned by the public at large. Noting the unwillingness of the United States and other countries to forego expected military and commercial advantages from space research, some critics advocate that internationalization and demilitarization of the field be combined with a sharing of expected

[9] Howard J. Taubenfeld, *Space and Society* (Dobbs Ferry, N.Y.: Oceana, 1964), p. 14. Arnold W. Frutkin and Richard B. Griffin, Jr., "Space Activity in Latin America," *Journal of Inter-American Studies*, X, No. 2 (April, 1968), 185-93.

benefits, thus paying the less-developed countries for not establishing a military capacity in space. UN operation of communication satellites is suggested by those who fear the use of space for unregulated propaganda. Many other forms of international cooperation are suggested by scientists anxious to use the frontiers of knowledge beyond the stratosphere as a demonstration of peaceful UN activity and to publicize the feasibility of UN-conducted disarmament inspection. In the absence of actual American moves in this direction, the oft-repeated assurance that only international exploration makes sense does not sound very convincing. On the other hand, the United States has supported with increasing interest UNESCO-sponsored research in geophysics and hydrology. A change in over-all American policy may be suggested in Washington's espousal in 1968 of a vigorous UNESCO-designed multilateral exploration project in oceanography.

So far, at least, the main thrust toward more international interest in applied science developed from concern over rapid economic and social development. The advent of the Third World and the need felt by the industrial nations to meet more of its demands proved to be the crucial political stimulant to a different approach. Although the new emphasis dates only from the early 1960's, some early projects deserve mention. UNESCO has sought to stimulate, and undertake itself, several research projects with immediate relevance for economic development. Coordinated international research on the properties of arid lands was launched in the early 1950's, in the hope of discovering ways and means of making these water-poor areas more useful to man. The UN study of desalination techniques grew out of this interest, including massive research commitments on the part of IAEA to discover whether nuclear or conventional power sources are most appropriate for desalination plants. Technical assistance and research seminars are now featured in this area of concern. UNESCO has expanded its sponsorship of cooperative research by launching a ten-year global study of water resources, studies of marine biology, oceanography, and the properties of the humid tropics.

The breakthrough in relating science to economic development, however, came in 1960. In that year the General Assembly went on record as instructing the Secretary-General to do everything in his power to advance the application of science and technology to human betterment. As early as 1956 the Assembly had prodded the Secretariat to survey all efforts then underway to hasten industrialization; two years later it instructed UNESCO to make a similar survey of the natural sciences, resulting in the adoption by 1961 of a ten-year applied science program by UNESCO and the recommendation that the UN create a new specialized agency devoted only to marshalling science for economic development. The Secretary-General implemented his new mandate in 1962 by convoking the giant UN Conference on the Application of Science and Technology to Development (UNCAST).

The work of the conference and the optimism with which Secretary-General U Thant greeted it can be described only as "Science Rampant." There was some recognition that even though science and technology were considered benign agents of wholesome social change, their application in non-Western countries need not imply the wholesale imitation of the giant Western industrial-urban-scientific complex. In fact, the adaptation should be sensitive to what the local culture can, and will, bear without destroying itself in the process of modernizing. In the field of new sources of energy, this recognition led successive UN conferences to scale down their recommendations from the wholesale installation of nuclear reactors to reliance on existing sources of geothermal and solar energy. But such restraint was not shown in other areas of concern. The model of organized and government-financed scientific research followed in Western countries was held out as desirable. The main need was said to be more scientists, and crash programs for training scientific personnel in all fields were featured to increase their numbers. Another central need was the multiplication of research and research training sites, as well as the more efficient diffusion of scientific information. Training and diffusion are to be accelerated through the construction of regional science centers in the Third World, in which all fields of science and technology will be brought to bear on the creation of a new class of scientists and their subsequent employment in systematic national development programs drawing on new knowledge in oceanography, meteorology, hydrology, agronomy and demography.[10]

Who is to do all this? UNCAST rejected the idea of a new specialized agency and thought of UNESCO as the primary agent of the work, as well as of the existing UN regional commissions. There was little evidence that much thought was given to which governments, because of their financial position, would be crucial in directing the process. Few delegates realized that "planning" involves more than a listing of scientific fields that are short of manpower. In fact, the only major institutional step taken as a consequence of the conference was the creation of the UN Advisory Committee on

[10] United Nations Conference on the Application of Science and Technology, VII, *Science and Planning* (United Nations: New York, 1963).

the Application of Science and Technology to Development, a group of eminent scientists serving as individuals. In 1965 the committee established eight priority targets to be attacked internationally: food supplies, health, population, natural resources, industrialization, housing and urban planning, transportation, and new educational techniques especially suited for developing countries. It also specified potential research breakthrough areas useful in dealing with each of these, such as improvement of water resources or weather control. In 1966, the committee published a "World Plan of Action," a "planned international campaign to strengthen existing programmes and to add appropriate new arrangements to round out the total effort." [11] Specifically, the plan calls for massive manpower training programs and institution-building, more diffusion of technical knowledge linked to policies designed to make people accept innovation more readily, and the reorientation of scientific research toward meeting the special needs of developing nations. The number and kind of regional research and training centers are discussed, and 2,000 annual training fellowships are demanded. Science Rampant it is, with the undiminished optimism that this gigantic effort will automatically improve the lot of mankind and thereby contribute more or less directly to world peace. But so far, at least, the effort remains largely on paper, with each agency and each government continuing to follow development policies previously determined without the benefit of the "planning" of science and technology.

In the case of UNESCO, this emphasis did infuse the program with a new spirit of applying science more deliberately to development. The agency decided in 1961 to devote its entire program to the advancement of the UN First Development Decade, with heaviest emphasis on teacher training, the design of educational systems in underdeveloped countries, and helping the new nations foresee their future educational needs. But science found a prominent niche in this new programmatic structure. The organization is giving increased technical aid to countries seeking to set up national councils of scientific research, training centers, and special research institutes related to economic development and industrialization. In some cases, the institutions created are of a regional rather than purely national character, and UNESCO plans to set up hundreds more. The most advanced and modern methods are advocated for industrialization. "We have studied these questions in UNESCO and we have concluded that these things really are needed. The

[11] Economic and Social Council, *Official Records*, 41st Sess. 1966, Suppl. No. 10 (E/4206), par. 129.

economic reconstruction of the newly independent countries will have to be completed in the lifetime of one or at the most two generations—that is, very rapidly. Their present backwardness must be completely eliminated." [12] The organization has undertaken the development of quantitative indicators of national "scientific and technical potentials," which serve as a guide to the scientific development aid given by UNESCO. In short, we have a "scientific plan" which guides the organization in aiding the scientific planning of its members.

Underdevelopment is considered such a central evil that the stimulation of basic and applied science is subordinated to its elimination. While UNESCO acknowledges the importance of science as good in itself and wishes also to contribute to the free flow of ideas, the emphasis is nevertheless put on the development of *national* science in the member states. Although UNESCO admits that crash programs in science planning may entail unwanted social, psychological, and ethical consequences for peoples perhaps not desiring the sudden intrusion of a new and strange way of life, the organization still takes the position that it must present a series of optimal scientific development models to member states, stress demonstrated causal connections in development sequences, and then permit each member nation to choose its own road to salvation without excessive worry about making science into the agent of the next generation's toils and frustrations. Hence we cannot discern any central science plan that guides and controls the evolution of scientific knowledge among the members.

Much the same is true in the field of education. *Any* kind of education for *all* is the yardstick of action, irrespective of the unbalances and frustrations that can be caused by the wrong kind of education for those unable to rise to dignified positions in national life. A UNESCO affiliate, the International Institute for Educational Planning, recognizes this danger and consequently prepares national education plans that differentiate between the needs and developmental potentials of the member nations' populations. But it, too, merely prepares models of optimal development for various situations; authoritarian member nations may choose one scheme and democratic nations another.

Nevertheless, it is obvious that a firm link between applied science, planning, and international organizational activity has been forged in the policy nexus of economic development. The driving agents have been the governments of the underdeveloped nations

---

[12] Victor A. Kovda, "The Organization of Scientific Policy and Technological Research at the National Level," *UNESCO Chronicle*, 9, No. 3 (1963), 96.

and the international scientific community. But Washington was not slow to fall in line after 1961, acting with the enthusiastic support of much of the American scientific community. International science and technology were credited with ability to expand the world's food supply and combat famine by exploring the ocean bottom and cultivating oceanic resources. Exploration for new natural resources under joint auspices and internationally controlled exploitation of mineral deposits were stressed. President Johnson pledged American cooperation to all international scientific ventures designed to increase the world's fresh water. Weather was conceded to be an international phenomenon that ought to be studied by international agencies and controlled for everybody's benefit.

But it is equally clear that the area of applied science has not, so far, linked the United States to a chain of international commitments and obligations. The financial outlay devoted to these efforts is minimal compared to the funds devoted to the UN economic agencies. None of the specialized agencies or advisory committees has come close to acquiring powers of direction or control, though American diplomats have sometimes proposed such a role. Finally, as long as the belief persists that any and all aspects of applied science are good for peace and welfare, the mere proliferation of unrelated activities defies control and direction. Enmeshment becomes an issue only when men realize that not all science is benign, that the application of science to agronomy can undo its application to rural development. When "planning" becomes more than a euphemism for strengthening the national research potential of new countries, when it is an international effort to coordinate and direct conflicting, diffuse aspects of scientific inquiry, the web of scientific interdependence will be woven more tightly.

### 3. Applied Social Science and International Politics

Sociologists and psychologists, particularly, but many others in applied social sciences and the natural sciences think of their knowledge as transpolitical, offering solutions to tensions, hatreds, conflicts, and war—solutions that escape the political policy-makers who are concerned with only the articulation and defense of national interests. Some of them argue that these problems are caused by politicians in the first place. How then can the substitution of social science for politics be advanced by international organizations led and financed by politicians representing 130-odd national interests?

UNESCO's work in applied social science suggests an answer. Like other scientists, researchers associated with UNESCO believed that their findings could usefully be applied to specific social problems, notably prejudice, intergroup hostility, and war. Consequently, they undertook a series of activities loosely called the "tensions project," which prepared and distributed booklets describing various national ways of life. In addition, a four-country project compared sources of intergroup tensions, and other conferences were held to discuss causes of tensions and wars. Finally, research was done on ethnocentrism, xenophobia, race prejudice, and the psychological causes of aggression. For the most part, these efforts were a failure, either because they did not add to existing knowledge or because the results were ignored by the world. In other cases "research projects proved to be too delicate politically to be pursued, failing an official invitation from a government to carry them on." [13] When the implications of the social issues submitted to research ran counter to government policy, the research was stopped. Conversely, UNESCO-sponsored training and research on the social implications of economic development have consistently grown and have prospered because governments are interested in the results. Nevertheless, the very commitment to "peace" often cited by social scientists as basic to their work makes this activity suspect to governments unconvinced that their own interest in higher production, stable commodity prices, strong armies, or dedication to democracy has much to do with the links to peace seen by social scientists.

But when the IMF uses computer simulation, for example, to determine how international compensatory finance schemes affect national balances of payments, governments welcome this help in choosing their policies. Social problems are almost entirely infused with political values, whereas "problems" in the natural sciences are not so perceived at the moment. American policy has been particularly hostile to social science research under UN auspices allegedly related to world peace; Washington favors such a policy only when it is linked to the basic goal of advancing urban reconstruction, economic development, education, and the ability of a nation to plan its own future. Hence it is hardly surprising that the portion of the UNESCO budget devoted to applied social science has not exceeded 3 per cent.

Which social "problems" have managed to escape this skepticism?

[13] UNESCO, *Appraisal of UNESCO's Programmes for the Economic and Social Council* (Paris, 1960), pp. 105-6.

Again, programs clearly related to economic development demonstrate their capacity to legitimate themselves. The majority in the Economic and Social Council, as early as 1956, was happy to bestow scientific credentials on the social practitioner when industrialization was the problem. But actual efforts remained confined to scattered training institutes in economic planning, statistics, survey techniques, and studies of rural-urban migration and adaptation. The UN Research Institute on Social Development seeks to do research on the social correlates of economic development and the maximization of social benefits during industrialization. Demographic studies and population policy have provided another field in which applied social science has been accepted as an adviser to politics, if not a substitute for it. UN-sponsored population conferences and studies have gone on for years. The WHO has been concerned with child welfare as well as with population pressure and control—after many years during which certain member countries resolutely blocked a WHO role in birth control education. Today, WHO makes pioneering efforts to apply systematic social science to forecast the social and ethical side effects of medical change; it uses simulation and cost-benefit models to determine these implications of modernization measures in public health work, a daring innovation that no other UN agency has yet adopted. As for the United States, it has supported medical research, health and social service establishments, and the collection of information relating to population pressure. But for many years the American government felt unable to support WHO programs of family planning. When this reluctance gave way to support for informational programs, the United States nevertheless continued to oppose the distribution of contraceptives. American policy has only recently embraced international organizations as desirable agents for enabling man to couple medical knowledge with economic objectives.

The most serious effort to apply social science to the work of the UN itself is the work of the UN Center for Programming and Projection; there economic growth models for the whole world are being prepared, with clear implications for trade and investment decisions in the future. All of these efforts are now uncoordinated and decentralized; the specialized agencies are not clearly tied to such tentative steps toward planning, and the research work of the social science units is not usually taken into account in UN or in national policy-making. In fact, agencies created for the application of social science may come to languish in irrelevance. It happened to the UN Institute for Training and Research (UNITAR). Created in 1965 to train national and international civil servants in the skills of international economic development diplomacy and peacekeeping—thus sidestepping the exclusively national socializing process that prevails in fact—UNITAR was also given the power to undertake policy-relevant research in fields such as the evaluation of development aid projects, methods of pacific settlement and peacekeeping, the protection of human rights, and the transfer of technological skills to non-Western cultures. The terms "operations analysis, evaluation and planning" recur with sonorous regularity in the programmatic statements of UNITAR. They have not yet given a systematic character to the institute's work, nor has that work resulted in any strong link with the UN decision-making process.

## 4. Planning at the International Level

The link between basic and applied sciences and their planned integration with the life of the international society is complex. Planning can mean deliberate, self-conscious assignment of research and development priorities for the positive exploitation of the unknown on behalf of human welfare. But it can also mean the imaginative projection of unsettling and disturbing innovations, the avoidance of disruptive exploitation and its political consequences. If scientific advance is indeed inevitable, it is as likely to lead to "national science" and to national self-assertion as it is to result in the peaceful internationalization of knowledge. Conflict, indeed scientifically aggravated conflict, remains in the forefront of possibility—unless one of the unintended consequences of randomly applied science is the realization that it may be too dangerous to permit this process to continue without international regulation.

Obviously, the world is far from this realization. International planning—to the extent that the various UN commissions and conferences can be said to engage in it—is confined to assigning priorities to the positive exploitation of knowledge, particularly for economic development. But when internationally encouraged efforts to explore the resources of the ocean floor and the properties of outer space begin to pay off, the nations will be guided by rules they have made confirming the *national* component in science: the international Convention on the Continental Shelf greatly strengthens the rights of the coastal state alone to exploit the ocean bottom; the UN-negotiated agreement on the Peaceful Uses of Outer Space, by prohibiting annexations, establishes the right of each nation to explore safely, but it does not strengthen *international* planning or control.[14]

The timidity of the United States in relating the exploration and exploitation of the unknown to systematic international planning may be passing. This is well illustrated in the discussion regarding the future of the ocean floor. Many scientists are convinced that the mineral resources of the ocean floor are tremendous; many biologists think that the nutritional potentials of ocean life forms have not yet been fully explored and that ocean farming may be the key to the world's food and population problems. One might wish to vest new powers in the UN, to control, license, and supervise exploitation of these resources, if the UN would seriously consider *international* planning instead of *national* exploration of the unknown, which it underwrites through neutralization, equal access, mutual aid, and nonannexation agreements. Malta suggested to the General Assembly in 1967 that an appropriate UN agency be created and that the royalties and license fees collected by it be devoted to development aid. Further, following the precedent of the Antarctic and Outer Space agreements, the ocean floor would be reserved for peaceful pursuits. Washington at first greeted this initiative with great caution, stressing the need to consider military security while admitting that the exploration of the ocean floor cannot be permitted to follow the "treasure syndrome" of earlier unplanned and uncontrolled private forays into natural resources.[15] But in mid-1968 the United States formally asked the ENDC to take up the question of arms limitation on the seabed and ocean floor, to prevent emplacement there of weapons of mass destruction. Further, the United States asked for "internationally agreed arrangements governing the exploitation of resources on the deep ocean floor," in order to safeguard the potential benefits to be derived by technologically and economically underdeveloped nations. Finally, Washington suggested, as Malta had urged, that a portion "of the value of the resources recovered from the deep ocean floor" be assigned to "international community purposes." [16]

---

[14] "Man *is* going to colonize the oceans, and it might just as well be *our* men. To compete successfully we must be able to move faster in the sea, to go deeper, to stay down longer than anyone else." Athelstan Spilhaus, "Man in the Sea," *Science* (Sept. 4, 1964), p. 993. Copyright 1964 by the American Association for the Advancement of Science.

[15] Herman Pollack, "National Interest, Foreign Affairs and the Marine Sciences," *Department of State Bulletin* (Feb. 12, 1968), pp. 211-14; Arthur J. Goldberg, *ibid.* (Jan. 22, 1968), p. 125; Victor Basiuk, "Marine Resources Development, Foreign Policy and the Spectrum of Choice," *Orbis*, XII, No. 1 (Spring, 1968), 39-72.

[16] U.N. doc. A/AC.135/L.1, Annex III.

The United States has done little to encourage a consciousness of the dangers inherent in the random growth of science. The policy of believing in the benign character of science and in its positive implications for human welfare, peace, and freedom continues to prevail in international policy. It is only the isolated scientist in America, and an occasional social scientist, who is beginning to question these assumptions. Presidential adviser G. B. Kistiakowsky called for the evolution of "a new breed of citizen-scientist . . . continually aware that the scientific community must accept its share of responsibility for the intelligent and successful resolution of the challenges facing the world." [17] When he was Vice-President, Hubert H. Humphrey called attention to the problem-generating, as well as the problem-solving, potential of science in the "second" industrial revolution now engulfing the West. He warned that mankind cannot be expected to adjust to an accelerated rate of change indefinitely, though the Third World needs science to achieve the promise of the first industrial revolution:

> Perhaps what is needed in the international field is some . . .
> forum which would bring together under nongovernmental auspices
> men of wisdom and experience from the universities and founda-
> tions, science and industry, politics and the professions, who could
> systematically assess the implications of this second industrial
> revolution for the world of the 1970's. Their recommendations
> would invariably become an important guide to government
> decision-making.[18]

We grow conscious of the Janus-headed nature of science when one consequence of science considered benign at first produces later results recognized as being harmful: the example of medical and nutritional progress and of population pressure is the most telling. Here international concern has been aroused in scientific circles and government policy, though the answer held out calls for more science. American scientists and some political leaders are suggesting that air pollution, urban congestion, and unemployment provide other "problems" so visible and so clearly attributable to science that only science can deal with them.

And so the identification of "problem areas" caused by science and amenable to scientific planning emerges as a crucial question.

[17] G. B. Kistiakowsky, "Science and Foreign Policy," *Science* (April 8, 1960), p. 1023.

[18] Hubert H. Humphrey, "The Technological Revolution and the World of the 1970's," *Department of State Bulletin* (Jan. 30, 1967), p. 167.

So far the identification has come when an obvious and visible price was being paid by man: overpopulation and famine, mounting research and development costs because of space competition, the danger of nuclear proliferation and mushroom-shaped clouds. But the network of international organizations remains to be utilized for the identification of less visible problems. Why?

The very epistemology of planning is full of conundrums. Earlier we distinguished between the perspectives of the actor, the critic, and the observer. Stance also governs selection of problem areas that are singled out for attention: what is a problem to the critic is not necessarily so viewed by either the actor or the observer. The same discontinuity in perception applies when the observer is able to identify trends, imbalances, and disturbances that escape the interest-dominated vision of the actor or the ideological acumen of the critic. Moreover, the crucial role of scientists in the politics of research and the planning of research compounds the difficulty. Are scientists observers, critics, or actors? Which perspective informs their judgments and their policy recommendations to the executive branch, Congress, the military?

Scientists in and near government are themselves actors. Far from transcending interest politics, they are themselves very often defenders of interests. Whether it be space, the earth's crust, synthetic foodstuffs, genetic manipulation, or cancer research, scientists defend the research commitments they have made and justify them in the name of the national, even international, interest. Social scientists act no differently when called upon to justify their demands for public funds. Science begets its own intellectual and organizational imperialism that makes scientists act much like politicians in seeking to advance their objectives. Thus they resemble actors rather than dispassionate observers. Increasingly, however, the stance of the critic has been adopted by scientists dimly aware that their profession is indeed Janus-headed. But it takes the stance of the observer to spot even this development! Planning, in short, is made most difficult because the comprehensive balancing of the benign with the harmful in science and technology is so difficult to undertake for scientific decision-makers already committed and for lay politicians trained to think of science as "good," indiscriminately, for the nation and the world. But when in doubt on this point, American policy has clearly favored national science over efforts at comprehensive planning through the UN or elsewhere.

It seems to be true that the perspective of the impatient and even alienated critic is necessary before problem areas inherent to scientific knowledge can be identified. One must be more than a professionally competent soil chemist, hydraulic engineer, or molecular biologist to realize that the acquisition of knowledge itself can have social consequences deeply upsetting to people's lives and happiness, creating the conditions for a new utopia or a renaissance of barbarism, whether induced by the destruction of the physical environment or the manipulation of men's genes. And this observation also applies to planning: the desire to assign priorities, to think out the possible consequences of research, to simulate the social system after a hypothetical major factor is altered—all these imply concern, uncertainty, and distrust of the automatic character of progress based on unchanneled research. A critical stance is a prerequisite to planning at any level. Has such a critical stance developed with respect to the international system and its future?

While many pure scientists and social scientists have isolated pieces and patches of problems, very few have identified the nature of organized research itself as a problem for the world. Hence the notion of comprehensive planning at the international level is still in embryonic form. Our survey of scientific research, thinking and planning in connection with economic development, and sharing the fruits of technology illustrated the patchiness of "scientific-political vision." A few scientists are warning that scientific investments are growing at an exponential rate in the West, so that by the year 2000 the United States may be spending 20 per cent of its gross national product on research. This may not only strain the national budget, but it may call for an intolerable rate of human adjustment to physical and psychological change. Some social scientists call attention to the costs incurred by traditional cultures in industrialization, in opening themselves up to rapid and energetic modernization. A few demand of national and international agencies that they review their technical assistance and scientific sharing programs, to minimize unbearable rates and kinds of social change, that they gear assistance to man's ability to adjust without the suffering that has accompanied industrialization in the past. A scientist close to the United States government realized that scientists no longer merely lobby for research funds and advance knowledge, but that they increasingly "manage" the research to be done in the future on behalf of the nation.[19] If the scientific manager is a critic rather than an actor, he could be a powerful force for *social* rather than purely scientific planning.

[19] For example, James R. Killian, "Making Science a Vital Force in Foreign Policy," *Science* (January 6, 1961), pp. 24-25. Copyright 1961 by the American Association for the Advancement of Science.

Science is indeed international, and scientists do have global mobility. They form an international community in the sense that knowledge, if it is scientific, is amenable to the same procedures and reasoning processes everywhere; its fruits can be shared in any cultural setting receptive to these procedures—and almost all are. And they form a physical community because of the number of their meetings, exchanges, and publications. Since they also share a belief in the validity of the scientific method as a problem-solver, and a common optimism about the application of the method to human progress—even the critics!—why should we not consider scientists working in UN programs as the first global ruling class, the Platonic guardians alone able and willing to predict and control the future on the basis of their knowledge?

There are very good reasons why critically inspired scientific managers, conscious of the problems brought on by science, will play no such role in the near future. In the first place, the huge bulk of scientists are actors in government or lobbyists for government favors, not critics. It is by no means clear that the scientists working with international institutes and commissions are able to adopt a comprehensive view or depart from the tacit conviction that all problems caused by science can be solved by it too. Furthermore, the lessons we can learn from the behavior of a crucial set of planners in other settings are not likely to change our conclusion.

Perhaps for the first time there is underway in the UN now a political and intellectual process that aims at comprehensive and rational development planning, subordinating politics and short-range interest to knowledge—or so it looks at first blush. The effort in question is the deliberate analysis now being undertaken to plan the Second Development Decade, to begin in 1970. It involves professional economists as well as UN administrators, representatives of the interests of specialized agencies and UN regional commissions, lobbyists for organizational vested interests, and expert economic planners interested only in an optimal allocation of global resources.

The centerpiece of this planning effort is the UN Programming and Projection Center; there the world growth model that is to guide the allocation of organizational programs and resources is taking shape. The center's recommendations are then submitted for discussion to the UN Committee for Development Planning, a group of eighteen experts serving as individuals, called into being by ECOSOC. The committee has the task of collecting and projecting all available information and techniques that lead to the efficient implementation of national development plans. But in its work the committee has developed criteria and techniques for *judging* such plans in the perspective of UN principles. It now has the additional task of shaping and submitting to ECOSOC a world development plan, and perhaps exercising some powers of control in implementing it after 1970.

Once the model is accepted, it will be important in deciding which specialized agency will undertake what program in the execution of the plan. It is already clear that FAO—which has produced a long-range indicative plan for world agricultural development—will adjust its agricultural and commodity policy accordingly and that ILO will prepare and seek to implement regional employment and manpower training programs that fit the plan. UNESCO's work in educational development will be dovetailed with the employment projections, and WHO's public health work will fit in with the population and urbanization projections.

But the model has not yet been accepted as an authoritative guide. It is being widely criticized for being overconcerned with economic variables, to the exclusion of the social and human dimensions, of asserting the virtues of economic development as self-evident without regard for the social and political transformations that may be engendered unwittingly. The member nations and ECOSOC have not yet spoken; UNCTAD's role as the spokesman for the developing nations is being asserted but not defined; OECD, as the agent of the financial contributors to the Decade, has gone its own way with its own projections. Planning the Second Development Decade is indeed a giant first step in the rational allocation of world skills, resources, and talents for control; but it surely has not demonstrated any unique ability of science to govern.

Social scientists rarely act as Platonic guardians. They criticize liberally, and they make generous claims about their abilities to solve problems if only sufficient support were budgeted. At the national level, however, their political influence seems to be proportional to their agreement with nonscientific decision-makers: the more articulate the critic, the less influence he is likely to have in government. In his effort to make apolitical scientific knowledge take the place of the politician's tainted insights, the social scientist must become political; he has no other way of gaining attention.

Much the same is true of another kind of planner, the young economic development managers of the Third World, trained engineers, applied scientists, and economists. As a group they profess faith in the universal validity of their knowledge, its centrality in enhancing the welfare of their peoples, the identity of physical welfare with progress in general, and the conviction that all of this contributes to world peace. Consequently they brand as villains all political elites who stand in the way of the rigorous application of their knowledge; and if the masses are slow to respond to planned stimuli, the young managers profess contempt for the people they are trying to help. Their contempt for politics, also, makes this class of planners a priori political when their efforts go unimplemented. Inability to move their political superiors turns the possessors of universal knowledge into politicians—as judged by an observer, not by the planner himself! [20]

Planners in UN bodies can retain their legitimacy only if they maintain the universal validity of their knowledge as being above partisan politics. But since the planners remain very marginal to the political process, their desire to influence decisions makes them enter the political forum to become authoritative as well as legitimate. And by becoming authoritative, they run the risk of losing their legitimacy. For social scientists, whose claim to universally valid knowledge is dubious, the initial legitimacy is weak and unlikely to be strengthened if the planners in research agencies claim active political power.

And so the paradox is complete. The possessor of knowledge is impotent to make policy if he is unwilling to be political. But being political calls for compromising, negotiating, giving, and taking. And the sources of the compromises lie in the interests perceived by nations and by groups, not in abstract knowledge. To impress the contradictions of Science Rampant into perceptions in the minds of actors demands political advocacy on the part of the planner, thus exposing him as partisan. The international community of science is condemned to politics, even though its basic creed puts it beyond political consciousness and knowledge.

This conclusion on the observer's part seems to condemn any thought of comprehensive international planning for some time to come, even if the imperfect state of social knowledge were not enough to doom such a trend. Comprehensive planning is no more possible at the international than at the national level, no matter what pretense may be made. Man and his computers, not yet capable of articulating and linking all the variables, are much less able to draw political inferences from them. But in the meantime, scientific planners continue to engage in defining and linking the variables in odd corners and selected squares of the universe of knowledge. Moreover, they possess constantly growing international organizations and agencies to help them do so. While no comprehensive plan comes forth, bits and pieces of planning do emerge in this sector and that—plans that may be capable of successful im-

20 I am indebted to Warren Ilchman for showing me unpublished data substantiating this summary.

plementation because they appeal to political decision-makers. No total science with a total plan, but incremental science with small groups of planners tied to specific policy-makers may be emerging, producing new ties, new policies, and new changes unplanned and unanticipated by the governments that permitted the growth of the agencies in the first place. As one high American official noted

> International organizations exist simply because they are needed; we belong to them simply because it serves our national interest to belong—and because it would damage our national interest to remain aloof. So while nations cling to national sovereignties and national purposes, science is creating a functional international community whether anyone likes it or not.[21]

Will disliking enmeshment enable the United States to evade it? In recent years, OECD has been considering some of the ambiguities and dangers implicit in the random growth of science. Its memoranda have argued for a less incremental approach, a more self-conscious division of labor among the Atlantic nations, and a greater sensitivity to the economic and social implications of science.[22] But nothing has yet come of these efforts, and the United States has been among the most resistant members.

In the meantime, the logic of incremental thinking and partial knowledge tied to limited slices of perceived national interest suffices to keep the process of enmeshment moving. The commitment expressed by American Presidents and diplomats since 1961 can point only in that direction. Policy-makers continue to express the belief that international "problem areas" demand international scientific sharing and cooperation; they believe that this sharing will somehow lead to an "international great society" of peace; they argue that the problems of science will be solved only by science so organized. Even if the argument is faulty and the links of reasoning weak, the implication is that of continued gradual enmeshment. Those in government who believe in the work for peace that can be done by the gradual widening of joint and international scientific ventures, in fact, contribute to the enmeshment simply by translating their belief into policy.

---

[21] Harlan Cleveland, in the Foreword to Gardner, *In Pursuit of World Order, op. cit.*, p. xi.

[22] OECD, Problems of Science Policy (Paris, 1968). OECD, Third International Conference of Ministers of Science of OECD countries, "The Impact of Science and Technology on Social and Economic Development," *OECD Observer* (April, 1968).

# PART THREE

## The strength
## of the web of interdependence

### A Scenario of the Future

The major and perhaps the sole justification for using systems theory in the discussion of international politics is its ability to link the will of governments with the shape of the world to come. It is policy that produces the "system," though the system then goes on to constrain future policy or to dictate its limits.

"Discussion of whether or not we should be in the United Nations is about as useful as discussion of whether or not we should have a United States Congress," comments Richard N. Gardner. He continues:

> What we really need is to accept the fact that international organizations are here to stay and to turn to the much more difficult question of how we can use them better to promote our national interest. We need to discuss the UN and other international organizations in operational rather than in symbolic terms. We need to consider in professional detail just what these agencies do and how they could do it better.[1]

[1] Gardner, *In Pursuit of World Order, op. cit.,* p. 6.

Because of commitments here expressed, the multipolar hetero-symmetrical system of the current era resulted from the policies followed by governments in the previous tripolar era. Because of the persistence of these commitments, we assert that the policies followed by governments during the multipolar era will produce a new sytem we may label "multibloc asymmetrical."

Of course, the giant assumption we make here is that governments will simply follow the logic of the course sketched during the present system and expressed in Gardner's judgment, thus swimming with the tide already flowing. The system projected is what it is only because we now treat governments as the helpless victims of earlier decisions. This assumption may be wrong. Governments may deliberately refuse to float along with the current; and if they successfully assert themselves, they will be turning the tide or setting up a countercurrent. Indeed, such a choice may be desirable.

Our job first of all is the presentation of a scenario with probable future world trends *not* subject to easy human manipulation or social learning. Then we must describe the multibloc asymmetric system that will characterize international politics in such a setting, *provided* that present trends continue. Next, we must ask whether that kind of system is normatively desirable from the viewpoint of the United States. Finally, we must prescribe the measures of further enmeshment in, or energetic untangling from, international organizations that appear linked to the realization of American values. This is the task of the final part, our effort to pit the logic of self-fulfilling against self-defeating prophecies. Here we abandon the stance of the observer, and we participate in action—to the extent that the fruits of observation can ever be translated into warning and advice—to foil a self-fulfilling prophecy.

*　　*　　*

There can be little doubt that the world will be characterized for many decades to come by the "basic multifold trend." [2] This trend is made up of separate strands that are by no means mutually reenforcing; perhaps the opposite will be the case. Nor are the items that make up the trend subject to any social learning that is now discernible. They just go on, as if of their own volition. Thus, culturally, the world will be more and more sensate, preoccupied with empirical perception, secular, humanistic, utilitarian, and hedonis-

[2] Herman Kahn and Anthony J. Wiener, "The Next Thirty-Three Years: A Framework for Speculation," *Dædalus* (Summer, 1967), p. 706.

tic. People will be less and less willing to defer gratification; they will be bent exclusively on immediate enjoyment of whatever they value. Elites will tend toward both egalitarianism and meritocracy. Scientific knowledge of all kinds will accumulate even more rapidly than it does now. Society will change faster and more universally in proportion to the application of this scientific knowledge through technology and its diffusion. Industrialization will be worldwide, though its benefits may not be; both affluence and leisure will increase in proportion, but population will also continue to burgeon, thus giving us a continuing race between food supply and people. Primary occupations will decline even more in importance, and secondary occupations will begin a downward trend. Education and literacy will spread more evenly throughout the world, and so will the capability for mass destruction through war. Urbanization will reach the point of the megalopolis, if not the necropolis.

The major technical revolutions of the next twenty years will include a vast increase in computers, data retrieval, and their application, so that instantaneous factual information will be available to decision-makers on almost everything—but also to the increasingly literate and aware public. Developments in biology may result in control over heredity, motivation, and the length of human life. The oceans will be increasingly explored and exploited, and the weather will be subjected to manipulation. New forms of energy will be developed, making man less dependent on coal and access to fresh water, with wide implications for location of industries.[3] Some of the more obvious "social problems" associated with these trends—*not* necessarily capable of being solved by learned behavior such as forecasting and planning—include unemployment, status deprivation, and society's inability to assimilate an excess of educated, aspiring counter-elites. The race for food will imply agrarian unrest, and the reliance on cybernetic equipment will lead toward the meritocratic rule of communications scientists and technicians. Since more work will be done by fewer people, private life will become crucial; the home and the communal pad will be new centers of activity.

The dominance of these trends is likely to result in the arrival of a society now often labeled postindustrial. Almost certainly, it will come quite soon to the West and to Japan, and eventually to

[3] This sketch is taken from Nigel Calder, ed., *The World in 1984* (Baltimore: Penguin Books, 1965), Vol. 2, summaries after p. 190.

the successfully industrializing nations of Asia, Africa, and Latin America. The postindustrial society is characterized by very high per capita income, the dominance of tertiary and quartenary economic pursuits, and by effective floors on welfare. New social aggregates, neither "public" nor "private," will be the major source of innovation; and as cybernation reigns supreme, the market will decline in decision-making importance. Since most institutions will become obsolete within a generation, "learning" will be a continuous activity in the sense of making people adapt to change beyond their rational control; quite literally, everybody will be going to school most of the time. Work- and achievement-oriented values will disappear as the pursuits associated with a sensate culture predominate and group activity is legitimated as psychotherapy.

The role of government and foreign affairs in such a setting calls for a further comment. As accepted values erode, we can no longer expect a consensus on notions such as the "national interest"; perhaps the postindustrial nation will no longer be an object of value at all to its citizens. The government may become an agency taken for granted as the dispenser of largesse and physical security that one assumes to be his right. More and more people will be able to afford to behave as spoiled children, and American society could become a loose network of self-indulgent groups profoundly indifferent to the issues that make up this book. But someone would remain to feed and exploit the data banks, to design and deploy non-killing but lethargy-inducing missiles, to plan the curricula for the next generation of adaptive gene selectors and ocean ranchers. The ruling meritocracy would inherit government by default.

Can this sort of widespread alienation survive? Chances are that the alienated would eventually seek to influence public decisions once more and develop appropriate ideologies. The mood of soma-centered withdrawal from public values—and the withdrawal from world affairs implicit in this mood—may then give rise to a new chiliasm of mission, reform, overthrow, and involvement. And the commitment-withdrawal-recommitment cycle of the American foreign policy mood might remain intact even in a postindustrial setting.[4] Nor should we forget that while the West is working itself toward the satiation of the postindustrial psyche, whole nations in the less developed world will continue to be ruled by genocide, famine, guerrilla brutality, and messianic behavior.

[4] Kahn and Wiener, "The Next Thirty-Three Years," *op. cit.*

All sorts of "problems" will abound twenty years hence, problems bequeathed to us by the pace of change associated with the basic multifold trend. We do not know whether these problems are amenable to solutions other than "progressive adjustment." We cannot tell whether man will have a consciousness of danger, of a need to forecast and to plan early corrective steps. We must suspect that technological and scientific innovation will go on growing exponentially. We must be dubious of man's ability to learn to mold these forces according to his hopes and fears. Thus we can affirm the tension between the Third World's desire to modernize and be rich and the West's ability to help, but we do not know whether the tension will result in a race war or a welfare world based on a regional economic division of labor. Will the erosion of national values in the West bring about similar disintegration in the Third World? In time to avert a race war? Will preoccupation with shaping man's physical environment make all international policies of the past obsolete? Will total ecological planning yield a new mentality for the ruling meritocracy in Malawi, as in Sweden; in Cambodia as in Czechoslovakia? Economic growth may lead to bitter disenchantment; the sensate life may spawn boredom and crime. Megalopolis may prove to be unbearable, and public order may come to depend on the regular administration of new and powerful tranquilizers. None of this is certain; all is possible. The minor troubles associated with questions such as who controls the weather, what agency decides on the eugenic balance of Upper Volta and Ecuador and how this affects Uzbekistan and Montenegro seem quite bearable in comparison. So is the vexing question of whether the twenty new moderately industrial nations will soon have advanced weapons system at their disposal, thus creating among themselves arms races and deterrence patterns of the kind familiar to the superpowers in 1968.[5]

This is the evolving setting of world politics. It will determine the future of the web of interdependence if existing trends are simply accepted by policy-makers and if systemic learning continues to take the form it has enjoyed for the last decade. The details of these implications for American foreign policy must now be thrown into relief. And the choices still open to us may become clear in the process.

[5] Calder, *The World in 1984, op. cit.*

# CHAPTER TEN

# THE UNITED STATES AND THE FUTURE INTERNATIONAL SYSTEM

## 1. A Multibloc Asymmetric System

The characteristics of the era in which we are living are changing before our very eyes. Alliances are visibly declining in cohesion and purpose. The ideological struggle between the superpowers is being muted. New nations declare themselves nonaligned almost as soon as their flags rise in front of the palace of the government, as the North–South issue predominates in their minds over the East–West confrontation more familiar to us. Economics and economic blocs are therefore more important than many military and ideological groupings. This trend is well underway and it rolls on, whether willed or not by the United

States. What kind of configuration can we predict for the international system if the trend continues unchecked?

We must exclude certain kinds of futures as incompatible with any now visible aspects of the multifold trend, at least for the next twenty to thirty years. There will be no world government based on voluntary federation, and the logic of deterrence will prevent the evolution of a world empire. The large powers will not be sufficiently cohesive and purposeful to impose their hegemony in the form of a concert, and the small powers—while more energetically independent than in the past system—will still lack the unity of purpose to dominate. It is conceivable, however, that the nuclear powers might establish a "condominium" whereby they jointly guarantee the safety of non-nuclear powers, such as in the framework of a nonproliferation treaty. Nor can we count on a UN with a capacity for independent military action strikingly greater than is now incorporated in the familiar structure on the East River.

Totalitarian polities in Europe will become more benignly authoritarian as the process of bureaucratic *embourgeoisement* catapults them along the trajectory of the postindustrial society. The Western democracies will move further along the road they have taken, implying more internal division and less willingness to take energetic international action. In Latin America, a few countries will become left-wing totalitarian polities, nine or ten will succeed in modernizing as democracies, and the remainder will oscillate between degrees of authoritarianism, including many of the features we associate with the fascism of the 1930's. In Africa, the bulk of the nations will alternate between mild authoritarian and rigid totalitarian forms of government and national purpose, thus keeping alive ideological tensions on that continent after the demise of the present leadership. In Asia, things will be somewhat more stable, with an East and Southeast Asian radical communist bloc, a few successful democracies, and a large number of authoritarian polities trying to modernize in the more leisurely fashion of contemporary Pakistan. Under no conceivable circumstances can we count on more than fifty-odd democracies in a 125-member United Nations, but there may be as many as eighty authoritarian polities.

If the present ideological cleavages will not survive, how can these nations be grouped? The slight proliferation of nuclear weapons, the rise of a cohesive West Europe, and the arrival of a powerful Japan, first of all, will prevent the polarization of power we now associate with the United States' and the Soviet Union's leadership. Poles of power will give way to a more decentralized system of blocs lacking clear leaders. These blocs, moreover, will be organized functionally rather than geographically: economic objectives will dictate one kind of grouping for a country, military objectives will dictate another.

Thus we can imagine common markets functioning in West Europe, Latin America, and Central America; a self-contained communist trading system in Asia; an independent African bloc and one tied to Western Europe; and some kind of Asian "socialist" trading system for the noncommunist nations. In global terms, the Asian, African, and Latin-American economic blocs will be the "developing nations group" in UNCTAD and UNIDO, while West Europe, communist East Europe, Japan, and the United States–Canadian complex will constitute their negotiating partner. In terms of national and bloc objectives, of course, the underdeveloped appear as the challengers of the international economic status quo, and the developed as its defenders. If there is to be an international class struggle, it will follow the lines of cleavage here suggested.

Military objectives, however, dictate a different pattern of bloc formation. It is probable that some form of attenuated East European bloc will linger on as understandings between the United States and Germany continue, while NATO decays. West Europe will be a weak military bloc, therefore, with some of its members seeking unity in nonalignment and others continuing to look to the United States. The United States and the Soviet Union, however, will be more on their own than at any time since 1948. All these formations will in essence be defenders of the status quo, territorially and militarily. In the Third World, none of the conceivable groupings will possess the power, cohesion, unity of purpose, or strong central institutions required to challenge any of the industrial blocs. In Africa there may emerge a bloc of totalitarian states bent on intervention and subversion and a defensive bloc of authoritarian ones anxious to fend off such challenges: but these two are unlikely to be coterminous with the economic blocs sketched above. In the Western Hemisphere, the familiar pattern of the OAS is likely to change soon, as nations of the hemisphere split into Washington-oriented, Havana-inspired, and nonaligned blocs. The pro-American as well as the neutralist blocs will contain both democratic and authoritarian polities. In Asia, much depends on the future vigor of China. If Maoism remains forceful, we may imagine a defensive military grouping of authoritarian and democratic nations

(India, Indonesia, Malaysia, Iran, Thailand, Philippines, and perhaps Pakistan), an offensive grouping of China, North Korea, and Vietnam, and a bloc of genuine neutrals, such as Burma, Nepal, and Cambodia. If China were to become preoccupied with other matters, no military-ideological blocs need arise at all. In the UN, therefore, we would have a minimum of six or a maximum of ten military groupings, of varying cohesion and vastly different strengths, playing roles different from the economic blocs and offering a heterogeneous bundle of aspirations and demands as compared to past historical systems.

This very heterogeneity of blocs and objectives results in an untidy and confusing international distribution of power, which we label "asymmetric" because it lacks the more congruent, interfunctional bargaining characteristics of the current multipolar system. In that system, region, ideology, alliances, and modernity tend to covary. Nations will continue to use familiar means for attaining their objectives. But technology will give us more sophisticated devices than we now have for warfare, riot control, mind manipulation, technical assistance for economic development, mass education, and propaganda. Whether these imply a qualitative change in the nature of the system may well be doubted if we assume roughly equal access by all nations and blocs to the artifacts and techniques involved. The developing world will demand more aid of all kinds and more access to the markets of the developed. The industrial world will furnish more and more aid but also insist on spelling out conditions and limits. These transactions will go forward through bilateral as well as multilateral channels. As the West and the Soviet bloc tone down their respective propaganda campaigns, no such restraint will be observed between the West and the Third World and among the various blocs of developing nations. The entire range of social and human rights policy will be infected with these concerns and charges. Argument will continue over the conditions governing private foreign investment. More acrimony will be heard over the most "egalitarian redistributive" way of applying new knowledge to economic and social development; solutions may well confirm a decentralized and asymmetric pattern of accommodation, eliminating both superpowers as the sole font of action and ultimate authority. And, it almost goes without saying, the agitation for the complete elimination of all kinds of colonial rule will continue, as will sporadic warfare designed to hasten the process or defend against it.

This view of the future international system assumes further that the absolute military potency of the two superpowers will decline as the balance of nuclear terror continues between them, buttressed perhaps by additional but equal power in ABM systems and multiple warhead missiles. But nuclear proliferation would also continue, despite the existence of the nonproliferation treaty. Perhaps as many as twenty countries would acquire the capacity to produce hydrogen weapons; but only six or seven would also have the incentive and political motivation actually to do so. To the extent that such weapons are available to countries other than the five nations now brandishing them, the logic of mutual deterrence would apply in their relations with each other and the superpowers. The over-all military situation will remain untidy and unstructured, however, because of the unpredictable security aspirations of non-nuclear nations. If the now familiar congruence of economic, military, and ideological blocs is certain to fall apart, it will be replaced by a multilayered international system fragmented by separate national objectives.

Will these objectives, alignment patterns, and methods imply more enmeshment—or less—in multilateral processes? Economic development, decolonization, world trade, the status of human rights, and the diffusion of scientific and technological knowledge will almost certainly involve continuous international negotiation, even culminating in confrontation—whether verbal or financial. The nature of the evolving human environment leaves little room to expect anything less. The exception to this projection is the preservation of peace itself: the different character of the blocs and the asymmetric confrontation pattern between demands and means suggests that the bargaining pattern between collective security and decolonization or economic development objectives is a thing of the past. To have UN peacekeeping, we must have an independent commitment of member nations, who accept it as good and desirable, not expediential, dependent on pay-offs in other issue areas. Such a commitment is unlikely to exist in the multibloc system.

And this has immediate implications for the tasks the UN will be expected to carry out. The members will insist on using the organization for the completion of decolonization, for energetic industrialization policies, for social modernization, for the regulation of world trade and finance, and even for propaganda broadsides in the field of human rights. It will almost certainly be used increasingly for social and economic planning and for the diffusion—controlled or not—of new knowledge. The point is, however, that each of these activities will be legitimate in its *own* right, with positive expectations attaching to *each* and little dependence on other issues or tasks. Therefore, the preservation of peace and the facilitation of peaceful change among the nations, *unless it also becomes an autonomous and legitimate task*, will not become legitimate by association with nonmilitary activities. There is nothing in the nature of a multibloc asymmetric system that gives us the right to expect such a development. As the tasks of the UN become legitimate, they also become self-encapsulating and self-sufficient, preventing the more precariously established tasks to profit from the success of the legitimate ones.

## 2. The Multibloc System and the United States: 1970 and 1990?

In an earlier chapter we described American public opinion as passive, reactive, and permissive except in time of great turmoil and crisis; then the mood of the public tends to swing back and forth between the pole of withdrawal from the world and the pole of deep and violent commitment to it. The systems through which we have passed since 1945 have avoided the kind of deep and painful crisis that could have challenged the permissive setting. Each successive system was accepted by the American public as more or less inevitable. Can we expect the multibloc system to become equally legitimate? In 1965 people were asked whether they expected, in 1985, that the West and the Soviet Union will be living in peace, whether communism will have collapsed, whether H-bombs will no longer be manufactured, or whether civilization will be in ruins. The results were as follows:

51% do *not* think that Russia and the West will be living in peace
61% do *not* think that Russian communism will have collapsed
61% do *not* think that the manufacture of H-bombs will have ceased
74% do *not* think that civilization will be in ruins

These responses certainly suggest a tolerance for ambiguity that might imply America's passing beyond the wild oscillations in basic mood. Yet the responses of the public to Vietnam, to crises in Africa and the Middle East, to foreign aid, and to dramatic social change in general suggest the rise of a crisis mentality. Linked to this is the growing polarization of the public into various passionate groups demanding sharply different foreign policies, ranging from the embrace of Maoism to its envelopment by the mushroom-shaped cloud, a distinct novelty over the "consensus" that has prevailed since 1945. In short, we cannot take for granted that the withdrawal-commitment cycle in the American mind has been outdistanced by an inevitable acceptance of "world responsibility."

Nor can we take for granted that the next international system will be accepted automatically. A good deal of uncertainty remains. In 1962 a full 83 per cent of the American people believed that it was *very* important to make the UN a success, and another 9 per cent thought it was fairly important.[1] Yet this generous sentiment means very little when we match it with more specific expressions of attitudes. When asked in 1966 whether Communist China should be admitted to the UN, 67 per cent of the sample responded negatively (the lowest percentage giving that answer in the decade during which this question was asked regularly); but when asked whether the United States should "go along" with a UN decision to admit Communist China, 47 per cent answered affirmatively while 41 per cent did not.[2] During the same year, the sample was asked what it thought of the submission of the Vietnam issue to the UN or the ICJ, with the stipulation that the United States accept whatever decision was made; 49 per cent thought this a good idea and 36 per cent did not.[3] But the comparison with opinion in earlier periods also suggests that the public may now be less permissive of

[1] Gallup Poll, Februrary 4, 1962.
[2] Gallup Opinion Index, Report No. 8, January 1966, p. 15. Some roughly comparable figures for 1954 are interesting. When asked whether or not the U.S. should remain in the UN, affirmative answers were given by 72 per cent of the "very satisfied," 58 per cent of the "satisfied," 57 per cent of the qualifiedly "satisfied," 53 per cent of the qualifiedly "dissatisfied," and 45 per cent of the "dissatisfied." Survey Research Center, The University of Michigan, Ann Arbor, Mich., 1954.
[3] Gallup Opinion Index, Report No. 9, February 1966, p. 7. In 1946, 57 per cent did *not* think that the U.S. should have the right to keep out a UN committee to investigate a border dispute with Mexico; but only 44 per cent thought that the U.S. should *not* turn down the substantive recommendations of the committee; 51 per cent thought the United States should not have the right to prevent the use of American troops to stop war in Europe and Asia (presumably if the UN ordered the use of such troops). National Opinion Research Center, The University of Chicago, Chicago, Ill., October, 1946.

automatic and inevitable enmeshment than it was earlier. The growing trend toward internal alienation and dissensus gives a sharply
ideological flavor to the choices involved, thus making the outcome
less predictable. In short, the increasingly postindustrial character
of American society no longer enables us to postulate as eternally
valid the relationship between opinion, elites, and government
sketched in Chapter 3. And so the observer accepts as real the complaints of the critic in forecasting the future setting in which foreign
policy will evolve.

This being the setting, we shall present a scenario involving mass
and elite frustration flowing from overcommitment in the early
multibloc system, attempted withdrawal from the system spurred by
American conservatism, defeat abroad and increasing turmoil at
home, and eventual recommitment with greater violence than that
which erupted during the multipolar period. In the postmultibloc
world, this recommitment, in turn, could lead to a totalitarian America waging ruthless war and establishing a world empire, or a
defeated America accepting the empire of the victorious communists
instead.

As domestic dissent increases, liberals increasingly question the
idea of a national interest that opposes "progressive" forces abroad.
Total "dropping out" from American society becomes both legitimate
and simple. Vietnam drags on, perhaps including even a few in-
conclusive nuclear exchanges with China, stopping short of the ultimate escalation by the mutual fears of the antagonists. New left-
wing revolts break out in Brazil and Venezuela; the United States
intervenes in force on behalf of an authoritarian regime in one case
and in aid of a democratic one in the other. The revolts are aided
by Havana and Peking. China threatens India; and as Pakistan
joins in, warfare breaks out over Kashmir, leading to an American
commitment there, too. None of these conflicts lead to nuclear
escalation, but none are settled, either. In the meantime, and partly
in deference to the domestic New Left, aid to developing nations
is stepped up and greater attention is paid to the Egyptian, Cam-
bodian, and Mali charges of genocide against Negroes in the United
States. Overcommitted militarily, economically, and propagand-
istically, the United States elects as President in 1972 the candidate
of the new Conservative Party. He withdraws troops from abroad,
shuts down bases, neglects alliances, reduces foreign aid, and
threatens to withdraw from the UN unless the genocide charges are
dropped. Mexico then goes communist, all of West Europe turns

neutralist, and Canada asks American business and missile bases to leave the country. Conservative policies of isolation in the United States are discredited by 1980 because they lead to defeat, stigma, and ridicule in the increasingly bellicose and industrializing Third World, spurred on by successful Maoism in China and in Southeast Asia. A coalition shouting "Let's get America going again" unites two American groups: one threatened by constant cybernation and automation; the other, the nationalistic-meritocratic professionals. The coalition also includes liberals sympathizing with the Third World's aspirations and disappointed by the previous eight years of withdrawal from aid to the developing nations. This heterogeneous alliance elects a charismatic Democrat who now proceeds to recommit the United States to world affairs, economic growth, increased trade, and universal respect as the oldest and most successful post-industrial nation. Since he encounters resistance from other countries with a vested interest in American weakness, an arms race ensues, extending to outer space. Soon his nationalism disappoints the Maoist New Left in the United States; policies of repression and control are instituted and increased, especially at the demand of the population groups endangered by continuing technological change. The result is a dual catastrophe: nuclear war abroad and totalitarianism at home.[4]

The world in 1990 might thus be a totalitarian American empire, a radioactive shambles, or a congeries of communist satrapies. The multibloc world with its intolerable demands for accommodation and learning might lead to such an outcome simply because nations—and especially the United States—are incapable of handling the frustrations implied. Is isolationism the answer *now*, instead of awaiting further enmeshment in the multibloc system and further inevitable hard choices? Is bilateralism a better answer, enabling us to jettison the alliances? Should we encourage other people's regionalisms, and pick and choose whom we wish to support where and when? Is an upgraded UN a better choice when we are almost certain of exercising less control over it in the future? Some analysts, conscious of the present drift and doubt of statesmen and

---

[4] In preparing these scenarios I found much stimulation in the papers of F. E. Armbruster and R. D. Gastil in Herman Kahn and Anthony J. Wiener, *The Year 2000* (New York: Macmillan, 1967). For an argument that it is too late for basic choices, see Horst Mendershausen, *Trans-National Society, Sovereignty and Leadership: the Environment of Foreign Policy* (Rand Corporation Report P-3662, August, 1967).

the looming dangers of the multifold trends that are not yet recognized by them, feel that the United States lacks the ability to analyze and choose, to reappraise and adjust to the new system. Perhaps they are right, and the multibloc asymmetric system will engulf us with the inevitability of foreordained history, while we continue, unconcerned, with the same unexamined policies. But even if the outline and basic character of the system are already upon us and beyond available choices, all the possibly catastrophic implications of the system are not. The decay of the current blocs and the continuation of rapid environmental change need *not* imply continued warfare, American controlled counterinsurgency, nuclear blackmail, foreign aid programs with ill-defined objectives, self-defeating approaches to world trade, and unceasing intervention by all in everyone else's domestic politics. If the system is indeed inevitable, we still have the time and the duty to seek to make it bearable for ourselves, to arrange the world so that some of America's interests will prevail without nuclear war and without totalitarianism at home.

### 3. What Is the American National Interest?

Outside the circles of the Extreme Right it is no longer fashionable to attribute unique values and special qualities to the United States, its political style, its way of public and private life. The special qualities sometimes admitted are more often the object of derision than of praise. Yet, there *are* such values, and they demand protection in a world of very rapid and quite unprecedented change. Change may be largely inevitable; but inevitability does not make change desirable by definition; nor should change be subject to the exclusive will of the Third-World modernizers. As long as there is some chance of influencing the rate and pace of change in the interest of creating or preserving something uniquely American, that chance ought to be seized. Its articulation constitutes the essence of my definition of the national interest.

Two admissions must be made at the outset. I do not argue that my definition is truly "national." My own scenario leads me to the conclusion that the future will include little domestic agreement on a joint or common purpose; hence we are talking of "my" definition: an interest that appears both moral and feasible to me. I concede that in many ways we are approaching rapidly the state of a genuine "world society" with many more universally shared aspirations and structural features than there have been at any time in human history. But I contend that these shared features are confined to the artifacts of welfare and modernity; they do not as yet include much common ground on the aims and purposes of private and public life. Matters of personal freedom and choice, temporal or spiritual values, dropping in and dropping out remain very much subject to pronounced and even growing differences. Even though the Third World is committed to energetic modernization, the values underlying these efforts are a far cry from those informing the emerging postindustrial society. Because of the growing value gap, I take a very dim view of visions of world government or of world federation by stages. I prefer to accept and even foster a genuine sharing of objectives as it arises; but I wish to protect and expand the area left for personal choice, common voluntary action, personal initiative, and the dignity of the *individual,* rather than that of racially or socially defined *groups* or manipulated *strata* of people. What is uniquely American at the present time, or Western at any rate, may of course be diffused more generally later. Then I will be ready to reconsider my position. In the meantime, I am preoccupied with using the American nation as the basis for anchoring the values I wish to preserve and extend. My quarrel with successive American Presidents since 1945 is their lack of judgment in indiscriminately seeking to spread the American gospel abroad. Foreign aid and military interventions, collective security and premature decolonization are very blunt instruments for spreading values that, perhaps, are not even desired abroad. Because I am strongly impressed by the limits on foreign policy—in and out of the UN—I advocate a prudential withdrawal from and a selective recommitment to the international system, in the service of the values I hold.

What are these values? In the face of ever more potent governmental and private bureaucracies, soon to be reenforced with the perfection of automated data retrieval, I wish to preserve a large area for individual freedom from manipulation by government, corporation, trade union, political party, social club, suburban clique, and computer. In the face of increasing capacity for control over all forms of life—whether through weapons or drugs—I wish to affirm the need for maximum respect for human life itself. Individual fulfillment and nonviolent modes of regulating large human aggregates take precedence over *any* social or economic doctrine, over *any* form of government, over *any* vision of modernization. Therefore I regard many of the policies followed in the Third World and in communist countries in the early stages of industrialization as reprehensible and inconsistent with the twin objectives I pose. These policies seek to manipulate the individual as he has hardly ever before been manipulated; they all opt for violent means of social control when they are defied by local groups that do not share the policy-makers' vision of the future. Not every form of manipulation can be justified by higher living standards; but since the trend opposing my preferences is very solidly launched, the state of mind of much of the world is running against the aims here described. Hence it behooves the United States to act prudently and consistently, to preserve the autonomy of the area in which freedom from manipulation is still conceivable—though hardly a certainty.

The first duty of American politics is to work toward the perfection of American society itself, to save what is unique and to ward off what is detrimental, whether triggered by domestic or by foreign events. Since the world resembles nothing less than a well-attuned orchestra, American policy should forego the desire to convert, to proselytize directly. We are not able to make the world "safe" for anything without paying a prohibitive price in our own values and institutions. Our duty is to perfect our own society; our foreign policy should seek to (1) enlarge the scope of universally shared values, (2) foster nonviolent means of resolving conflict, and (3) make the preservation of individual freedom abroad the criterion of support, rather than economic or political "development." This commitment requires that the United Nations and regional organizations be given a different emphasis. It also means that drastic changes must be made in certain bilateral policies. But most importantly, it requires a "prudential withdrawal" from the exuberant world mission featured by the Truman, Eisenhower, and Kennedy-Johnson administrations, to be followed immediately by a "selective recommitment" to avoid the dangers implicit in the historical cycle that describes the American foreign policy mood.

My espousal of prudential withdrawal and selective recommitment is governed very heavily by my conclusion that much of American post-1945 policy has been an investment in erroneous liberal analysis, unexamined and uncorrected until the challenge of the Vietnam intervention coupled with the domestic urban and race crisis engulfed us. Claims that the twentieth is "the American century" may be exaggerated, but the essentially American character of the first decade following World War II is a simple fact. Although the hegemony declined after 1955, American influence remained greater than any other nation's. World trends and policies took shape within an active American hegemony based on an articulate ideology of protecting the world from communism, whether that world was actually or only potentially "free." One architect of this policy feels that the New Deal-Great Society generation of policy-makers created the postwar world by building the infrastructure of an armed peace with communism, decolonization, and the beginnings of world industrialization. These leaders, he argues, kept the new barbarism at bay and made it possible to do the rest of the job of refurbishing the world in the image of American material progress. One major obstacle only remains, he says: the Vietnam war must be won, to demonstrate to China the limits on the attempted subversion of the American Dream. What is the new agenda for action after Vietnam? The completion of the various political, military, and economic policies described and criticized in Part II of this study—the ushering in of the multibloc asymmetric system.[5]

Unlike the liberal generation of policy-makers, I do not believe that economic development necessarily fosters democracy and that democracy is necessarily a force for world peace and order. I do not believe that active world trade suffices for economic development, that foreign aid is necessary to keep neutrals neutral and anticommunists firmly on our side. I do not see why and how the network of UN agencies necessarily mirrors or advances the American conception of the good international society. The UN is not the Great Society writ large. I do not understand why it is important to "sell" superficial and self-limiting international resolutions to the UN Afro-Asian majority and then claim to have demonstrated the oneness of UN objectives and American policy. And unlike the liberal, I see no reason to espouse the alleged eternal virtues of national self-determination even if lauded by that same Afro-Asian majority. A policy of generous encouragement and use of the United Nations should not automatically be linked to belief that the American way will inevitably be victorious abroad.

The application of liberal ideology to world politics "worked"

---

[5] W. W. Rostow, "The Great Transition: Tasks of the First and Second Postwar Generations," *Department of State Bulletin* (March 27, 1967), pp. 491-504. For a scathing criticism of this thesis by two aspiring members of the "second generation," see Policy Memorandum No. 33 of the Princeton Center of International Studies, September, 1967.

only in the case of West Europe and Japan, industrial nations in which modernization was well launched before the American presence was generally felt. Further, a substructure of shared values on a wide range of issues already existed in American-European relations. And even in these instances, the ideology merely accomplished economic rejuvenation, continued peaceful modernization, and military alignments against a commonly feared enemy. With the transformation of that enemy, however, a phenomenon perceived differently in Paris and in Washington, even the military and political alliance is headed for decline. It will not do, therefore, to advocate simply more of the same kind of policy. More economic aid will not necessarily advance the community of like-thinking nations; a limited consensus on world health problems is unlikely to influence trade and payment, armaments, or peace-keeping forces. Espousal of the Covenants of Human Rights will not guarantee democracy, shore up world peace, or usher in the rule of law for the whole world. Everyone is in favor of stability—except the nations that produce the turmoil. The President and the Osagyefo agree to the need for world order—each on his own terms. Individual dignity is an objective dear to many politicians, but they differ widely in the institutions chosen to enshrine it. American military and political security measures are not necessarily served by claiming that they also advance the legitimacy and authority of the UN. American prosperity and security needn't be congruent with the encouragement of all types and varieties of regional organization abroad. "The chief purpose for which our foreign policy operates is to develop an international environment in which we can enjoy our prosperity and cultivate our internal societal values without excessive disturbance or threat from the outside. . . . The international posture that results from this goal is one of discouraging rather than fomenting or encouraging violent changes by war, revolution or other dislocation or upheaval." [6] Yet we pretend also to be revolutionaries; we ought to make plain that humane progress takes precedence over the unthinking demand for change, even if we do fly in the face of evolving opinion in the developing nations. And most of all, we should observe in our own policy the prudence and rectitude that are implied by a respect for individual freedom and nonviolence and cease speaking of "liberating" this country or "reversing a revolution" in that one.

We are almost certain that the multifold trend of quasi-involun-

[6] Bloomfield, *United Nations and U.S. Foreign Policy, op. cit.,* p. 30.

tary technological, urban, scientific, industrial, and economic change will go on. One of the most dangerous liberal illusions, therefore is the conviction that improved education for pre-industrial groups and peoples and modest increases in living standards will produce social contentment, political stability, and world peace. The opposite is likely to be the case. Improved education unaccompanied by higher-status jobs will breed frustration and resentment. When Telstar enables the remote hamlets of Chad, Bolivia, and Bhutan to compare their slightly rising standards of living with the steeply ascending consumption in postindustrial nations, the contrast will not produce contentment.

It seems overwhelmingly clear to me that the cycles of development in Europe, the Soviet orbit, the Third World, and the United States will *not* coincide or overlap to any appreciable extent. The multifold trend will strike different societies very differently, turning the already industrialized nations increasingly inward, but the developing countries to the world scene and against each other. As the more developed nations increasingly acquire the ability to solve some internal social problems—while experiencing new ones—the late developing nations will have a far different experience. Coming decades hold the promise of increasing unrest, discontent, demands that cannot be easily met, and further cumulative change that tends to add new explosive charges to those already triggered. It is the height of folly to suppose that the economic, military, and cultural policies of even the strongest nation can hope to bend, shape, and form these forces to conform with American values of what is just and desirable. The development programs presently favored by American and United Nations initiatives tend to increase unbalance, disharmony, and internal unrest; they are more likely to produce the fuel for new wars and revolutions than result in a universal pursuit of welfare and progress based on democratic participation, and thus incidentally produce world peace.

These illusions exposed, we must examine the details of a policy of prudential withdrawal and selective recommitment. Our objective is to help build the kind of peaceful world in which our values will be accepted—but not to destroy the world or ourselves in the process. Our objective is the building of a world community based on what truly is able to unite men: the dedication to shared hopes for the future and the exclusion of commonly recognized dangers, whether military, technological, or demographic. The strategy underlying the prudential withdrawal and the selective recommitment, then, is to bend the facets of the multifold trend and to exploit the properties of the multibloc system so that we perfect American society *and* strengthen the global foundations of an eventual world community. This, however, demands that we turn our attention to the concrete jobs of bilateral and multilateral policy, jobs that recognize shared hopes and fears.

Our alternatives are few. To continue with the present policy of unthinking commitment and enmeshment will exacerbate the destructive implications of the multifold trend and the disintegration of American society. To abandon bilateral elements in our policy and deliberately to commit all our resources to a UN-centered approach would be to surrender to many world forces whose interests are diametrically opposed to the values that make up the national interest. A frank confrontation of the moderately satisfied West and the stridently discontented Third World illustrates clearly the deep clash of values at the world level. The opposite alternative suggests the abandonment of the UN and the reinvestment of our energies and resources in regional organizations faithful to our objectives. The difficulty with this choice is that there are no such organizations, nor will there be any in the foreseeable future, and this frank policy of Balkanization would be a hindrance to the attainment of the nonviolent world to which we attach overriding importance. Richard Gardner is clearly correct in urging that "both supporters and critics of the UN should avoid an either/or philosophy." [7] But he compounds the errors of our present course in blandly assuring us that

> We have many important institutions for the promotion of our
> national interest. We have the Strategic Air Command. We have
> Polaris submarines. We have NATO. We have the OECD. We
> have the Alliance for Progress. We have the Peace Corps. We have
> programs of foreign aid, technical assistance, and cultural exchange.
> We have the OAS. We have the UN. There is no inconsistency
> in our use of all these and other instruments of national policy.[8]

Separate programs do not add up to a finely orchestrated ode to the national interest when each exacerbates a different strand in the multifold trend of change. Nor is much help offered in vapid sermons by an outspoken critic of American policy who claims that

[7] Gardner, *In Pursuit of World Order, op. cit.,* p. 41.
[8] *Ibid.*

the answer lies in dismantling national sovereignty.[9] Nationalism and its clashing values cannot be banished by having the United States tell the rest of the world, which still cherishes its national myths, that all men are really brothers.

To head off some of the dangers to our values and yet come to terms with the multibloc system, we must practice a prudential withdrawal from *both* regional and universal organizations and in addition cut back unilateral and bilateral policies. Then, after stocktaking and an examination of the national conscience, we must selectively recommit *both* at the regional *and* the universal level. Simply to list dangers to peace—nuclear proliferation, intervention, violations of human rights, and the imbalance between real and voting power in the UN—and to expect the present policy of the United States to deal with them is to rely on the automatic forces of transformation in the present system and to assure the victory of the destabilizing forces implicit in the next. Surely *homo sapiens americanus* is still sufficiently sapient not to resign himself to the blind forces of this fate.

[9] J. William Fulbright, *Old Myths and New Realities, op. cit.,* pp. 140, 146-47.

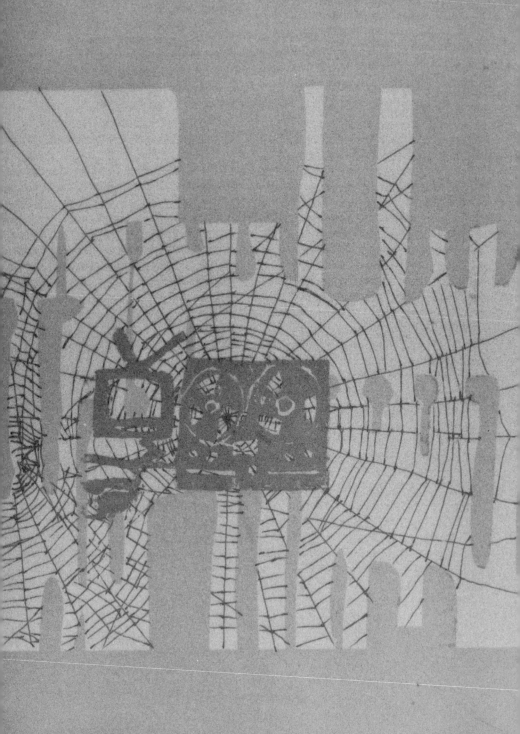

CHAPTER ELEVEN

# THE WEB OF ISSUES

It may be morally reassuring to assert our dual imperative: to minimize American involvement in violence and to assure mankind's physical and spiritual welfare, with minimum stress and strain on established ways. It is quite another thing, however, to translate this maxim into concrete policy issues that characterize the web of interdependence. The preference for nonviolence may clash with the commitment to progressive welfare. The attainment of higher living standards often collides with the enjoyment of human rights—particularly when people and nations clash over the distribution of welfare benefits while the contestants are exercising their rights to speak, vote, demonstrate, and organize.

We slipped into the strands of the multibloc asymmetric system as the unwitting heirs of the policies we had ourselves fashioned and advocated during the preceding period. These policies have included measures designed both to increase and contain the international level of arms. The resultant setting is one in which the chances for general war are low, but the likelihood for limited conflict remain very high, with the further considerable possibility of escalation by miscalculation or error in judgment. Our policies also featured unilateral or collective intervention in the civil wars of emerging nations when we feared for the survival of indigenous leaders opposed to communism, but we showed little consistent concern for the ability of our protégés to assure physical and spiritual welfare in their nations. Hence we sometimes found ourselves in this situation:

> Foreign policy is the delta formed over time by a multitude of seemingly minor decisions governed by national predilections, political discretion and personal caution. One day men find themselves trapped in the alluvial mud of their past. As long as the United States seeks to vindicate its own social and political priorities by the undiscriminating suppression of alternative cultural enterprises, we may in the act of extricating ourselves from the ooze of any given instance say with some confidence that we will return.[1]

We must now extricate ourselves from issues that will be traps during the multibloc era; but we cannot, with confidence, say that the extrication will be complete. It has been estimated that today the politically "active" segment of the world population amounts to 3 per cent, whereas the number in 1915 was 0.5 per cent. The relatively and absolutely much larger elite today is the beneficiary (or victim) of almost instantaneous world communications, shrinking travel time, and exposure to increasingly shared norms and symbols. At the elite levels, at any rate, people are growing more alike all the time in their images and beliefs. Yet this trend does not necessarily foster peace, relaxation of tensions, or world brotherhood. Nations are being fragmented *internally* more rapidly than in the past decades; they become harder to govern as the multifold trend gathers momentum. "Anxiety, disappointment and frustration often breed resentment and an aggressive mood and cast of mind. It is with such a cast of mind that many elite members—and indeed large sections of the population of some countries—are turning to the old

---

[1] Tom J. Farer, "The Enemy: Exploring the Sources of a Foreign Policy." Reprinted from The Columbia University *Forum* (Spring, 1967), 10, No. 1, p. 17. Copyright 1967 by the Trustees of Columbia University in the City of New York.

images of conflict. . . . Some of them will select images that lead to war. Others are retaining or adopting images that may lead to actions that may promote peace."[2] Science, trade, technology, the media and the creation of sets of converging elite attitudes across national boundaries all imply *more* interdependence; yet they do not spell increasing responsiveness at the same time. The issues must then be analyzed in a fragmented, multilayered, and asymmetric setting of demands and responses. If indefinite entanglement is to be avoided, there must be respect for the reality of interdependence.

## 1. The Issues: Withdraw from Where? Recommit to What?

Most Americans cherish thoughts of a world that is a global federal republic of like-minded, moderate, sober nations, each intent only on peacefully perfecting its own society, more or less along the model of a Western nation. The first step we must take is to discard that image. Among nations—internally and externally—there is little consensus on specific values. The human rights cherished in one country constitute the basis of treason in another; a war that appears wholly just to one is an abomination to another; a trading system that seems right and natural to the wealthy is considered exploitive and neocolonial by the poor. The dual moral imperative must be realized in a world ruled by dissensus, weak law, grossly dissimilar institutions within nations, and weak structures among and above them. The challenge facing us is to make the dual imperative prevail in our consciousness *despite* our fragmented world, *despite* and *because of* the limits on the power of any nation, even the United States. The acceptance of the imperative means that we must settle for less than Utopia in the middle run, in the hope that we can still build the infrastructure for a livable world when the multibloc system will have run its course.

Hence we must affirm that "communism" is not the enemy to be faced by the United States everywhere and at all times. No specific foreign regime or ideology is the enemy. No single problem is the enemy. No defined policy is the enemy. Violence and the manipula-

---

[2] Karl W. Deutsch, "Changing Images of International Conflict," *Journal of Social Issues*, XXIII, No. 1, p. 105.

tion of man by man *are* the enemies. Yet there is no blinking the simple fact that the world is made up of an increasing number of nations and groupings of nations that are divided by many basic conflicts. To intervene in each tension spot that offends our values is to engage in violence most of the time. Intervention in the service of man's dignity and freedom from manipulation makes sense only if the price of the intervention is less, in terms of violence and death, than the harm being done abroad; it makes sense only if there is evidence that the bulk of the victimized population welcomes an American, Western, or United Nations presence. To act otherwise is to stumble into the quagmire of mindless imperialism, to become the neocolonialists that the Chinese Communists accuse us of being.

These should be our guidelines in deciding when and where to permit the web of interdependence to enmesh us. We ought to discourage the use of violence, but we should support resistance to manipulation while we look after man's welfare—always weighing whether our intervention does more harm than good. We should foster institutions and build up policies that create shared concern for these things. We have the right and the duty to seek to influence other nations to see things our way by example, by persuasion, and by money. We do not have the right to force them to see the world as we do. If the web of interdependence in international organizations results in ever-growing ripples of shared consciousness, of common concern, of problems and values defined in more and more similar ways, so much the better. But then we shall achieve this cooperative welfare world by example, by natural growth, and not by violence or manipulation on our part.

### a. Democracy, Intervention, and Peace

Do we not then have the right or the duty to defend democracy abroad? What if the violence of a communist or fascist regime threatens a society professing the same values we cherish, governed by institutions like our own? In this situation we should come to the assistance of democratic regimes requesting our aid. Even though we do not and cannot expect Western democracy to become the predominant way of world life, we certainly need not tolerate its destruction where it does exist. And though we should not foster democracy by violence abroad, we should protect it more energetically where it does exist. This would mean that we would *refrain from unilateral* intervention when two Latin-American oligarchical or authoritarian regimes collide or when a Southeast Asian communist regime challenges an authoritarian one. It means that we may consider cautious and contingent *collective* intervention in such instances, to limit international violence. But it also means that we must be ready to defend the institutions and territorial integrity of democracies everywhere, not only in Europe and Australasia. And this doctrine, finally, implies that *whenever larger and indiscriminate violence is not a risk*, we should aid truly democratic insurgent movements in their attacks on totalitarian and authoritarian regimes. Wider violence was a threat in Poland and Hungary in 1956; it might not be in Czechoslovakia in 1970.

Alliances with other democracies are desirable when there is a demonstrable threat to them from nondemocratic nations; during the multibloc system there is unlikely to be one. But alliances with weak and new nations, most of them indifferent to democracy in the Western sense and unlikely to cement its institutions, are not desirable. Such ties make the non-Western alliance partner overdependent on military structures and supplies, which often detract from energies being devoted exclusively to domestic welfare. The United States concerns itself intimately with the domestic affairs of such nations, a process which cascades into an ever-growing sense of involvement justifying additional expansion of military ties in order to protect the initial position staked out. Reversing such a trend is a most complicated business in the decision-making process of America's imperfect pluralism.

This implies a much more consistently selective and cautious approach to the issue of insurgency and counterinsurgency than is presently featured in American policy. Our policy now is certainly selective. It implies "closing an eye to externally caused disruption in the Communist world and in non-Communist regimes we do not favor, while insisting on the principle of nonintervention in areas chosen as targets by Communists and other forces as well as in countries with undemocratic regimes with which we find it convenient to deal." [3] To avoid this much "pragmatism" clearly calls for a withdrawal from many types of operations assumed by the Central Intelligence Agency and for restraint in UN forums in castigating other nations' interventions simply when they may be directed against any ally.

We should live in peace—though not necessarily in close friend-

---

[3] Bloomfield, *United Nations and U.S. Foreign Policy,* op. cit., p. 88.

ship—with all established governments, whether or not we approve of their values and institutions. We should attack none. Neither should we defend a nondemocratic regime when its legitimacy in the eyes of its own citizens is thrown into doubt by large-scale civil unrest. Intervention on behalf of unstable, unpopular, and undirected governments in the Third World is wrong even if such regimes *do* profess to be anticommunist. We should not judge the degree of "goodness" inherent in the styles of oligarchic, totalitarian, and authoritarian governments in the Third World; we should treat them as democracies when they show signs of accepting democratic values and institutions (as in Venezuela, India, and Costa Rica); we should treat all others with nondiscriminating coolness as long as they do not threaten world peace (as in Brazil, Burma, and most of Africa). We should deny all Third World nondemocratic countries military aid, provided we can convince other developed nations to do likewise. But we should provide arms when this seems necessary to support an established but struggling democratic regime (as in the Philippines or Chile, but not in Pakistan or Guatemala).

A judicious withdrawal from present American positions thus seems indicated. Our direct and indirect military presence in Africa, the Middle East, and Southeast Asia should be minimized. Bases should be given up, troops withdrawn, and military aid eliminated. Civil strife should be left alone, with the new nations forced to fight their own internal battles *unless* international peace is threatened in the process. Decolonization should be completed as soon as possible in Africa, even if this implies American support for sanctions against Portugal. But as far as the territorial future of the diminutive slices of land and picturesque islands in the Pacific and the Caribbean is concerned, we should continue to deny the world community any direct role. We should give these peoples the opportunity to join neighboring nations if they wish, or continue in their present status if they prefer. We need not indulge the abuse of the principle of national self-determination indefinitely, especially not in the case of ministates.

The withdrawal from unnecessary alliances with Western democracies and useless alliances with Third World countries, however, must be balanced with other types of American military measures. Pending a comprehensive arms control pact, the bilateral nuclear balance of terror must be retained; conventionally armed striking forces must also be kept in a state of readiness; their deployment abroad must remain possible even in the multibloc system, whether in defense of a democratic nation against external attack or to help

it deal with totalitarian-inspired domestic violence. A selective recommitment to universal collective security procedures also calls
for the maintenance of such striking forces.

## b. Peace and Collective Security

The comprehensive principle of collec-
tive security written into the UN Charter has failed to withstand
the tide of systemic evolution as member states have refused to
live by the rules they wrote in 1945. Nor can we realistically expect
a sudden reconversion to that principle in the multibloc system. We
can, however, seek to have as much collective security as possible
in the current division of the world and the clustering of rival values.
Selective recommitment for American policy, therefore, should be
governed by the maxim of splitting up big conflicts into many little
ones, in hope of more effectively defusing violence, of dealing with
economic and social issues by appropriate means and separating
them from military and territorial ambitions. To "fractionate conflict" rather than subsume it under some comprehensive legal
formula should be the central aim. Hence the approach would be
applied to various types of conflicts, roughly classified in the following paragraphs.

The UN is not capable of deterring or intervening in a general
thermonuclear war between the major powers. At best, the powers
may wish to make use of the UN to aid in stopping such a confrontation or in defining issues in a way that will limit recourse to
thermonuclear war. This was in fact done in the Cuban Missile
Crisis and in past crises over Berlin. We should enable the UN to
continue doing this, but we should not expect more.

The UN has been used successfully by the United States—in
Korea—for countering and defeating a limited war launched by the
communists. This use enmeshes the United States in the UN, because it mobilizes many kinds of restraints on American preferences
concerning the kind of political settlement such wars entail. In view
of the fact that the United States no longer commands a two-thirds
majority in the General Assembly, this practice is dangerous unless
we are faced with an unusually clear-cut case of unprovoked aggression. It is better not to count on using the UN in such situations,
unless the aggression is indeed flagrant. The UN should continue
to be used as a peacekeeper in conflicts among small nations, par-

ticularly in the Third World where the bulk of the conflicts that can be "fractionated" originate. It should be the primordial task of the UN—and of our policy in it—to keep conflict localized. But the United States must reserve its right *not* to contribute financially and *not* to give its consent otherwise if it feels that a particular peacekeeping operation runs counter to the dual imperative that ought to guide our policy.

Regional organizations should be used increasingly, not as anti-communist alliances but as agents of peaceful settlement and negotiation within Africa, the Middle East, Southeast Asia, and Latin America. In fact, UN-sanctioned regional organizations may contain the key to the limitation of aggression in these parts of the Third World. Neutralization and guarantees for the maintenance of neutrality appear central. American support for peacekeeping forces mounted to enforce regional neutralization pacts should be obligatory.

Recent American policy toward disarmament and arms control issues has begun to reflect a recognition of escalating and uncontrollable danger. Indeed, the United States took the initiative in demonstrating to the Soviets the economic and human implications of existing overkill capacity and argued that it was unnecessary for the preservation of the nuclear balance of terror. We should continue to seek fields in which arms control measures can be inaugurated: the sea bottom, for example, and the elimination of underground nuclear weapons tests. We should take most seriously the Soviet proposals to prohibit flights of bombers carrying nuclear weapons beyond national borders and the idea that navigational zones for nuclear-armed submarines should be limited. Along with this we should intensify the ongoing discussions on cutting back nuclear stockpiles and refraining from building ABM systems. Most particularly, these discussions should not be undercut by simultaneous American policies of building small ABM systems and space weapons. Only thus can we approximate the promises made when the Nuclear Non-Proliferation Treaty was negotiated: continue progress toward more general disarmament and devote more resources to world economic development by supporting the peaceful application of nuclear energy in the Third World.

The Non-Proliferation Treaty also highlights some less obvious policy issues. The non-nuclear nations foregoing the acquisition of nuclear weapons were given some assurance of protection by the Security Council's resolution empowering the nuclear powers to extend their umbrella over a nation threatened with nuclear blackmail. It remains unclear whether this guarantee, legitimated by the

Charter's authorization of unilateral self-defense measures, creates a nuclear hegemony of the two superpowers or whether, instead, it compels these powers to seek the support of smaller nations through bargaining and special coalition-building. In all likelihood, a *de facto* hegemony will be recognized only if the superpowers make collateral concessions to restive smaller nations able to denounce the treaty at any time and resume their work on nuclear weapons.

Which is the most desirable policy for the United States: to work toward nuclear hegemony with the Soviet Union or to share control with the smaller nations? It is better to be realistic and to recognize that only the two superpowers possess both the lethal capacity and the chilling diplomatic experience to deal with the issue of brandishing these weapons with restraint. Regrettable as the situation may be, the genie is out of the lamp and refuses to go back in; our task should be to make certain that he does not fly too far, to spread his favors. In holding the nuclear guarantee umbrella over third countries, the United States should not seek to share control with anyone except other nuclear powers; but we shall have to pay *quid pro quo*. In order to be able to retain bilateral control, we must make speedy progress in other fields of arms control and step up greatly the internationally controlled application of science to economic development, thus once more upgrading the powers of the UN in other areas.

### c. Trade Policy

But the implementation of our double imperative demands more than a military and territorial security policy: it calls for an approach to trade and aid that is different from the hit-and-miss procedure we have favored since the mid-Fifties. Our objective must be to advance economic modernization of the Third World in a way that will minimize disruption of society, keep frustrations at a low level, and restrain the propensity of leaders and revolutionary political parties to bully and manipulate their citizens. Our objective therefore must be redistributive, must be the gradual reduction of the tension between North and South. Clearly, this conception of our national interest does not deny that the United States and the industrial world also have legitimate economic objectives of their own. The task, therefore, is the reconciliation of the redistributive aim with the protection of living standards in the West. It can be carried out only if aid and trade policies are considered jointly, as part of a single package, rather than as separate and competing strands in the web of economic interdependence.

Decolonization may very well prove to have been a cruel hoax on the developing nations. As they become independent, direct responsibility of the industrial nations for their welfare has declined, because independence included the right and competence to plan and execute national economic development. But at the same time as the revolution of rising expectations triggers demands for higher production and greater consumption, the technological-scientific aspect of the multifold trend constantly increases efficiency of the rich nations, their trade with each other, and their autonomy from the primary exports of the developing nations. Far from being exploited by the rich, the poor are simply becoming irrelevant to them.

> The exploited could always strike against those who were making a profit on them; what recourse is there for the unexploitable, locked out of the market by the shift of prices? I can only predict the intensification of resentment, the evolution of new ideologies to express this resentment. Since by the very nature of their situation the independent poor cannot strike militarily at the rich, they may show resentment by striking at one another. . . .[4]

Trade and aid policy, then, must overcome the isolation of irrelevance, in order to satisfy rising expectations without triggering the wholesale destruction of nonindustrial values and institutions. This victory, however, is dependent upon the West's acceptance of a doctrine of redistribution in which indefinite growth of productivity is unnecessary, even dysfunctional. The West must be willing to forego the introduction of synthetic materials and automated production, to decline to make use of innovations just because they are available and cheaper.

American and European industry, and Japan's as well, must learn to subordinate their production and export policies to the needs of the developing nations. American and European industry can absorb losses when Indian and Chilean industry cannot. The first duty of the wealthy nations must be to protect and expand the prices and volume of the exports offered by the developing nations. Only thus

[4] Nathan Keyfitz, "National Populations and the Technological Watershed," *Journal of Social Issues* (January, 1967), p. 76.

can the poorer nations build up their own capital for industrialization. Only thus can trade take the place of aid that might well stifle indigenous adaptation and entrepreneurship. Hence, using some foreign aid funds to help adjust American producers who are adversely affected by the mass importation of textiles, shoes, and processed food from the poor nations makes more sense than investing that aid in stemming hunger or starting unproductive heavy industries. The demand for tariff preferences favoring the Third World should be heard with sympathy; claims for protecting commodity markets—in terms of price stability and market shares—should be examined equally sympathetically, provided only that protection is combined with powerful incentives to the exporting nations to diversify their supplies. Still this is not enough. Unless the industrial nations also learn to forego the application of technological breakthroughs, these measures will not suffice to create capital and entrepreneurship—public and private—in the developing nations. The deliberate and rational building up of the Third World's trade with the wealthy nations also demands a willingness on the part of the rich to curb their propensity to innovate, produce, and consume.

Such an attitude, however, also calls for certain devices to protect the industrial nations from the possibility that a united Third World will blackmail individual developed countries. In addition, certain Western nations may be able to derive undue advantage at the expense of others unless care is taken to avoid this. Hence concessions to the Third World and self-restraint in the West must be determined jointly: UNCTAD should become the forum for making trade rules, but OECD should be greatly upgraded to become the institutionalized Western caucus within UNCTAD. Nor is this enough. The recommitment pattern suggested here calls for a much more effective world monetary and payments system than we now have. In order that trade and aid can be linked more efficiently, a true global central banking system is needed, with authority over monetary problems going beyond the protection of the members' balances of payments.

### d. Aid Policy

If we stress policies of economic development that proceed at less than breakneck speed and that seek to preserve as well as to modernize, a number of the misconceptions and disappointments that have grown up with the practices of foreign aid can be laid to rest. Does foreign aid foster the evolution of democracy in the Third World? Americans are led to think so by their government. The answer is as murky, conceptually, as the evidence is dubious, factually. When is democracy expected to set in? During the process of development, or after a plateau of productivity and consumption has been reached? As the industrial infrastructure is built, or some time after the education, skills, new managerial and administrative groups have become dominant? The theory of foreign aid employed by the American government is mute on the subject. The facts suggest that *less* democracy is in evidence as development is accelerated, *perhaps* to lead to something more benign much later in the process—perhaps. We know only that aid—military and economic—is necessary to shore up the independence of new nations, and independence is a prerequisite to democracy. But we are not entitled to argue, though successive American aid agencies have done so, that somehow aid is systematically related to democratization in the Third World.[5]

Foreign economic aid, therefore, had best be liberated from all considerations other than to spur production and consumption as effectively as possible without victimizing the premodern peoples by massively destructive innovative policies, as in China. Donor and recipient alike must forego the desire to use aid for short-run political, military, or propagandistic purposes. Donor and recipient alike must consider as the *only* goal the most painless and least upsetting methods of increasing production and consumption. This requires the kind of central coordination of funds, approaches, and techniques that are best taken from sovereign states and vested in an agency that enjoys the confidence of donors and recipients and is capable of achieving some detachment from short-run politics. In brief, foreign aid should be almost entirely multilateralized. It should also be liberalized by freeing the recipient from the donor's special restrictions on how funds should be spent. Donors and recipients could then engage in a permanent dialogue about the purpose and the direction of aid, thus giving the recipients the opportunity to appreciate the longer-range and nonpolitical implications of the choices confronting them. A greatly centralized UN Development Program is necessary. Our approach thus implies a sagacious withdrawal from helter-skelter, unplanned trade and aid—bilateral

[5] For a systematic discussion of this issue see Charles Wolf, Jr., *United States Policy and the Third World* (Boston: Little, Brown, 1967), chapters 2, 5, and 6.

and multilateral—funneled through competing and uncoordinated agencies bereft of a common purpose; and it calls for a selective recommitment to a differently arranged set of international agencies.

### e. Human Rights and
### Self-Determination

Our policy in the area of human rights and national self-determination should be one of partial withdrawal. Absolute national self-determination is a deceptive cliché: independence solves few real problems and tends to create new frustrations for small, underdeveloped, and isolated nations. New nations find their independence almost immediately negated when trade and employment continue to be dependent on more powerful or developed neighbors. To fetishize absolute national self-determination as a primordial right is to create hardship for nations and the international society, thereby re-enacting some of the tragedies of the earlier part of the twentieth century. The United States should not join in enshrining self-determination even if it can do little to discourage the faith of others.

Nor should the United States indiscriminately encourage or join in active human rights programs in the United Nations. Withdrawal is advocated *not* because human rights are undeserving of protection but because in the multibloc system their protection will be hit-or-miss, subject to propagandistic charges and countercharges. A true consensus of the kind that appeals to our values is most unlikely to develop. On the contrary, the stringent needs of developing nations will create more indifference to the substance of individual rights and increasingly cynical use of the existing international machinery. Desirable though it would be to use international pressure to spread the gospel of human rights as understood in the West, the world aura for such a crusade is as unpromising as our lead is suspect. It would be better to abandon the game for the moment, rather than cheapen the ultimate values to be protected. Before we can match the deed to the word we must put our house in order, not preach to Pakistan, Ecuador, and Poland. Selective recommitment is recommended only in instances of rights in which we have an active interest and which can be dealt with outside the propaganda limelight, rights that stress *man, the individual* as resisting the manipulative power of the state, the party, the corporation, the media, the hidden and public persuader who shouts loudly or burrows subliminally.

Human rights programs, therefore, should stress seminars and technical assistance for those who genuinely want to improve human rights. We should distinguish between very general rights—such as those defined in the two Covenants—and more specific rights, dear to already organized private groups eager and able to seek help from international agencies. These specific rights include freedom of association, collective bargaining, and the instrumental rights associated therewith, such as the right to assemble. By identifying with such rights, the United States can actively support the growth of human groups that are relatively free from state manipulation. But the nuclei of such groups must already exist, to make this approach feasible. A specific right that should be stressed far more than it has been stressed in the past is the right to privacy. Here, too, support can be garnered from existing groups of lawyers, trade unionists, and businessmen dependent on privacy for the exercise of other rights. The United States should initiate an energetic UN program for privacy, and the program should include conventions and supervisory machinery.

Education, both basic and advanced, should be downgraded as a social development activity until mobilization "plans" for specific underdeveloped countries can give us insight into the need for the appropriate number and kind of skilled people at various points in time. American enthusiasm for crash programs of basic education result from a misplaced optimism in "knowledge" as a harbinger of political stability and democratic progress. Programs of human betterment involving the organization, staffing, and financing of widespread social services in developing nations should also be subordinated to comprehensive mobilization planning. But we should continue to support *ad hoc* programs of refugee relief, resettlement, and narcotics control.

## f. Science, Technology, and Planning

No withdrawal is possible from the realm of science and technology. Here, immediate and passionate commitment is required to sensitize the world to the implications of the multifold trend, commitment that goes far beyond the application of technology to more rapid economic development. We must awaken mankind to the truth that technology is not always benign, that science is not necessarily the guarantor of progress. We must accustom the world to think in terms of plotting the various, diverse, and mutually opposing trends of evolution in various fields. We must train the world to think in terms of possible consequences and to weigh whether these are acceptable if man is to determine his pace of adjustment to technology, rather than technology cutting man to its measure. But withdrawal is to be preferred when, as in UNESCO, we participate in an organization whose programs do not clearly dovetail with ours simply in order not to leave the field to the communists.

Much more energetic recommitment is required in the general area of "planning," in order to make a success of nonviolent and gradual human betterment in the Third World and in order to keep us from being victimized by the implications of the multifold trend. Planning is the key to rationalized and more effective aid and trade policies; it is equally crucial to the harnessing of science to development and to the preservation of individuality and free choice in industrial society. Indirectly it even influences peacekeeping, because of the possibility that the number and intensity of conflicts may decline if economic and social development are approached more rationally than by the tripolar and multipolar systems.

Not all programs now being "planned for" in various UN agencies are deserving of American support. Some that contribute to a continuation of the helter-skelter approach should be discouraged, such as social planning that proceeds independently of economic planning. On the other hand, human values—such as free choice, privacy, autonomy, the ability to understand and harness abstract forces, the proper balance between the public good and private rights, or the legitimacy of traditional values rejecting these modern notions—should be included and stressed in all planning much more than they are now. Technical feasibility is only one—and a very subordinate—aspect of rational planning.

## 2. The Issues: The Government's View

Does American policy in practice adhere to this—or any—consistent line? No. *Pragmatism* and *flexibility* are the universal official clichés that describe our policy.

Far from following a principle of concerted and restrained use of regional security organizations geared to the UN, we follow no principle at all. Our approach is "pragmatic": we seek to use the UN purely expedientially for the maintenance of peace. Disputes concerning the United States directly, especially when they occur in the Western Hemisphere, are kept out of the UN if possible; they are usually given to the OAS in the hope that a settlement favoring an anticommunist solution may be more readily attained there. Confrontations with the Soviet Union are submitted to the UN only when this appears to be a useful way to reduce tensions and facilitate a settlement that was unattainable by more direct means. Like other nations, we submit cases to the UN and to regional organizations only if we feel that they will be solved to our advantage in these forums. In other cases, we follow our own counsel. During periods of reliance on the UN, NATO, or the OAS, we therefore attempt to strengthen these organizations; but during periods of unilateral dominance, we neglect them, go our own way, and expect our allies to follow. When we advocate general principles of UN predominance, as in the crisis over obligatory payments for peace-keeping operations, the world never knows whether we mean to adhere to our principle when the immediate need for the UN has passed. American policy here, it must be stressed, is no different from that of all other major, and many lesser, powers: Russia, France, India, Britain, Egypt, Israel, Mexico, Pakistan, Indonesia, and many others have used regional and universal organizations just as "pragmatically," and some much more so.

Because American policy-makers have preferred this pragmatic approach, no "grand design" for Atlantic union, Pacific security, or global peacekeeping has ever grown beyond the rhetorical stage. And this approach has been justified, over the years, by the need for a "flexible response" to communist probes and unrest in the Third World, likely to be exploited by the communist bloc. With the waning of the Cold War in the consciousness of some American policy-makers, there is also some evidence of a reconsideration of this hit-or-miss approach to collective security. If the North–South conflict is taking precedence over the East–West confrontation, there is some point in thinking of a loose "northern" bloc—a united West Europe, the Soviet bloc, and the United States—dedicated to economic improvement and the protection of the dignity of the individual. Such a bloc of blocs could also use the UN for the maintenance of peace among regions, to preserve a regional balance, without having to intervene in every future nationalist revolt. On the other hand, voices in the Department of State have also been heard advocating the use of NATO as a collective negotiating device to continue the process of all-European *rapprochement*, thus preventing the confusion and competition that might result from separate French, German, British, or American dealings with the Warsaw Pact nations. NATO has also been described as a device for coordinating aid to the Third World, to help unite West Europe, and to facilitate "partnership" between a United Europe and the United States. Still, the same voices also and simultaneously advocate the military strengthening of the alliance and the need for Soviet–American negotiations *à deux!* [6]

Pragmatism also characterizes trade and aid policy. Foreign aid is meant to serve political as well as·economic purposes. It is supposed to make the world safe from the communist threat by demonstrating how life can be better without totalitarian solutions; but it is also supposed to demonstrate the virtues of democracy, even though the recipients of the aid are variegated oligarchies and authoritarian polities; and aid is to be given *without* telling the receiving nation how to run its internal affairs. Both economic and political development are objectives, but nobody knows how these two aims are related. Foreign aid is given to help certain American exporting industries dependent on foreign markets, and it is expected to support the military postures of American allies in Latin America and Asia. Finally, we expect our aid to pre-empt other approaches to economic development, particularly the Third World's reliance on heavy contributions from the Soviet Union and China, contributions that are expected to pull the recipients into the communist orbit (though why this should be so is not always clear). And while we certainly rely on UN agencies to make available some of the more "nonpolitical" aid, we prefer to keep the lion's share under our own control. Thus we blandly assume that multibillion-dollar programs of the UN Development Decade, involving all of the UN specialized agencies and commissions, somehow contribute to making a wealthier and hence a more peaceful world. We rarely stop to wonder whether American policy is not likely to increase expectations and hopes—as through UNESCO's programs—faster than they can be satisfied by aid programs, thus exacerbating frustration and unrest instead of promoting peace.

The all-purpose notion of "stability" is frequently invoked by

[6] The conviction that the pragmatic approach is good and sufficient to serve the American interest is well expressed in Gardner, *In Pursuit of World Order*, Chap. 3. For thinking in the State Department suggesting the newer approach, see Zbigniev Brzezinski, "The Implications of Change for United States Foreign Policy," *Department of State Bulletin* (July 3, 1967), pp. 19-23; and Eugene V. Rostow, "Concert and Conciliation: The Next Stage of the Atlantic Alliance," *Department of State Bulletin* (October 2, 1967).

American spokesmen as the basic objective of our aid policy. At times, this is taken to mean the ability to develop, free from disturbances such as rural insurrection, strikes, student uprisings, military intervention, and oppressive or exploitative economic policies on the part of traditional elites. At other times, however, *stability* seems to mean "noncommunist," and the need for stability is then used to justify American aid—economic and military—to any local elite considered able to maintain stability, but especially aid to the military. At one time we admit wisely that aid

> should not . . . be thought of simply as a bribe or a carrot or a stick. It is rarely effective when given as a reward or withheld as a punishment. It should not be expected inevitably to procure gratitude—which, incidentally, is hard to define when applied to nations. It should not be expected to produce the same effects in different countries, and it should not be expected to "Americanize" everyone it touches.

But in the next breath the government also asserts that aid

> can and does provide the basic stability necessary for economic growth. It can be and is a deterrent to Communist expansionism. Most importantly, it can often provide the crucial margin of resources and skills needed to bring a nation's economy to the self-sustaining point. It can assist in the development of institutions which make a free society function and grow.[7]

If our trade program were geared to the aid objectives, things might go better. But it is not. Instead of dealing with tariff preferences, commodity prices, and loans in terms designed to stimulate economic development without massive coercion and manipulation of sluggish populations, we treat matters of trade as if an economically rational world division of labor were attainable and good for all. The free trade doctrine still underlies our GATT policy of dramatic and nondiscriminatory tariff cuts, recognizing the demands of the late industrializing countries only in the promise not to seek immediately reciprocal tariff concessions from them. Free trade is held to be in our interest and in that of the industrialized countries of the West; the Third World can be made to benefit equally if

---

[7] Nicholas de B. Katzenbach, "Foreign Aid: An Essential Element of United States Foreign Policy," *Department of State Publication* 8309 (October, 1967), pp. 11-12.

the slight concessions made by GATT's Action Program are faithfully implemented. GATT remains preferable to UNCTAD. While the United States does not openly attack the UNCTAD demands for tariff preferences favoring the Third World and commodity prices protecting the exporters of primary commodities against deterioration in the terms of trade, it certainly is not doing anything dramatic to advance them, either. Trade is designed to benefit the American businessman even if that objective clashes consistently with our desire to help development abroad, thus sacrificing once more to the push of the immediate and ignoring longer-term policy planning.

Nor does our monetary policy further our foreign aid objectives. Short-term balance of payments considerations predominate here. Our monetary policy since 1958 has increasingly stressed tied foreign aid, military orders placed at home, curbs on tourist purchases abroad, limits on private lending, prepayment of debts and artificial stimulants to American exports. All of these steps can be defended on balance of payments grounds; none of them makes sense if we wish to have a coordinated program bettering the lot of the Third World while making minimal sacrifices in our own standard of living.

American leaders are anxious to use the UN to advance human rights everywhere. But they see our advocacy of human rights as part of the Cold War, as a necessary step in unmasking communist and communist-leaning modernization programs in other parts of the world. To build and defend democracy, our argument runs, we must see to it that individual human rights are not submerged in the drive to modernize. To have peace, we must make sure that no totalitarian tyrannies arise. Hence the Administration continues to go along with the drafting of human rights conventions and even advocates the ratification of some by the United States. To the argument that American racial discrimination practices would be highlighted and perhaps punished in the UN, State Department spokesmen have countered that little additional adverse publicity is imaginable: the United States is sitting in the "hot seat" already. It is time that we take the offensive, they urge, and use the human rights machinery to put others in the same position.

Pragmatic uncertainty and the pretense that everything that is done is really for the best also predominate in the field of scientific cooperation. All our contributions to UN scientific and social service agencies are justified not by humanitarianism and generosity but by their being in the national interest of the United States—even though that interest is sometimes no more than the childish wish not to let the Soviet Union get the credit for some program or operation. There is widespread recognition now that the population explosion, if not actively combatted with birth control measures, will undo the UN Development Decade; but as far as we are concerned, that recognition is of recent vintage. We recognize, too, that unlimited and unplanned urbanization the world over may generate frustrations, neuroses, riots, and revolutions; but we still feel that the sum of specialized agency programs somehow is capable of dealing with this threat. Even though UNCAST is likely to intensify the implications of the multifold trend for the Third World, we continue to profess belief in its work. In matters relating to outer space, we believe in international cooperation but not integration of programs; in global, orderly, and noncompetitive communications systems but not in government control over private space enterprise; in the peaceful uses of outer space but not in the prohibition of military experiments and military satellites. We speak of the rights of all to explore in space and of the common benefits which cooperative research will bring; but we also assert the need to maintain American "leadership" in meteorology and in the deployment of communications equipment with military as well as civilian uses. American policy has been so "pragmatic" that it espoused and justified all these items, avoided assigning any management or control responsibility to the UN or to groups of nations, and preferred to keep space "open" to untrammeled national programs.

## 3. The Issues: Elite Preferences

The positions just described are those of the Department of State and of the Executive. How do they compare with the conduct that important elites wish the United States to demonstrate in international organizations? First of all, we ought to note that the UN is taken for granted by American elites today:

> If there are fewer people today who regard the United Nations system with the sentimentality that one might lavish on his favorite charity, there are also fewer people who see in every act of the organization the hand of a dark conspiracy directed at themselves. Americans instead are beginning to accept the United Nations system as a vital working part of international diplomacy—one which

deserves to be taken seriously and to be regarded with professional care.[8]

Still, propositions concerning "the American elite" should be put into the proper context. We have in mind a cross section of people who are interested in, concerned and informed about American policy in international organizations, people who at the same time occupy positions of influence and high prestige in the major American interest groups. Such people include representatives of both major parties and independents; however, spokesmen for radical dissenting groups on the right and left are not included, because they do not normally occupy positions of influence and prestige. Further, such a cross section tends to hide much reserve or dissent concerning specific policies, but it comes to the fore in discussions and activities of interest groups focusing on very specific issues: immigration of Mexican farm labor, cotton imports from Japan, investment in business machines in Europe, for instance. Our summary makes no effort to include these specific arguments and demands. It abstracts the generally agreed upon propositions.[9]

Thus there is no question that the UN is accepted as the prime and legitimate organ for inducing nations to settle their disputes peacefully, to be used by all nations before and even after hostilities are begun. Any method likely to increase the capacity of the UN to achieve peaceful settlements is defended, including the repeal of the Connally Reservation. As for peacekeeping by the UN itself after the failure of peaceful settlement, elite opinion favors energetic institutionalization of UN peace forces, excluding direct big power participation, with greater powers for the Secretary-General and greater logistical support to be given by the United States, including access to American overseas bases. The United States government is urged to follow a consistent policy of financial support to *all* UN peacekeeping operations, not a pragmatic one,

---

[8] L. D. Battle and Harlan Cleveland, "UNESCO and U.S. Policy," *Department of State Bulletin* (November 5, 1962), p. 700.

[9] The following discussion is based primarily on the resolutions adopted by the 1965 White House Conference on International Cooperation, as summarized in Richard N. Gardner, ed., *Blueprint for Peace, op. cit.* The conference also called for the more systematic use of social science and social scientists in advising government officials in conflict resolution. It included several hundred officials of all leading American private organizations in business, labor, agriculture, religion, education, transport and communication, the arts, charitable activity, social planning, all cultural media, and academic life.

and to use foreign aid as a means of strengthening peacekeeping forces to be supplied by small nonaligned nations. Further, at the elite level there was much more willingness than in the Administration to adopt a flexible and nonobligatory method of financing UN peacekeeping, as opposed to the unflinching insistence on binding assessments featured during the Article 19 crisis.

Elites also regard existing regional arrangements and alliances less expediently than does the Administration. They prefer to subordinate the use of these organizations to the primacy of the Security Council, and they note that the major regional organizations are far from reliable, cohesive, or linked to American objectives. Commitments and recommendations far in excess of official policy are also evident in the disarmament field. Regional nonproliferation pacts to bar nuclear weapons from Africa and Latin America are strongly advocated. NATO not only should be used to prevent proliferation in Europe but might be "disarmed" by having it conclude a nonaggression agreement with the Warsaw Treaty Organization. While restricted arms control arrangements of this type would continue, the search for general and comprehensive disarmament would go on as well, culminating in the creation of the special UN Disarmament Organization proposed by the United States some years ago. Moreover, these elites strongly favor the inclusion of Communist China in all these efforts.

American elites show no lack of enthusiasm for much more energetic measures fostering economic development—provided only that private enterprise, private investors, private educational centers, and private service agencies are given a much greater role than they have now. The target of an annual aid contribution rising to 1 per cent of the gross national product is commonly accepted; five-year disbursement authorizations are favored, to be given by Congress to the President. Elites feel that military aid should be separated from economic aid; technical aid should include measures to stabilize populations and feed them better; investment guarantees should be worked out by the UN to protect private enterprise against political risks; all UN development agencies should be improved in terms of staff, personnel, coordination, and the participation of private groups; local managerial skills should be improved through all kinds of internship programs as well as joint private and governmental financial participation. Finally, a general increase in the multilateral share of American aid contributions is advocated.

On the trade and finance side, elites express satisfaction with the existing monetary system, provided the world's nations exercise more internal discipline. Regional development banks should be supported even more strongly, the International Development Association must be enlarged and strengthened, and the IBRD is favored as the central coordinating mechanism for all development aid. While American elites generally favor the ideal of maximal free trade and a gobal division of labor, they are far from doctrinaire about this; special concessions to satisfy the UNCTAD program are also endorsed and put forth in terms that surpass actual American policy in conciliating the Third World. Yet there is no doubt that when asked to choose between the GATT approach and free trade on the one hand and systematic protectionism in favor of infant industries on the other, American elites—like their government—choose the first. Indeed, they are more consistent than the government, because they also demand the elimination of hidden subsidies, distortions, and gentlemen's agreements not to trade, the gentlemen's agreements, particularly, favoring high-cost American producers.

The field of human rights also illustrates the willingness of elites to accept enmeshment in excess of government policy. The United States is urged to assume the leadership in a more stringent UN human rights program, including American ratification of the various conventions on discrimination and their international complaint procedure. A UN High Commissioner for Human Rights is to be endorsed and accepted by the United States. And regional arrangements for the protection of human rights are to be supported, particularly to enable the United States to "set an example" in the Inter-American system.

This brings us to science and technology. Unplanned, rapacious exploitation of world resources worries American elites enough to make them favor a new, specialized agency to analyze and plan allocation of those resources. Recognizing the destructive implications of unplanned, uncontrolled urbanization in developing nations, they advocate UN study centers for providing solutions. To bring about these solutions, multilateral and bilateral aid programs would implement UN studies. The elites demand little scientific cooperation that is not already government policy, however, and they recognize the minimal facts that science is expensive, that it respects few frontiers. They support all ongoing schemes of nuclear cooperation and are committed to a stronger and more autonomous IAEA; but so is the U.S. government. There is little evidence that many members of the American elite are yet conscious of the powerful role that unplanned, uncontrolled, and aggregated technology is likely to play in the coming system. Most people still think in terms of single problems to be solved piecemeal—with more science. This is especially true of new ventures into outer space. In that area, all ongoing programs—though not necessarily their timing and financing—are accepted as essentially desirable, and more scientific refinements are suggested to make them more effective. That the effort as a whole could be destabilizing or that it could interfere with more urgent tasks is not given much attention.

The first section of this chapter advocated the policy that we *ought* to follow if we wish to maximize our own values in the next international system, if we wish to restrain the coercion of man by his government and curb the use of violence—realizing that the achievement of these aims often imposes the kind of self-restraint on American power that will let coercion and violence in other countries continue without intervention by us. We then saw where actual American policy fails to recognize or deliberately departs from these norms. Finally, we also saw that elite opinions—on peacekeeping, disarmament, human rights and, to a much lesser extent, aid and trade—are willing to accept more enmeshment, more financial and political responsibility in the network of international organizations.

From the viewpoint of our dual norm, this willingness is far from constructive. Prudential withdrawal and selective recommitment require *less* enthusiasm and *more* restraint with respect to enmeshment than the American elite displays. International organizations are not necessarily good, wise, and benign merely because successive learning experiences of America have resulted in greater acceptance of them, even commitment to them. We need not make idols and fetishes of international organizations. They exist, they grow, they envelop nations because nations certainly have demonstrated their need for them by their past policies and hopes for the future. But we must not assume that these hopes are identical for all or that international organizations are the only methods for realizing them.

The notion that the American ideal of world harmony requires us to support the UN, come what may, is as primitive as that which denounces the UN as a communist conspiracy. Because international organizations are part of the system of international relations, we must *support* as well as *oppose* them if we wish to fashion the future system to our liking. The art of doing this resides in knowing what to support when, where to withdraw, and where to recommit. The uncritical enthusiasm displayed by the American elite in favor of international action is as unwise as is their government's pragmatic policy.

Is this insistence on a realistic appraisal of international policies and institutions not an invitation to a new isolationism, a full-scale withdrawal to a new Fortress America besieged by forces, ideas, and demands that we cannot accept? It need not be. I do not deny the reality of transnational politics, the reality of dependence on international institutions to deal with issues that defy national solution. I do not revere the nation–state any more than the UN or the OAS or NATO. All are means to the same end: the perfection of human life. If we decide which *tasks* require a common effort and common institutions, the implementation of the task will yield habits, procedures, and people who can carry it out and carry it further. Even if the general symbol of the United Nations or of NATO were to lose some of its limited luster, progress could continue, for it is not the organization that is of lasting importance but the habits formed in carrying out needed, common tasks. Truer communities among men will be fashioned from the continuation of these task-oriented habits and procedures than from highly visible organizational symbols that tarnish easily. To these institutional issues, we now turn.

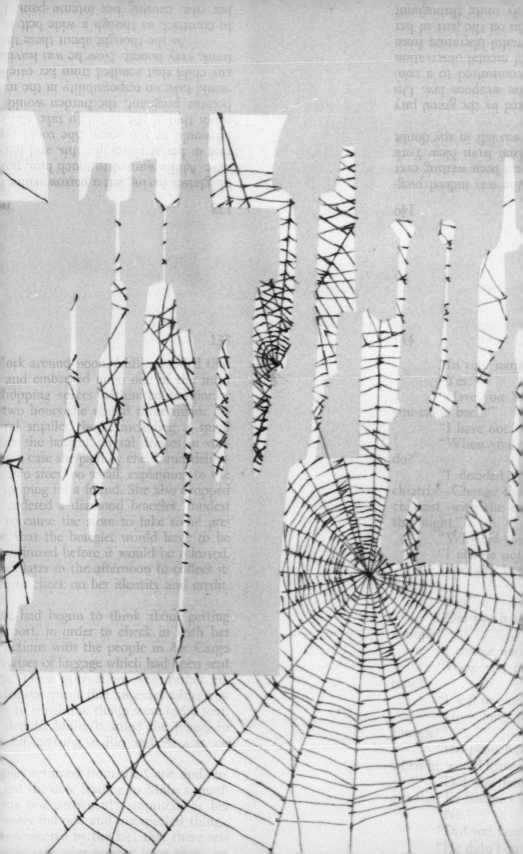

# CHAPTER TWELVE

# THE WEB OF
# INSTITUTIONS

Americans tend to overestimate the importance of institutions, largely because they think of assemblies, committees, debates, and rules of procedure as devices for civilizing the immature and the irresponsible. Discussion, confrontation, and voting are considered educational devices as much as they are ways of making decisions or committing resources to programs for action. Hence, what better way of pressing a sense of responsibility on new nations, devoured by their own problems and demands, than to give them a greater share of power in a global institutional web in which they are "part owners"? Peaceful and sober ways of resolving future conflicts would thereby become routinized, and the stridency of the confrontation between black and white, poor and rich would be toned down.

Such an approach calls for a generous revamping of international institutions, to upgrade their prestige and competence. It runs directly into the argument of those who say "the United States should use but not rely upon the UN; it is an avenue, not a cornerstone." [1] Upgrading international institutions implies that *any* strengthening of the UN is a way of defending the American national interest, but such a policy affronts those who would take a much more instrumental stance toward the UN and use it only when we may obtain a clear-cut endorsement and strong support for whatever policy we demand. Both attitudes are inconsistently and unevenly reflected in our actual policy in international institutions. Neither is calculated to implement the policy of prudential withdrawal and selective recommitment.

## 1. International Institutions and United States Policy

Government spokesmen are less sanguine than they are expediential in their defense and use of the UN. When they speak of the civilizing function of the UN, they usually do so in the context of a concrete policy problem that the UN is asked to solve in line with American interests—connected, perhaps, with compulsory assessments for peacekeeping operations or the virtues of the most-favored-nation clause. The government feels that it was "irresponsible" for the UN to create various committees on colonialism that endorse an extreme principle of national self-determination, but it was "responsible" to permit the OAS to handle disputes that some parties wished carried to the UN instead. Yet it was the United States who, in defense of Charter principles, wanted the Hungarian crisis solved by the Security Council and trade union rights protected by the ILO. Nothing was heard then of the more "responsible" use of regional or bilateral channels.

American government spokesmen are not indifferent to the larger issue of habituating new nations, even Communist regimes, to the constraints of international institutions. But they often subordinate this objective to the use of the UN and its agencies purely and simply as instruments of American national policy, a policy which

[1] George E. Taylor and Ben Cashman, *The New United Nations* (Washington, D.C.: American Enterprise Institute for Public Policy Research, 1965), p. 14.

may, at any one time, reflect little of the longer-range concern for more civilized international practices.

For approximately a quarter of a century, the official American attitude toward international institutions has reflected a sentiment that assumes an American "civilizing mission" and regards the UN as a component in the realization of the American world dream, of making the world like America writ large. The UN, the OAS, NATO, and the specialized agencies were considered separate bulwarks in the big fortress that was holding back the forces of communism, left-wing nationalism, and "unsound" schemes of social and economic modernization. As former U.S. delegate to the UN, Ernest Gross, put it:

> Those in our own country who may be led by fear or frustration to urge American withdrawal from the United Nations should likewise ponder the risk that such action on our part might not relinquish leadership, but indeed transfer it to the enemies of freedom.[2]

This attitude continues to predominate now. In Vietnam and elsewhere, American effort is credited with holding back the forces of aggression and barbarism. America is said to hold the balance of world power in favor of peace and civility. Moreover, America has the supreme responsibility for holding the balance: withdrawal and isolation are held out as irresponsible abdication of a moral imperative. In short, the duty of *homo americanus,* in the current international system and in the next, is said to be the creation of a world resembling the political community known as the United States of America. International organizations are regarded as servants in this act of creation. They are both a school and a process for launching programs designed to create that community—by gaining endorsement for American initiatives and by blocking the uncivilized efforts of Communist and youthful Third-World nations.

This view of the world is both wrong and dangerous. International organizations may well be regarded as a school, but neither of democracy nor of the American way of life. They are a school for demonstrating the unwanted and unplanned consequences that flow from systemic interdependence. They may conduce to civility by making painfully obvious the constraints under which all governments operate. But the United States is the victim almost as

[2] Ernest Gross, *The United Nations Structure for Peace* (New York: Harper, for the Council on Foreign Relations, 1962), p. 4.

much as is Mali or Nepal or Ecuador. It is inaccurate historically to see international organizations simply as one of several instruments of policy available to the United States; it is dangerous to regard these institutions as a one-way learning process. International institutions are indeed instruments. They should be used when appropriate for realizing the dual imperative that ought to form the basis of the American national interest: to minimize the use of violence and to underwrite man's freedom from manipulation. But institutions should be avoided and even side-stepped when they fail to contribute to those ends. It is naïve to expect that the UN can be used indefinitely as if it were a slightly bulky advance guard of the Department of State. Because our expectations in the past were excessive and our demands for the future too extreme, our commitment to institutional growth must be cut down to the specific tasks and policies that we wish to accomplish through international organizations.

## 2. The United Nations and Collective Security

American enthusiasm for regarding UN peacekeeping and occasional enforcement activities as a tacit extension of the Pentagon suffered a great blow during the prolonged crisis over the financing of these operations. Initially, the American position had been the insistence that the support of peacekeeping activities is the shared responsibility of all UN members and that all should obligatorily contribute to them by way of regular assessments. Countries refusing to accept this responsibility—legitimated by an advisory opinion of the International Court of Justice—should be deprived of the right to vote in the General Assembly. The policy was a failure: too many UN members were simply not prepared to accept the blanket commitment, and most were unwilling to punish noncontributors (especially since these happened to be the Soviet Union and France). This situation emphasizes the weak global consensus regarding the norms of peacekeeping, and it certainly shows that the membership does not go along with the American penchant for thinking of obligatory peacekeeping operations as one of the civilizing ventures to render the world safe for the American way of life.

Paradoxically, there is now good reason for actually upgrading the task of the UN in peacekeeping. Before the Article 19 crisis, such upgrading would merely have shifted American military objectives to the UN, which was generously supported by American financial and logistical inputs, even though no American forces were involved. Now that the crisis has occurred, an upgrading of the UN's role would help to create a firmer international consensus in favor of peacekeeping and would probably inculcate a sense of responsibility in nations that are not now among the few regular contributors to the blue-helmeted police operations. (The Scandinavian countries, India, and Canada are now regular supporters.)

"Letting the UN do it" is a futile cry if the UN is considered a substitute for American policy. It is less futile if we put the slogan in the context of the need for a prudential withdrawal. Such a posture on our part calls for the maintenance of strong national military forces, both nuclear and conventional. No military threat to the United States and Western Europe will be warded off by UN operations, anyway. We must retain the unilateral and bilateral capacity to come to the aid of threatened democratic regimes if an appeal to the UN falls on deaf ears. But we do not have to be concerned about the outcome of every dispute and crisis among nondemocratic regimes; hence we stand to lose very little by "letting the UN do it" in Latin America, Asia, Africa, and the Middle East. If the UN fails, we are no worse off than before. If it wins, we will indeed have struck a blow for the institutionalization of regulatory and constraining international procedures and law. This stance, however, does *not* require advance and blanket commitment on our part to contribute to such operations either financially or otherwise. Rather than insist on uniform and obligatory commitments for all, it makes more sense to use the UN frankly and openly for instrumental purposes and to regard as a pleasant and desirable surprise any accretions of authority and responsibility it manages to acquire on the way.[3]

This precept implies some sharp institutional lessons for the United States. We should continue to stress the difference between collective enforcement and peacekeeping. Enforcement should require the *unanimous* support of the permanent members of the Security Council and should be used, therefore, *only* when the big powers agree on coercing a smaller nation. There will be few such

---

[3] This has become the announced position of the United States with respect to peacekeeping operations. See the statements of Ambassador Goldberg and Assistant Secretary of State Sisco, reported in Arthur M. Cox, *Prospects for Peacekeeping* (Washington, D.C.: The Brookings Institution, 1968), pp. 18-20, 135-39.

episodes. But the door should be left open for the use of the UN
as a mechanism for legitimating enforcement against South Africa
or China or any other nation whose policy threatens all the major
powers—democratic and nondemocratic. And the Soviet Union's
proposals for reviving the dormant Military Staff Committee—perhaps giving it regional subcommands with standby authority to deal
with local outbreaks condemned by all big powers—should be very
seriously considered by the United States. In an age of détente and
an increasing multibloc system, there will be many occasions on
which the interests of the major powers will converge. Standing
military machinery under their exclusive control, properly subject
to the veto of any one of them, thus makes good sense. Enforcement is, and should be, properly the prerogative of the Security
Council.

Peacekeeping, however, is, and should remain, a less awesome
operation. The UN should have the power to establish and patrol a
truce line, observe infiltration and stop it when insurgency is supported from across the border, and interpose its own forces to keep
combatants apart. The United States should exercise the right not
to participate in such operations when they are contrary to American policy, and to refuse payment as well. Normally, the United
States ought to support peacekeeping, irrespective of the character
of the participating regimes, whenever a dispute threatens to esca-
late. We should resolutely avoid making the UN define the situation as "indirect aggression" or illegitimate insurgency. Instead, we
should support peacekeeping operations to protect a nation against
domestic insurgents when that nation requests UN help. Moreover, we should support peacekeeping operations that become desirable because domestic insurgency has been internationalized by
aid from abroad. Both types of counterinsurgent operations are thus
made dependent on a consensus among UN members. When the
consensus arises, institutionalization will result; when it does not
arise, no harm will be done.

The country that is victimized by insurgency must be able to
arouse the concern of the UN and trigger its intervention, thereby
freeing the United States from the onus of unilateral and contrived
measures. But this formula also creates the risk of making the
United States the object of UN verbal intervention if we decide to
participate in insurgent operations such as those featured in the
past—as in Cuba and Guatemala.

In what forum of the UN should all this take place? The exclusive
role of the Security Council, bound by the unanimity requirement,
must remain intact with respect to enforcement operations under

Chapter 7 of the Charter. But what about peacekeeping? What about the disputed role of the General Assembly and of the Secretary-General? In view of the frequently sharp differences in national interest between the United States, Communist, and Third-World countries, it would be a mistake to follow the earlier policy of entrusting large military powers to the General Assembly. It makes very little sense to give final power over peacekeeping to a random two-thirds majority, which might be made up largely of sometime consumers of security without real interest in deliberately institutionalizing the practices of maintaining peace. In short, peacekeeping operations should be authorized by the Security Council but not necessarily subject to the veto. More and more often, the major states with doubts about a given operation tend to abstain rather than veto the resolutions concerned. This practice is to be encouraged and even followed by the United States. It preserves the possibility of action but compels prior negotiations among the major interested parties. The Secretary-General should have the powers to organize, send, and deploy peacekeeping forces—much as he does now—but *not* exercise them until given the right to do so by the Security Council. Nevertheless, residual powers for the General Assembly to concern itself with peacekeeping cannot be legislated out of existence simply because no state can stop a two-thirds majority from asserting itself in the Assembly. We can recognize such residual powers without catering to them. In the future, our security will depend on our working in concert with major nations and spokesmen of minor nations on the Security Council, more than on our attempt to organize an elusive and unreliable world consensus in the Assembly.

With this understanding, the Secretary-General should be encouraged to be less restrained by Soviet criticism and to enlarge his staff of advisers on peacekeeping. He should be encouraged to revive the UN field observer panels, the panels on inquiry and conciliation, and the peace observation commissions. These groups, all the fruit of previous Assembly resolutions, have languished from disuse as *ad hoc* machinery was improvised in each new crisis. There may well be new use for them as the older rifts and divisions pale into obscurity and far more complex divisions arise in the multibloc asymmetry of the future. And the Secretary-General should have far more discretionary power to move these groups into action. In principle we are already committed to such a position. Why not carry it out in fact?

Should the United States participate in peacekeeping operations directly? There can be little reason for abstinence if the general principle of balanced big-power participation is generally accepted. If we participate, we must be ready to recognize Soviet participation as well. We are already accepting the use of East European personnel in some peacekeeping activities. So long as no single major power dominates a given operation, there need be no objection to American or Soviet participation. Again, it will be up to the diplomatic skills of the Secretary-General to manipulate the kind of consensus in the Security Council that would permit such balancing of influence. The United States should support modest plans to create UN-financed training to perfect peacekeeping skills of national contingents previously earmarked for UN service and composed exclusively with that purpose in mind. It should use bilateral military aid funds for reward and encouragement to Third-World countries who set aside troops for this purpose and participate in UN-operated training activities. Further, the United States should participate in purchasing and equipping bases around the world for training UN troops, perhaps even donate American-constructed bases for this purpose.[4] Certainly there is no bar to the earmarking of American forces for UN duty.

The model for reserved and cautious participation in such ventures has already been set by the Scandinavian countries. They have evolved rules that govern the availability to the UN of the combined Nordic Force. Earmarked and specially trained troops are available for peacekeeping only, *not* enforcement. A decision or recommendation to use troops must have been lawfully adopted by the UN, whether by the Security Council or the General Assembly, *or* the Secretary-General acting on their behalf! Presumably, the Scandinavian countries themselves are the judge of lawfulness. Further, the four governments individually reserve the right to appraise the situation and to decide whether they wish to take up the task offered them by the UN. Finally, the consent of the nation on whose soil the operation is to take place must be obtained.[5] This is a far cry from an automatic commitment to aid in any peacekeeping resolution adopted by the UN. Why could not the United States agree to participate on identical terms?

The financing of peacekeeping must remain tied to the formula of voluntary contributions. Although the disproportionately heavy American contribution of more than 40 per cent is not excessive in terms of the American share of the global income, it is excessive in

[4] These suggestions were fully worked out by Lincoln P. Bloomfield. See his "Peacekeeping and Peacemaking," *Foreign Affairs* (July, 1966) and *International Military Forces* (Boston: Little, Brown, 1964).

[5] Per Haekkerup, "Scandinavia's Peacekeeping Forces for the UN," *Foreign Affairs* (July 1964). Also Cox, *op. cit.*, pp. 139-47.

terms of the dependence of the world on American largesse. To inculcate a sense of responsibility also involves the creation of a willingness to pay. Committed to a voluntaristic formula, we should diminish our contribution to it and induce others to take greater interest in making UN operations more efficient, cheaper, and routine. For the longer run, we must seek an independent base for the UN budget, a base that generates enough income to make peace-keeping operations independent of the miserly whims and fancies of the governments of the moment. Without great loss of income and with a very considerable gain in prestige, the United States could offer to internationalize the Panama Canal by confirming day-to-day control in Panamanian hands, creating a UN supervisory body and splitting the tolls between the UN and Panama. The UN should be given the competence to sell rights for mineral exploitation in Antarctica and on celestial bodies. It should become the grantor of licenses for those who wish to farm or mine the ocean floor, though it is too late to give the UN a financial stake in the exploitation of the continental shelf. Finally, some have even suggested that the fees earned by the IMF in the more ambitious currency stabilization operations of the future could be plowed back into the UN to finance peacekeeping. A prudential withdrawal for the United States would be aided by all such measures.

### 3. Alliances, Regional Organizations, and the United Nations

During the bipolar epoch, American policymakers conceived all the major multilateral alliances, with the partial exception of the OAS, as bulwarks against the Communist tide, stronger and more predictably amenable to American influence than the UN. Bipolarity has passed into history; peace-keeping has taken the place of the more ambitious doctrine of collective enforcement action; formal alliances seem to avail little in wars against insurgents in underdeveloped and new nations. And so the invocations of the litany of loyalty to allies and responsibility for their defense sounds increasingly hollow. Often alliances are justified as "the defense of freedom" at the frontier of civilization—whether along the Mekong, the Euphrates or the Elbe. In an age of missiles it is a little hard to believe that guerrillas in the rice paddies of Vietnam and radical junior officers in Damascus endanger America's and freedom's security.

To minimize the current importance of the existing alliances is not to argue that the world has now reached an epoch in which all coalitions and pacts outside the UN are useless. In the multibloc system, new and different alliances will no doubt be formed. These will coexist with new and different regional organizations, and all will dance the eternal minuet of maximizing influence and neutralizing power in the family of UN organizations. Our argument, then, addresses itself exclusively to the utility of the *existing* alliances in the emerging system and to their possible function in realizing the imperatives of coping with the multifold trend.

The institutional aspect of our policy should aim at abandoning or rebuilding alliances in order to arrive at the progressive disarmament of military frontiers, particularly in Europe. It should also, and more importantly, aim at the neutralization of particularly volatile areas of the world, above all in Southeast Asia, Africa, and the Middle East. In short, SEATO should be abandoned so that it may give way to a new organization for establishing and guaranteeing the sovereign independence and neutrality of the states of the region. The same is true of CENTO.

NATO poses a more complex problem. Its purpose, over the years, is explained only in part by the desire of the fifteen allies to contain Soviet military might in Europe; for many of them, NATO also provided the answer to the German problem: how to rearm Germany, maintain the division of Germany, and control German might by enmeshing it inextricably with that of the United States and the other major Western nations. Specifically, NATO made it possible to persuade the Germans—and have the Germans persuade themselves—that they did not require nuclear parity with Britain and France. The French policy of all but abandoning the military aspects of NATO makes sense only if Germany really foregoes hopes for military equality or if alternative arrangements are made to deal with the German problem.

The military case made by the French against the utility of NATO is a strong one. It receives backhanded support from the United States when we strengthen our global missile capacity and progressively thin out our conventional forces in Europe, while encouraging further arms control agreements with the Warsaw Pact nations. We should have the courage to draw the institutional inference from our policy. We should strengthen the diplomatic organs of NATO while permitting the military structure to fade away—with the exception of the integrated air defense system. We should use the Council and its many committees as a means for collectively negotiating with the Warsaw Pact, to arrive at an all-European security arrangement. Collective negotiations will assure each NATO nation of a voice and prevent suspicions of separate bilateral dealings and deals. The security arrangement may involve subregional guarantees of the territorial integrity of West and East Germany and Poland, to be given by NATO and the Warsaw Pact, respectively, to their own members. The two alliances may then negotiate collective arms reduction agreements and continue the process of razing the Iron Curtain until the division of Germany, while accepted as a political fact, will be made bearable by the increase in trade and human exchanges. NATO, in short, would continue to solve the German problem by becoming the servant of a gradual East–West *rapprochement* that ought to result in the military defusing of Europe.

This argument should be examined carefully for what it does *not* say. East–West *rapprochement* involving a dismantling of NATO may also result in the evolution of an integrated West European nuclear force that would pool British and French nuclear capacity and include Germany as a client. Such a development is not necessarily inconsistent with our argument. A system of nuclear defense that decentralizes decision-making while leaving control in the hands of cautious, responsible, and restrained governments is not inevitably a step toward nuclear proliferation; this is all the more true if the British and French deterrents are to be merged, while the inclusion of Germany and Italy under the umbrella would deprive these nations of the desire to acquire their own nuclear arsenals (which they could easily do now). If such an integrated deterrent does not emerge, separate German-American nuclear understandings might evolve instead of NATO. They would not necessarily interfere with the other portions of the détente if they were matched by bilateral Soviet guarantees for Poland and East Germany. In short, NATO is sufficiently obsolete militarily and diplomatically to permit its use for the initiation of a different security arrangement in Europe, an arrangement that might include more arms control and perhaps even a nuclear-free zone *without*, however, resulting in guaranteed neutralization. The nations of the two blocs in question are strong and independent enough not to require such assurances from the Third World or the UN.

The UN, however, is crucial in assuring a different institutional arrangement in the Third World. The Arab League, the Organization for African Unity, and a new Southeast Asian body should be used to neutralize the respective regions and assure them against extraregional intervention. The states' members of each organization must reaffirm their respect for one another's independence, subject to change only through the free consent of the parties. They must also affirm their desire *not* to invite the intervention of extraregional states for the solution of regional military, territorial, and political disputes. Violations of any of these assurances would be brought to the attention of the UN Security Council by any nation *or by the Secretary-General.*

The nations in each regional organization—true regional security organizations—must perfect their own techniques for the peaceful settlement of disputes. Indeed, the records of the OAU and even the Arab League suggest a definite capacity for peacemaking on the basis of commonly accepted doctrines, even though these involve a heavy dose of distrust for the extraregional world. But these organizations will not have a capacity for organizing and mounting their regional peacekeeping operations, as indeed they do not have now. Following the example of declarations in Africa and actual treaty arrangements in Latin America, these regional security organizations will have made themselves into nuclear-free zones inspected by the IAEA, thus foreclosing the possibility of nuclear proliferation into the many parts of the Third World. But they will have done this only because they expect to have their territorial integrity protected by the UN's peacekeeping and enforcement responsibilities.

That brings us back to the UN. Because most Third-World countries are weak militarily, they cannot show the kind of self-reliance on which our prescriptions for NATO and the Warsaw Pact rest. For them there is no alternative to protection from the UN if they wish to avoid an open client–patron relationship with a great power. Hence the UN, and particularly the Security Council, must become the guarantor of the regional neutralization and nuclear nonproliferation agreements. The UN takes the responsibility of restoring the *status quo ante* when violations occur. The peacekeeping arrangements suggested above can be used for this purpose. Furthermore, the UN can prescribe acceptable methods of pacific settlement, appropriate to each regional organization but consistent with the Charter. The exhaustion of these must be stipulated before a dispute will be heard in New York, unless an act of aggression or a threat to the peace has already occurred, thus triggering the military clauses of the UN guarantee to the regional organization.

The principle of UN-guaranteed regional neutralization is so crucial in the national interest of the United States that we might well depart from the principle of "no blanket commitment to peace-keeping" advocated above. If such agreements are concluded in each region and between the region and the UN, we should commit troops and services to UN forces mobilized to enforce the agreements, even if the ideological strictures on intervention discussed above are not applicable to a given situation. However, the normal control organ for this system of guarantees should be the Security Council.

In all this, the OAS constitutes a somewhat special case. It has an important economic function as well as military and political responsibilities. It has been used as a security organization to protect the hemisphere from extraregional challenges, but it also functions as a device to protect the members against threats from each other. It combines the features of a multilateral military alliance, a regional collective security organization, and an economic development forum. These three functions are perceived as mutually interdependent by most member nations. But one main reason for the perceived interdependence is the hegemonial role of America in each.

Consensus in the future is less likely to obtain as the members of OAS develop along different lines and at different rates. The institutionalization of collective security through peacekeeping forces and firm procedures is not to be expected as the purposes of the member governments diverge further and further. Agreement is not to be expected on the treatment of insurgencies, civil wars, coups, and ideological conflict of left against right. United States' initiatives are likely to be suspect. On the other hand, a good deal of consensus can be expected whenever the threat to the hemisphere is a clearly defined extraregional effort, as it was during the Cuban missile crisis of 1962. This contingency may be remote during the early 1970's, but is to be taken seriously in terms of the scenarios that might obtain by 1975.

The nature of inter-American relations precludes the use of the present OAS as a regional security organization that would neutralize the hemisphere; the presence of the United States prevents this. On the other hand, an organization of South American states dedicated to neutrality and one another's territorial integrity is desirable. Chances of agreement on such a scheme are remote in the near future, but its utility for American policy is clear, once we give up the thought of always being able to manipulate Latin-American relations to suit our purposes. Once established, such an organization could have the same relationship with the UN as that of the Organization for African Unity or the Arab League. A similar arrangement might be concluded among the Central American and Caribbean nations if they do not federate around their common market.

I suggest that we confine the use of the OAS to peacefully settling intrahemisphere disputes. I suggest that we give up using the OAS for the creation of an inter-American *cordon sanitaire* against communism. When insurgent action pits one nondemocratic regime against another, we should not intervene through the OAS or alone, but reserve our right to participate in UN operations. When a democratic regime is being endangered by insurgent action, we should support it through bilateral means if necessary. Hence much of the standing machinery of the OAS can be abandoned without great loss. The major institutional reforms launched in 1967 are likely to be unproductive because they do nothing to change the hegemonial role of the United States or to rechannel the activities of the OAS into generally accepted directions. The economic and developmental tasks of the OAS have not been well carried out in the past, though the incorporation of the Inter-American Committee of the Alliance for Progress in the Inter-American Economic and Social Council might make some slight difference in multilateralizing the examination of aid programs and social reforms.

If we accept the principle of neutralization as preferable to inconsistent and often ineffective American manipulation of Third-World regions, we should welcome the emergence of Latin-American blocs of genuinely neutral nations dedicated to economic progress. We should then quietly abandon the OAS. And we should seek to strengthen the emerging South American common market institutions by vesting in *them* some of the powers now associated with the Alliance for Progress, while making of the Inter-American Development Bank the main institution for reviewing results and deciding on policy. But our over-all economic policy must be subject to the global institutions to be fostered.

## 4. Human Rights and Social Development

Let us restate the principles that ought to guide American policy in the field of human and social development: support legal and supranational institutions that gain strength from the already existing political culture of the people to whom they relate, institutions that command the support of established private groups, no longer the creatures of governments or single parties; support only technical assistance programs when these preconditions are not met and when the creation of new machinery will simply serve the symbolic and propagandistic needs of nondemocratic governments. This double principle gives us an Occam's Razor with which to judge the existing and suggested institutions in terms of their relevance to American aims.

Clearly, we ought to support and encourage regional mechanisms for the protection of human rights when these correspond to flourishing commitments of governments and private citizens' groups, as in Western Europe. In such contexts it makes great sense to create international conciliation panels, ombudsman offices, and even courts. In Eastern Europe, Latin America, Africa, and the Middle East, this makes considerably less sense.

With respect to UN programs, we also ought to support those institutions and mechanisms that address themselves to rights and aspirations that already command support at the grass roots level in many parts of the world. Such rights include the legal prohibitions against slavery, forced labor, and genocide. We ought to support these by ratifying the appropriate conventions and submitting reports to the UN supervisory bodies—and submitting to litigation or conciliation if we are accused of violations. Further, we ought to ratify the ILO conventions on freedom of association and collective bargaining, in order to strengthen the grass roots processes implied by these rights and thus aid in constructing the infrastructure for democracy and pluralism. We ought to submit reports on our implementation of these rights and submit to international complaints and investigations. Our actions can only strengthen these institutions in the United States and provide an example for budding pluralism elsewhere.

We ought to take the initiative in calling for conventions, studies, and investigatory institutions concerning yet another right, the right to privacy. The development of computers and all-powerful bureaucracies increasingly endangers man's ability to be alone and unharassed by society. Because the technology of communications today makes purely national regulations inadequate, America should initiate an international code including submission to UN institutions of investigation and conciliation.

Our guiding principle, however, suggests that the United States should provide no more than technical assistance to a long series of "rights" that constitute the stock in trade of superficial international propaganda exchanges. Rights such as having a family, full employment, instruction in one's own language, and the like are often unenforceable and are actually considered undesirable by many regimes and ideologies—but that does not keep them from invoking such principles if propaganda mileage can be gained thereby. We must favor and encourage greater concern for the observation of minimal standards in housing. Social justice would hardly be enhanced were we to increase economic productivity while health is neglected, tenants are exploited, food prices are rigged, and families are prevented from determining the number of children they wish to have. In short, we ought to work for the elaboration of social programs—not "rights" in any meaningful sense —that make industrialization bearable and that preserve human dignity while they increase productivity. But the means for this are world planning and technical assistance programs, not UN covenants and declarations. And if we support the single principle of freedom of association, we will be aiding the developing nations in the evolution of private groups increasingly able to defend themselves by political means against the inhumanity of purely economic development programs.

Support for technical assistance programs relating to human rights does *not* imply support for new legal institutions designed to protect rights not rooted in political culture and grass roots commitment. UN conventions dealing with civil and political rights will not help in creating proper national practices in nations committed to nondemocratic ways, but they will give such nations the weapons for attacking democratic states remiss in the application of these rights. These institutions, however, create a double standard of international and national morality most obvious today in the use made of the "right" to national self-determination: the West is accused of violating the right, but the Third World is free to treat its citizens and subdivisions as it pleases. There is no reason to submit to this pattern. The United States should not ratify the UN Covenant on Political and Civil Rights, the UN Convention on Racial Discrimination, or the UNESCO Convention on Racial Discrimination in Education. We should always work against discrimination and cement our civil rights, but not as the result of the criticism of nations who seek only to find fault with the West while they do little for the civil rights of their own peoples. Hence, the United States should not continue its support for the creation of a High Commissioner for Human Rights, since it has little assurance that such an office would work against the continuation of the present double standard. Building stronger international institutions makes sense only if they will be used symmetrically by all kinds of regimes in nations, if the embarrassment that they can generate falls impartially on all culprits. The international environment is a long way from supporting such a pattern in the field of most human rights.

This approach, finally, suggests a way of rationalizing and cutting down to basic concerns the burgeoning and uncoordinated social development projects of the UN and of four of its specialized agencies—ILO, FAO, WHO, and UNESCO. Social development programs should, above all, conform to our dual imperative, not scattered to suit this or that short-term need. There is a tendency to launch attractive crash programs designed to deal with a single ill or take advantage of a single boon, such as the World Food Program which seeks to use food surpluses to aid development. Social development programs should not be judged by criteria of immediate advantage or benefit. Instead, they should be self-consciously geared to the kind of integrated human and national development thinking that shows awareness of the dangers and possibilities of the longer-range multifold trend. Hence, ILO should concentrate exclusively on work mitigating the rigors of industrialization and urbanization; it should aid worker housing and the formation of voluntary groups. FAO should show more concern for creating peasants' cooperatives and mutual aid societies. Instead of stressing agricultural productivity or commodity control agreements as ends in themselves, FAO should examine practices of agricultural marketing and production that will obviate the development of synthetics. WHO should concentrate its resources not on single diseases—no matter how important to certain countries or groups—but on the treatment of health conditions that will make modernization more readily bearable. For instance, more work should be done in the fields of mental health, birth control, and environmental medicine in a total ecological perspective of social change. Finally, UNESCO should concentrate on *one* major activity: aid to technical and higher education geared to the social mobilization and development plans of African and Asian countries. It should de-emphasize basic education that is not related clearly to a controlled and humanized development program. The United States, for its part, should discontinue budgetary supports for programs other than these and perhaps cease supporting the specialized agency budgets.

Clearly, such rationalization is not possible without much more comprehensive social planning than is now done. We shall return to this theme in the next section.

## 5. Science, Technology, and Planning

We saw in an earlier chapter that there is nothing approaching comprehensive planning in the UN system, either in the realm of social and economic development or in the field of science and technology. Separate committees, commissions, and institutes seek to isolate priority areas, to define the kind of effort that ought to be made in spurring general goals of the Development Decade. The dangers of perilously unbalanced social and economic trends, of breakthroughs in one field of endeavor checking those in another and making man more subject to manipulation by blind technological forces are not being faced when the UN Advisory Committee on the Application of Science and Technology simply recommends such things as cheap and simple generators in villages, regional technology centers, and mass education via telecommunications satellites. How these things will effect social ties, expectations, and the structure of future elites ought to be taken into account first.

The episodic, gimmick-dependent, and uncoordinated efforts at planning suggest the need for two kinds of institutions to engage in systematic forecasting: one for economic and social aspects, another for science and technology. These organs would not "plan" in the sense of setting future goals for education, industrial production, agricultural output, and the size of cities. Such planning is beyond the scope of human ability at the moment. Where it has been tried, as in the Soviet Union, it has failed to yield satisfactory results. The forecasting bodies would not plan definitively, so much as they would think out the probable consequences of innovations on social and economic structures, impartially weigh alternative paths of development, warn politicians and administrators of the implications of policies already being planned, and advise them on the choices open to them. But this self-conscious attitude toward the possibilities and risks of innovation should be broken down into economic and social forecasting as opposed to dealing with innovation growing out of scientific and technological change. The machinery created for planning the Second Development Decade falls lamentably short of these objectives. The attitudes and expectations inspiring the machinery show little evidence of being conscious of the needs for candid forecasts. We shall return to social and economic forecasting when we talk of institutions appropriate for trade and aid. Here we are concerned with science and technology.

Two kinds of scientific self-awareness already are institutionalized in the web of international organizations. When nations have recognized that control over the physical and man-made environment can be obtained only by joint effort, appropriate agencies have been created: the International Civil Aviation Organization, the World Meteorological Organization, the International Telecommunications Union, and the Intergovernmental Maritime Consultative Organization. IAEA and UNESCO also reflect this concern. Governments have done next to nothing in joint exploration of the physical universe and mapping its resources; but efforts have been made by numerous private associations of scientists united in ICSU. They have been carried farthest in the field of coordinated space research under COSPAR. It is here that an international community of functional specialists has grown most rapidly. But few links have been created between discovery, assessment of the results of discovery, control over the environment, and implementation of that control. The need is for institutions now to forge such links before it is too late.

The United States should take the initiative in creating a UN Science Advisory Council with a mandate to examine areas of impending scientific breakthroughs and to assess their social implications. This Council should be composed of eminent scientists selected by ICSU and should meet in almost continuous session. Eventually it might be given the power even to prohibit lines of research found to be overwhelmingly harmful to human dignity and contentment. It might also be given the power to license risky kinds of research for limited periods and reassess results periodically.

The United States should also take the initiative in creating a second body, a UN Conference on Environmental Control. This organ would consist of national ministerial delegates charged with responsibilities such as water and air pollution control, urban planning, rural reconstruction, and resources management. Panels of experts chosen from scientific unions associated with ICSU would be permanent advisers on trends and problems in each area of environmental control. With this advice, the conference would eventually issue instructions governing environmental control, to be implemented by the existing UN specialized agencies and any new ones needed to deal with pollution of the oceans, with weather control, and migration.

The implementing agencies would have to be reformed in order to make possible their coordinated efforts under a UN Conference, and in response to a panel of UN Wise Men. They would have to cease being sovereign agencies, each ruled by its own intergovernmental conference. The temptation to create a specialized agency for world resources management should be resisted and opposed by the United States. Further, the United States should put teeth into the policy of scientific planning and forecasting by sharply curtailing its contributions to the budgets of ITU, WMO, IMCO, and ICAO. Unless such pressure is brought to bear, Parkinson's Law will continue to operate, unabated, in institutional proliferation.

## 6. Trade, Aid, Monetary Policy, and Planning

Institution-building in the economic field must accept the principle that the neocapitalistic notions on which the GATT system is based do not conform to the needs of heading off the economic and social imbalances implied in the multifold trend. Trading on the basis of the most-favored-nation will not help Africa develop. Investments in labor-intensive manufactures will not raise living standards unless the products find a market. Stabilizing commodity prices will not help unless the mass flight into synthetics is halted. A world currency based on a shaky dollar is not calculated to facilitate orderly economic growth.

The GATT rules—or a maximum degree of international laissez faire—are obsolete. GATT remains relevant, including its machinery for the peaceful and judicial solution of trade disputes, for the commerce among industrial nations. But since tariffs cannot be cut much more in the Atlantic area, even here the continuing negotiating function of GATT might have run its course. In short, American policy is wrong in continuing to invest in GATT as an institution or a program. GATT's role should be to prevent nations from going back on their tariff bargains. Our job, instead, is to design new institutions for coordinating a world trade and aid policy that will permit relatively painless change while we deal with the underdeveloped world's impatience.

Let us recapitulate the main objectives and policies that the United States ought to follow in a coordinated approach to trade, aid, and monetary policy. American aid ought to be largely multilateralized, to avoid the need for constant—and inconsistently implemented—choices regarding who ought to receive what kind of aid, and in order to stimulate recipient participation in the planning of aid measures. Availability of UN aid funds should be multiplied, perhaps, by a factor of ten over current resources; more if other donor nations follow the American lead. Ampler funds will allow the mounting of more and different kinds of aid projects, permit fuller evaluation of results, and finance additional training facilities. They will also permit the UN to devote more human resources to the supervision of projects. Most specifically, the funds will make possible the creation of large corps of career UN aid supervisors and administrators, in expanded and specially trained groups of resident representatives and deputy resident representatives. The rationalization and reorganization of development aid proposed here could not possibly succeed without their services. Furthermore, such services would continue to give experienced national aid officials the opportunity to offer their skills to the UN system.

Moreover, a coordinated approach implies the reduction of American support to social and economic activities in the specialized agencies that do not qualify. On the other hand, it also requires that the United States as well as all other industrialized nations engage in serious soul-searching, to determine whether their trade policies aid or hinder the economic development of the Third World. It may turn out that the GATT approach remains relevant to trade among industrial countries, whereas a different set of rules ought to be worked out for trade among developing nations and between them and the industrialized world. Moreover, since the trade among industrial nations accounts for so much of total world trade, special rules departing from the principles of equal, competitive, and nondiscriminatory treatment must sometimes be observed even in trade among industrial nations. Special rules are particularly necessary for the introduction of new products competing with the exports of Third-World nations. Trade rules geared to development needs thus require some kind of planning, a periodic survey of what ought, or ought not, to be done along purely commercial lines. A coordinated approach also calls for new institutional devices such as special preferences and commodity agreements that may be actually uneconomic from the Western viewpoint. It calls for easier credit terms and new kinds of credit to finance more uneconomic projects. It calls for a world monetary policy that respects aspirations in addition to the payments and liquidity needs of the West. *Above all, it involves a consciousness of the possible effects of innovation on the earning and growth capacity of the poor two-thirds of the world, a subordination of further economic growth in the North to the desirability of letting the South catch up.* We ought to be ready to tolerate an untidy world-trading system, the growth of many new common markets and free trade areas that derogate from GATT principles and fail to meet the stringent criteria of the optimal economic growth doctrine. We are well launched toward such a "system" anyway. Finally, the institutionalized confrontation between rich and poor—in UNCTAD and similar organs—is a fact of life. No world rules aiming at the realization of the dual imperative can operate outside this confrontation. UNCTAD must therefore become the centerpiece of a coordinated and rationalized approach to aid and trade.

Placing UNCTAD in this position implies two very major institutional innovations. First, it means that the principle of majority voting must be abandoned wherever it may be permitted constitutionally. Since the first sharp splits at the 1964 conference, UNCTAD wisely makes all decisions by "consensus" and "conciliation"; that is, votes may be taken in each of the caucuses but over-all agreements are negotiated until general agreement is reached, and voting is avoided in plenary meetings. This procedure ought to be the general rule in all UN aid and trade bodies. Majoritarianism makes no sense at all when some twenty-five countries provide the aid and markets for about one hundred other countries. Second, the principle of sovereign autonomy for specialized agencies, the UN Development Program, and the UN Industrial Development Organization must go, as must the separate status of a half-dozen planning and forecasting bodies. All these bodies must become subordinate to a centralized and coordinated approach to trade and aid, in which UNCTAD will be the centerpiece. They must give up their autonomous intergovernmental conferences and policy-making boards.

Coordination and rationalization demand the following major institutional changes: (1) In each government, creation of machinery that will be better able to make and absorb trade-aid policy and better able to participate in UN decision-making. What is to be avoided is the uncoordinated and decentralized way in which most governments participate in the General Assembly, the Economic and Social Council, the Development Program, and each of the dozen specialized agencies—especially the IBRD and the IMF. (2) For each government, a single spokesman must be able to state his nation's coordinated views. All spokesmen would sit in a reorganized ECOSOC, a UN Welfare Council with clear and sole jurisdiction over the aid–trade–money nexus. (3) The creation of a nongovernmental UN Social Planning Board merging all the present planning groups, to advise the Welfare Council and UNCTAD. (4) Elevation of UNCTAD as the central decision-making body for

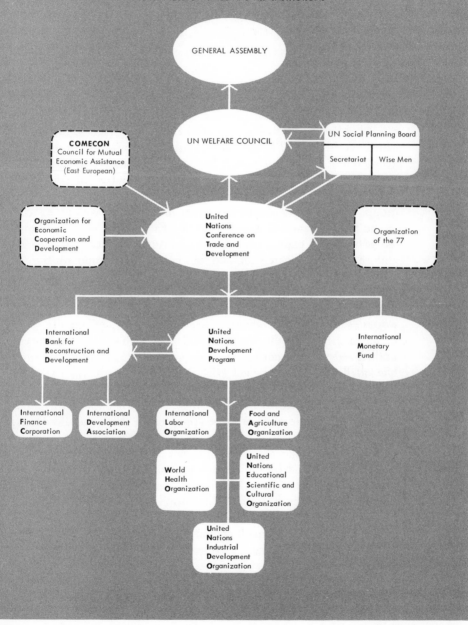

trade, aid, and money, accountable to the Welfare Council in principle, but powerful in ruling the totality of UN economic and social bodies. (5) Subordination of IBRD, IMF, and the Development Program to the directives of UNCTAD. (6) The subordination of ILO, FAO, WHO, UNESCO, and UNIDO to the Development Program's policies and funds. (7) Sharply increased powers for UN Resident Representatives in implementing aid policies at the national level.

Obviously, institutional tinkering is meaningful only if it provides channels of expression for existing and nascent political groupings with identifiable common interests, opposing the interests of other blocs but converging with them as well. Hence, just as the Third World in 1967 fashioned a standing organization to represent Third-World views in future UNCTAD negotiations, so should the West. The United States should take the initiative in converting OECD into the West's (and Japan's) spokesman and pressure group. Since we are reconciled to an untidy and overlapping economic bloc system, this would give the European Common Market its institutional expression while permitting the same to LAFTA and the East African Common Market in the Group of the 77. OECD would serve the purpose of perfecting and supervising the GATT rules that the industrial nations wish to retain for trade among themselves, including GATT's arbitral competence. OECD would also work out a common "negotiating package" for the West, to be presented to the Third World. The rich nations' sensitivity to the needs of the poor nations does not include an obligation to be blackmailed. A strengthened OECD can prevent the Third World from playing one Western country against another; it can also bring great pressure to bear on single Western nations to join in fashioning a single and sensitive approach to the trade–aid–money needs of the developing nations. Moreover, the rationalization of policy in each major camp will also have repercussions in the policies to be followed by the Inter-American, African, and Asian Development Banks. These institutions, while continuing to be financed independently from UN aid sources, will then nevertheless fit into an over-all policy pattern.

The UN Welfare Council should have a membership larger than the present ECOSOC and smaller than the General Assembly, to which it would report. The council is not conceived as a major policy-making body. Its purpose is to review, at high-level, negotiations and policies elaborated at lower levels, and thus be able to socialize governments into the habits of coordinating trade, aid, money, and development planning. The *raison d'être* of the council is the socialization function; unless governments also reorganize appropriately at the national level, it will be as marginal to UN operations as is the now familiar ECOSOC. Voting should be avoided here, as in UNCTAD.

A UN Social Planning Board is the social science counterpart to the UN Science Advisory Council. Like its counterpart, it should be made up of a number of generally respected and impartial social scientists, serving as individuals, able to weigh and judge the *interaction* of economic, social, technological, and political trends. The Wise Men will be aided by the present UN Secretariat staff scattered over the existing planning bodies, and they will maintain close links with international social science professional associations. The board will advise and carry out studies for UNCTAD as well as for the UN Welfare Council. It might well include specialized panels drawn from international professional associations, particularly in fields such as housing, demography, and education.

The center of gravity, however, rests with an UNCTAD now made legitimate by our recognition that the world will not necessarily be shaped entirely in the American image—at least not without lots of future Vietnams. Trade, aid, and monetary policy will be *made* in UNCTAD; that is, it will be negotiated continuously. UNCTAD, where every government will be represented, ought to become the superspecialized agency with competence over the entire development nexus. The UN Developmnt Program could then shed its present Governing Council and simply become the executing organ of the technical aid and pre-investment part of the package negotiated in UNCTAD. It should use for this purpose the major specialized agencies and UNIDO; but these bodies would have to lose their independent budgets and policy-making organs too. It therefore behooves the United States, as the major contributor, to change its policy, throw its annual bilateral and multilateral aid contribution into the UNCTAD negotiations, and go along with an UNCTAD-determined allocation for technical assistance as opposed to capital investment.

UNCTAD would also acquire control over the general policy of the IBRD, though much discretion would have to be left to the bank's staff in making specific loans. By gaining large new funds for grants and interest-free loans, IDA would be the main beneficiary of the multilateralization of American aid. Certainly, IDA's attitude toward development would be expected to infuse the bank, more and more. Finally, the IMF would have to be brought under the control of UNCTAD as well, thus implying some loss of power for the national central bank governors who now quite autonomously make IMF policy. The special role of the dollar, sterling, and gold should be curtailed further. New drawing rights of the kind now proposed for the IMF should be created and administered autonomously by the fund's staff, in line with over-all UNCTAD directives, rather than in response to the central banks of the world's major trading nations. The rules governing the use of IMF reserves should be liberalized to permit the fund's participation in commodity stabilization agreements, balance of payments difficulties associated with structural readjustment of economies to new production and employment patterns, and even for peace-keeping expenses.[6] The IMF, in short, ought to become a world central bank, responsive not only to short-term balance of payments troubles associated often with national monetary mismanagement, but to the long-term liquidity needs of developing as well as industrial nations.

## 7. World Government or Splendid Isolation?

The American recommitment to the economic and social program of the UN thus implies considerably stepped up enmeshment into the web of interdependence, but the prudential withdrawal from certain kinds of collective security and human rights issues suggests a loosening of institutional links as well. Does this imply a step toward federal world government, a gradual enmeshment that can lead only to the disappearance of the United States as a separate nation? Or does it imply a release from the entangling network of international obligations, a recovery of national initiative outside the UN?

The probable future system we have conjured up—even if America does adopt the policy suggested in these pages—is not one that permits such clear-cut choices. "The value of the United Nations for the future lies not in any prospect that it will become stronger but in the promise that it may become more useful, and useful in more varied respects. . . ."[7] Thoughtful advocates of the rational

---

[6] I am indebted for many of these ideas to Robert Triffin; see his *Our International Monetary System: Yesterday, Today, and Tomorrow* (New York: Random House, 1968).

[7] Inis L. Claude, Jr., "Implications and Questions for the Future," *International Organization* (Summer, 1965), p. 846.

and consistent use of the UN as an instrument of the American national interest in opposing communism above all still concede that the improvement of various economic and social agencies remains desirable. Although the United States should block UN resolutions and efforts inconsistent with the anti-Communist purpose, they urge that such opposition stop short of withdrawal or boycott.[8] Our recommendations in the peace and security field are equally cautious. On the other hand, the main attractiveness of the UN to American public opinion is its image as a community of nations working together for a common goal: peace and welfare. No matter how naïve the image actually is, it bears enough resemblance to the visible world to afford a built-in public opinion base in favor of continuing the policy of encouraging gradual and task-directed accretions of competence to the UN.

The issue, therefore, is not "more" or "less" United Nations. No thoughtful person can imagine doing without gradually growing international organizations in a world faced with the multifold trend and with the political problems of modernization and decolonization. In that sense, the web of interdependence cannot be broken. But not all strands must be equally strong. Not all tasks are equally relevant to the kind of world that the United States has every right to foster. There is no need to sacrifice our very real role in world affairs in deference to a principle of world federation that is neither feasible nor palatable in the foreseeable future. But the opposite pole, withdrawal, is equally undesirable and quite unnecessary. Let institutions that meet the national purpose grow as they acquire a consensual base in the UN and a task that is wanted. Let institutions that fail to acquire such a task gradually wither, and let American initiatives hurry along their demise. And let the United States safeguard its status as a great democratic power in the international system. Because the United States *is* a great democratic power, more depends on our policy than on any other nation's.

---

[8] See, for example, Franz Gross, ed., *The United States and the United Nations* (Norman: University of Oklahoma, 1964).